"...isn't it ironic?"

"It's like rain on your wedding day"

"Can you handle this?"

"What do you take me for?"

"I still have a thing or two to learn"

"Swallow it down...what a

way you are

ct"

"Does anyone hear me?"

"I'll make you what I never was"

"It's a free ride when you've already paid"

jagged little pill

my nails

se's back

RECEIVED
JA - - 2021
BY:
NO LONGER PROPERTY
SE - - LE PUBLIC LIBRARY
IT'S
EASY
NOT
TO

nter"

everything's gonna be
fine, fine, fine"

"Why are you so petrified of silence?"

about me?"

"These are my words
This is my voice"

"This is the first wave of my white flag"

"We had to believe in something"

It's a bla

THIS BOOK BELONGS TO

jagged little pill

The Healys

YOU LIVE, YOU LEARN

the stories behind the iconic album
and groundbreaking musical

ALANIS MORISSETTE,

DIABLO CODY,

and the complete cast & crew

Foreword by Rachel Syme

Principal photography by Matthew Murphy

GRAND
CENTRAL
PUBLISHING

MELCHER
MEDIA

Denise and Mike Fulton
694 Sycamore Lane
Greenport, CT 06839

Merry Christmas

Merry Christmas from
The Healys!

Dear friends and loved ones, old and new: you probably guessed from the signature gold envelope that this is the annual Healy Christmas letter!

I always look forward to sharing the events of our year with all of you. I feel particularly cozy this holiday season—or "gezellig" as they say in Amsterdam. (We learned that on our tour of Europe this summer!) I can even hear carolers in the neighborhood.

Steve is now in his seventh year at The Pepperwood Group. He's thoroughly enjoying his new role as partner!

Moving on to the kids! The kids are outstanding. Frankie is 16 now, but she's still our little princess. She's very artistic. Always expressing herself. In fact, right now she's upstairs with her best friend Joanne working on a little craft project. I've always emphasized the importance of female friendships. I remember those endless conversations about clothes and boys. Fun stuff!

And then there's Nick, ah. My son Nicholas. He received the most incredible news today and so happy to share it here: Nick has been accepted early to Harvard! His dream school since he was ten, and now, that dream is becoming a reality. All those years of cello lessons, Connecticut Debate Society tournaments, Kumon, Mathletes, A.P. everything, and five a.m. swim practices are finally paying off!

As for me, it's been an interesting year. I've recovered from my little fender-bender in February—my car may have been totaled, but you can't total Mary Jane Healy! After a couple of surgeries, my body is stronger than ever. How did I do it? I've turned to natural healing solutions. Pilates, acupuncture, and anti-inflammatory foods like miso and blueberries.... Oh! And LOTS of hot yoga. Hot yoga is my favorite. It's so good for you. Really gets rid of those toxins! And after all these months of practice, I don't even notice the heat at all! It's amazing what you can get used to with a little discipline. The mind and body are connected in ways we can't even imagine. I've gotten to a point where I can't feel anything!

Wishing you and yours comfort, peace, and joy,
M.J., Steve, Nick, and Frankie

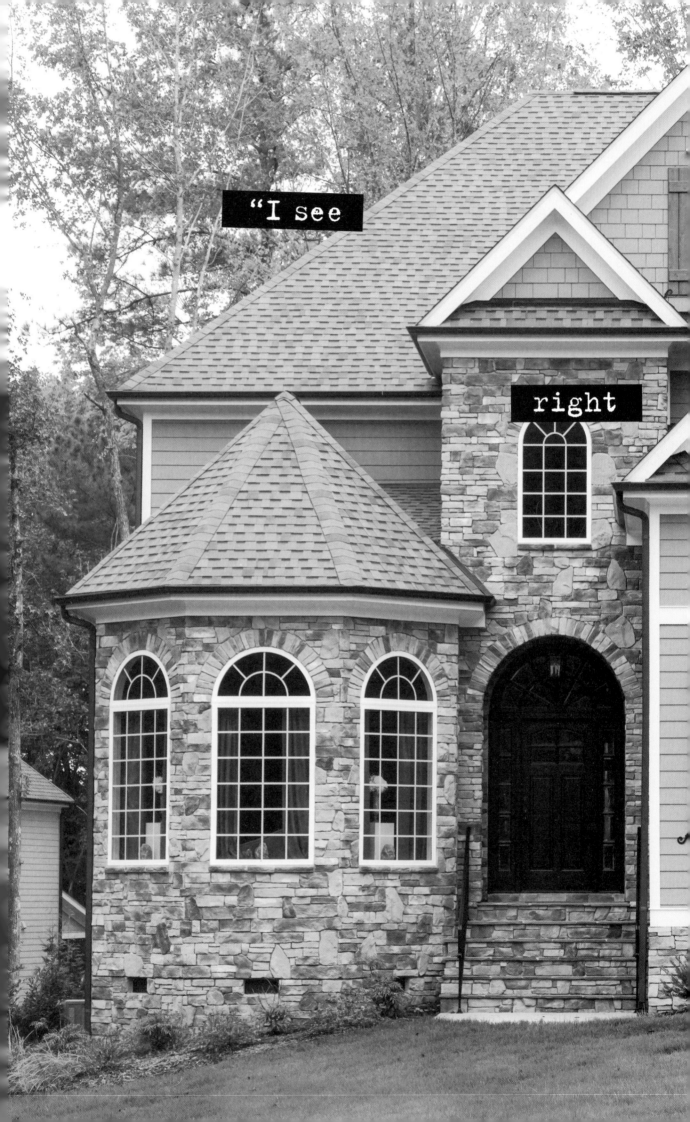

"And I keep on smiling...

can't stand still..."

Life has a
funny way of
sneaking up
on you.

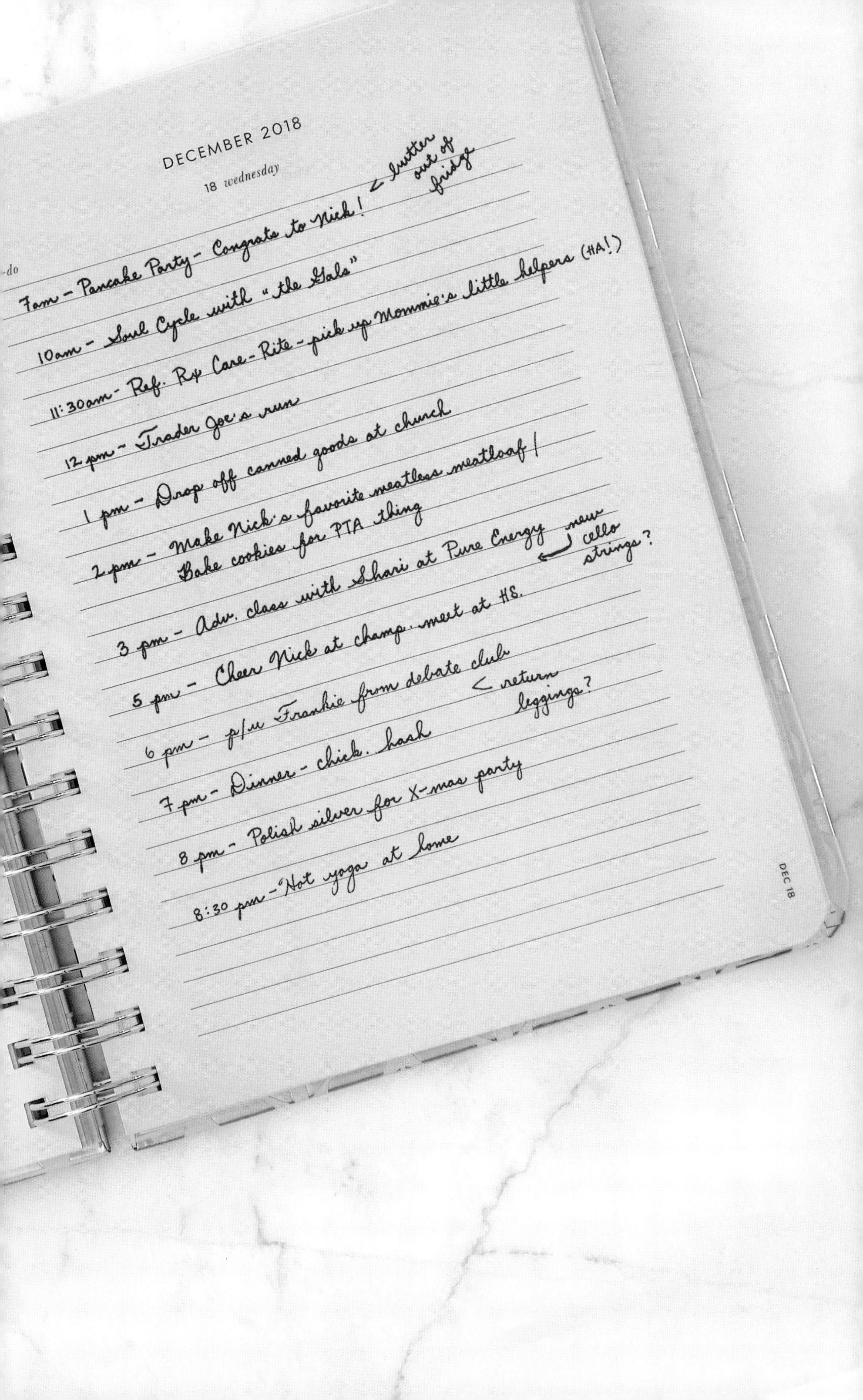

DECEMBER 2018
18 wednesday
-do
7am - Pancake Party - Congrats to Nick! < butter out of fridge
10am - Soul Cycle with "the Gals"
11:30am - Ref. Rx Care-Rite - pick up Mommie's little helpers (HA!)
12 pm - Trader Joe's run
1 pm - Drop off canned goods at church
2 pm - Make Nick's favorite meatless meatloaf / Bake cookies for PTA thing
3 pm - Adv. class with Shari at Pure Energy ← new cello strings?
5 pm - Cheer Nick at champ. meet at HS.
6 pm - p/u Frankie from debate club < return leggings?
7 pm - Dinner - chick. hash
8 pm - Polish silver for X-mas party
8:30 pm - Hot yoga at home
DEC 18

PERFECTLY IMPERFECT

MARY JANE HEALY

Played by ELIZABETH STANLEY

GOOD CATHOLIC GIRL, DEVOTED WIFE, HARVARD MOM, PTA PRESIDENT, SOULCYCLE STAR, TRADER JOE'S SHOPPER, CHRISTMAS LETTER WRITER, CONTROL FREAK, CAR ACCIDENT VICTIM, OPIOID ADDICT, RAPE SURVIVOR

Mary Jane Healy has the perfect life...from the outside. She has a husband who just made partner at his swanky Manhattan law firm, a big house in a Connecticut suburb, and she manages to make highly nutritional, paleo meals for her family and still squeeze in a hot yoga class every day. She has two beautiful children: Nick, her oldest, who just got into Harvard, and Frankie, her artistic, rebellious adopted daughter whom she loves dearly but feels might be slipping away. But she tells herself that's always what happens with teenage girls and their moms—they drift apart, but eventually come back together.

Mary Jane knows a thing or two about fitting in. She's been learning how to change herself to fit her environment since she was a young girl growing up in the Catholic Church. She tried so hard to be good. So why, when she got to college, was she held down and raped at a party? In the moment, she decided it was God's will. And she learned how to bury the trauma, deep down inside herself, so that she could live the kind of life she desired. She fell in love with and married Steve. She never told him about her assault. She didn't want to burden him—she wanted to *fit in*. Over time, she became the envy of her friends: the best at SoulCycle, the best at making class brownies, the best swim team mom. And then came the crash.

After getting into a bad car accident, Mary Jane doesn't take the time she needs to slow down and nurse her injuries. Instead, she decides to be the best at healing. She gobbles down antioxidant foods, does sun salutations, and tries homeopathic remedies. But what she's really doing is self-medicating (in secret) with the strong opiates her doctor prescribes. Soon, she is hooked on the pills. And worse, the car accident has triggered her college memories, and she stops feeling safe inside her own body. She doesn't want to touch her husband, and she nitpicks at Frankie about her clothes. She turns to Nick, her golden child, to be her best friend and surrogate caretaker. Suddenly, nothing makes sense anymore.

It takes an overdose—a near-death experience that sends her first to the ICU and then to rehab—to get Mary Jane to realize that honesty is truly the best way to heal. She opens up about her past, both to her husband and her children, and realizes that the demons that hold us back are often the ones we keep in the dark. Mary Jane may no longer be flawless, but she's finally free. As she writes in her final Christmas letter, she and her family are "perfectly imperfect people just like you. We don't have any secrets anymore."

"We get it, Mary Jane, you're winning at Candy Land."

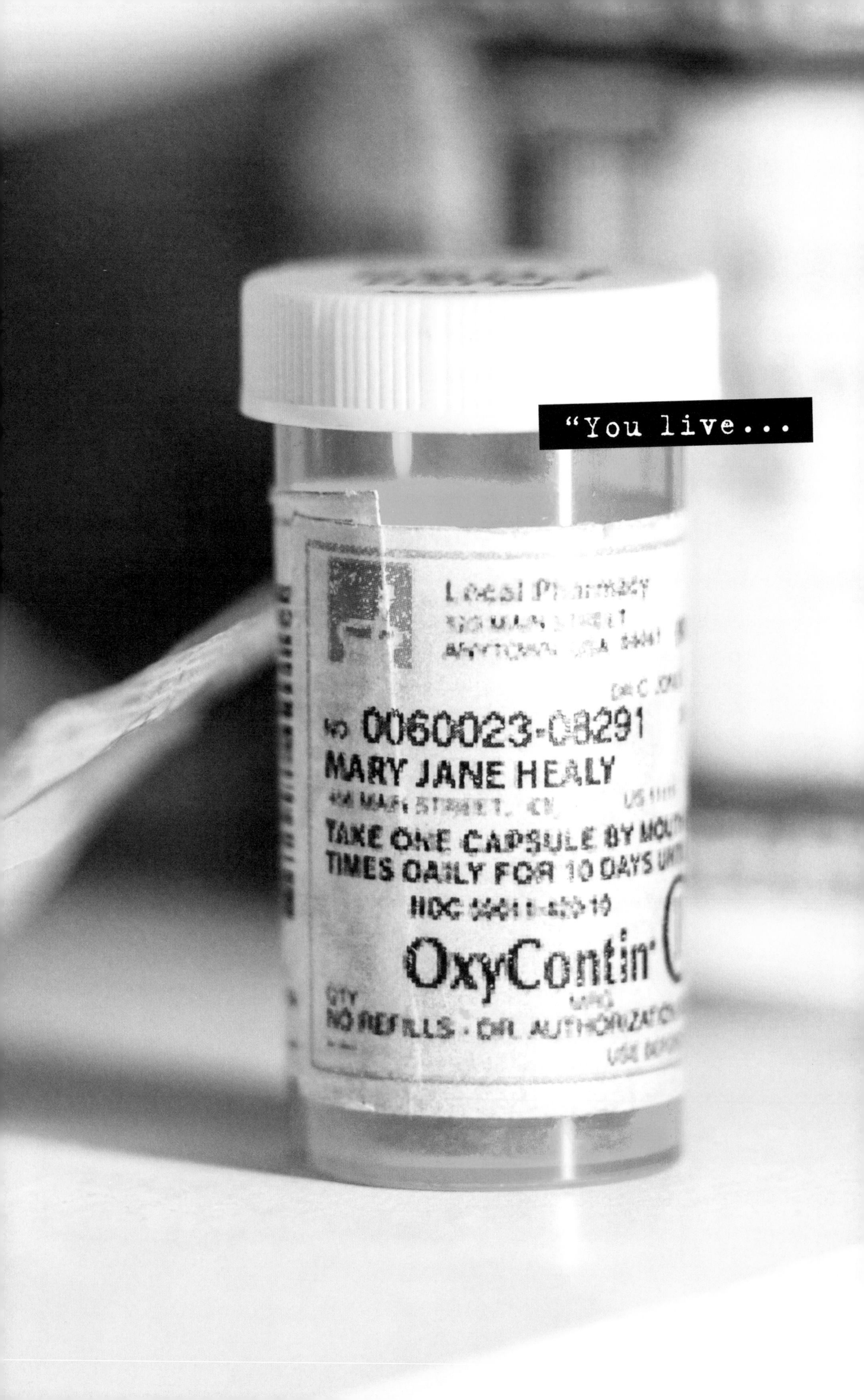

"You live...

Local Pharmacy

Dr C. JONES

0060023-08291

MARY JANE HEALY

TAKE ONE CAPSULE BY MOUTH
TIMES DAILY FOR 10 DAYS UNTIL

NDC 59011-450-10

OxyContin

QTY   MG
NO REFILLS · DR. AUTHORIZATION

USE BEFORE

KEYSTONE
REHABILITATION CENTER
PATIENT INTAKE INFORMATION

❖ **SECTION 1:**

Date: 01 / 10 /2019   Patient Name: Mary Jane Healey

Patient Address: 13 Buttercup Drive

City Greenport   State CT   Zip Code 06839   Email mamamj@hotmail.com

Home Phone #: 203-555-7028   SS# of Patient: 597-26-0038   Marital Status: married

Sex: M   F X   Birth Date: 5 / 15 /74 Age: 44   Referring Physician's Name: Dr. Juvenal Urbino

Date of Injury/Onset: 2 / 17/ 18   Date of Next Doctor's Visit: 1 / 21/ 19   Date of Last Doctor's Visit: 12 / 3 / 18

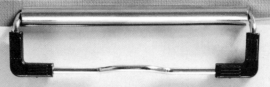

f patient is a minor): Self-Employed/homemaker

if patient is a minor): N/A

→ Have you received any physical or speech therapy in this calendar year? YES ___ NO X

If yes, where? ___

→ Are you currently receiving any home health services? YES ___ NO X

Emergency Contact Name: Steve Healy   Phone #: 203-555-7204

Spouse's Name: see above   Phone #: see above

List any ongoing health issues: Chronic lower back pain

List any medications you are currently taking: Ibuprofen

List any illegal drugs you have taken in the last 6 months: Oxycodone, Fentanyl

Hom many drinks do you have on average per week: 10

Do you smoke, and if so, how many cigarettes a day: No

Admitting Physician: Dr. Akara Woodson

❖ **SECTION 2:**

Auto Accident? YES X NO ___   If no to both questions, then please see the next page.

Worker's Compensation? YES ___ NO X   If yes to either questions, please complete section 3.

❖ **SECTION 3:**

Attorney's Name and Address (auto accident related injuries only): Stephen Barnes

420 Lexington Ave   City New York   State NY   Zip Code 10170

Worker's Compensation Company Name and Address (worker's comp injuries only): ___

___   City ___   State ___   Zip Code ___

Claim # (worker's comp injuries only): ___

**** Please keep copy of insurance card(s) with this form ****

"I just want our life to be normal again."

"I don't want to be resented when I'm just trying to provide."

"I don't want to be the filler
if the void is solely yours."

WORKING STIFF

STEVE HEALY
Played by SEAN ALLAN KRILL

SUCCESSFUL CORPORATE LAWYER, HARVARD DAD, TROPHY HUSBAND, WORKAHOLIC, CITY COMMUTER, ABSENTEE PARENT, PORN LOVER

When we first meet Steve Healy, he is at the office. Because Steve Healy is *always* at the office. As a partner at the high-powered Manhattan law firm, The Pepperwood Group, he puts in over eighty hours a week filing briefs and preparing litigation. This has made it possible for his family to have a bountiful life—a big clapboard house in Connecticut, posh handbags and fresh sneakers, summer vacations abroad—but it also means that he is almost never home to enjoy it. He has missed so much from his children's lives: school plays, swim meets, debate tournaments. He is proud of Frankie and Nick and what they have accomplished, but he barely knows them as people. Steve was so excited that Nick got into Harvard that he bought his "Harvard Dad" T-shirt before the acceptance letter even arrived—and yet he has no idea that underneath the surface his son feels empty and numb. He does not know that his daughter feels completely isolated at school, or that she is bisexual and in a relationship.

And as for his marriage, well, he has no clue what's truly going on. He loves Mary Jane, but he's not in *tune* with her; he does not see the obvious. He knows his wife is popping pills and acting strangely, but he cannot see that she is crying out for help. Perhaps he is just oblivious due to his crushing work schedule, or perhaps he just sees what he wants to see. If Steve faced the fact that his wife is falling apart at home, he may not be able to devote so much time to his job. He would rather work himself to the bone, spending nights in the city and chugging Pepto-Bismol, than slow down and take a long hard look at what's really happening inside his gilded fortress.

One thing Steve does recognize is that he and Mary Jane have stopped sleeping together. After her car accident triggered past sexual trauma, she stopped touching and even kissing him. As a result, Steve has turned to hard-core pornography in order to release the tension. He desperately wants to reconnect with his wife on a physical level, and even convinces her to go to couples' therapy. But in therapy, it becomes clear that Steve keeps MJ on a pedestal; he doesn't see her as a real person so much as an embodiment of goodness and perfection. Both Steve and Mary Jane have become married to idealized versions of one another, forgetting the passion and spark that united them in the first place.

MJ's overdose is a huge eye-opener for Steve. He realizes he hasn't been there—for his wife or his children—and he makes a decision to radically change his life. He cuts way back at work. He encourages Nick to go to the police. He starts *listening* to his daughter and his wife. He even takes up guitar lessons—and he's learning Alanis Morissette riffs.

> "I would describe myself as a beagle under a table, begging for scraps... And getting kicked in the head with a loafer."

"What Instagram filter should I use

for these pancakes?"

"Suburban Despair?"

MAKE US PROUD

NICK HEALY
Played by DEREK KLENA

SALUTATORIAN, ALL-STATE SYMPHONY CELLIST, MATHLETE, AP SCHOLAR, CONNECTICUT DEBATE SOCIETY CHAMPION, CAPTAIN OF THE SWIM TEAM, RESENTFUL SON, TIGHT-LIPPED WITNESS

"I like pain, but only if it doesn't hurt too much."

Up until now, Nick Healy has played life like a board game. He was raised to think that the world works according to a simple plan: You earn all the right chips, follow the rules, keep your head down, and in the end you'll prevail. That philosophy, ingrained in him by his parents and teachers, has served him well so far. (His milk-fed good looks and athlete's physique may have helped some too.) He's graduating high school at the top of his class and bound for Harvard University.

Since they were toddlers, Nick has been a close confidant for his adopted sister, Frankie. However, as Frankie has recently begun claiming her own stake as a person apart from the family, their relationship has started to fracture. Her awakening leads him to start questioning the structures around him. Then, when he is forced to face the ugly act that his friend committed at Lancer's party, his world turns upside down. He stood by and watched as his friend took advantage of Bella and he did nothing. Why did he freeze? Why couldn't he act?

Nick senses a simmering resentment boiling up beneath the surface: Why do his parents have to place so much pressure on him? Did their need for Nick to keep himself out of trouble lead to his inaction the night of the party? MJ and Steve projected so many of their own personal hopes and dreams upon him that Nick is starting to feel he doesn't have any hopes and dreams of his own. He feels like a marionette doll whose strings are being pulled by the authority figures around him. He's tired of coloring between the lines. How can he fall in line with expectations, but also strike out on his own? And how can he be his own person when Frankie has already claimed the role of "rebellious youth" in the family? It's hard to feel sorry for someone so privileged and seemingly perfect, but Nick shows that privilege—and patriarchy—can form a prison of its own kind.

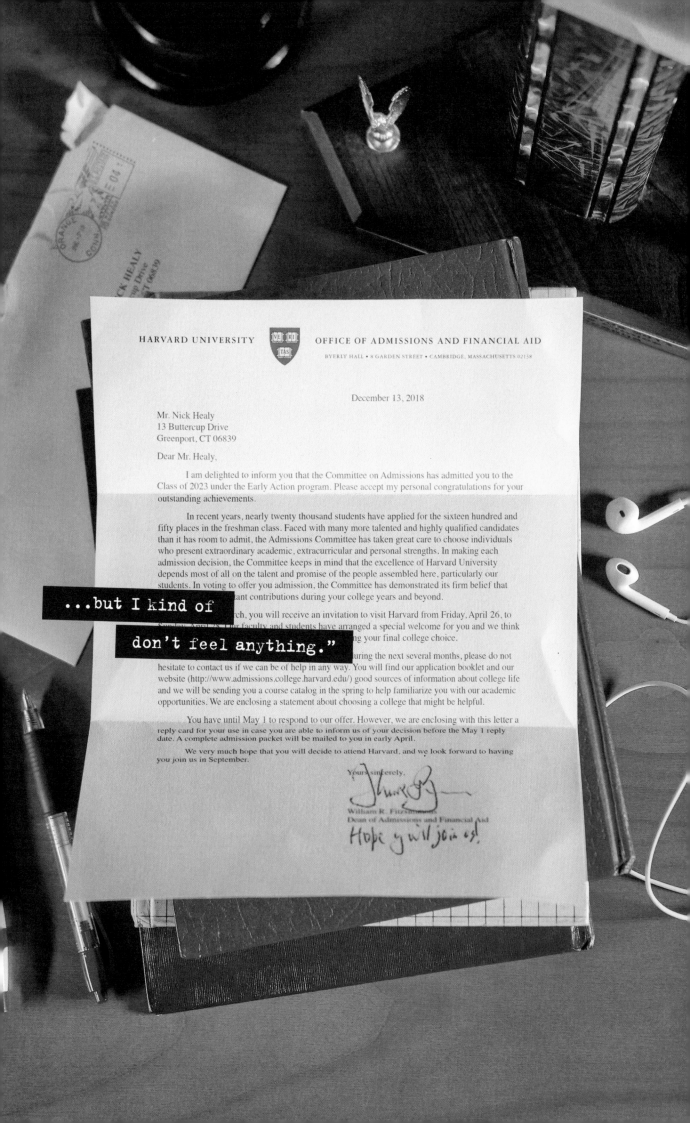

Sl. NO. 342/74

FORM 71/1184679 - F

STATE OF CONNECTICUT

Certificate of Adoption

DEPARTMENT OF PUBLIC WELFARE

DATE 02/02/01

This certifies that MARY FRANCES HEALY , born on 04/13/99

in HARTFORD, CT was brought into the adoptive custody of

MARY JANE HEALY AND STEVEN HEALY in the town of

GREENPORT, CT at the FAMILY OF HOPE CENTER .

VITAL INFORMATION

CHILD NAME	MARY FRANCES HEALY
SEX, AGE	FEMALE, 1 YEAR 10 MONTHS
GUARDIAN(S)	MARY JANE HEALY, STEVEN HEALY
ADDRESS	13 BUTTERCUP DRIVE
	GREENPORT, CT 06839

Certificate of entry in the Adopted Children Register maintained at the Connecticut State Department of Health,

United States of America, on behalf of the Registrar General of Vital Statistics. I hereby certify the above to be true

and correct. Verified by my hand and the seal of this Office, this 2ND day of FEBRUARY 20 01 .

K. Freeman

MRS. K. FREEMAN
CLERK NAME (PRINT)

CLERK SIGNATURE

PRINTED BY AUTHORITY OF THE REGISTRAR-GENERAL.

REBEL WITH A CAUSE

FRANKIE HEALY

Played by CELIA ROSE GOODING

ASPIRING POET, PRESIDENT AND FOUNDER OF SMAAC (THE SOCIAL MOVEMENTS AND ADVOCACY COMMITTEE), PROUD BLACK WOMAN, BISEXUAL FEMINIST, PERENNIAL TROUBLEMAKER, REVOLUTIONARY IN THE MAKING

Frankie Healy stands out in Greenport, Connecticut. Part of this is unavoidable—as one of the only black students at her uptight, privileged school, Frankie acutely feels the differences between herself and her peers. But she has decided to take her isolation and turn it into action. She founded SMAAC, the Social Movements and Advocacy Committee, in order to raise consciousness about pressing issues, including feminism, gender fluidity, consent, and racial justice. At the moment, SMAAC only has two members—Frankie and her best friend/girlfriend Jo—but it doesn't matter. Change has to start somewhere.

Still, Frankie has found that always pushing boundaries can lead to loneliness and misunderstandings, especially within her family. Frankie was adopted as a baby, and though her parents dote on her, she has never felt like a full part of their cookie-cutter world. She feels she cannot live up to her brother, Nick, the golden boy. Mary Jane and Steve have been so distracted with Nick's achievements that they barely know what's going on with Frankie. For example, they have no idea she is bisexual, that she has a girlfriend, or that she is exploring her sexuality. At family meals, Frankie butts heads with her parents; she feels she can never be "perfect" enough for Steve and MJ.

In addition to her confusion at home, Frankie finds herself lost at school. Her classmates mock her poetry and try to touch her hair. Jo is a source of comfort, but is going through her own struggles at home. Frankie finds a new friend in the doe-eyed Phoenix. Soon, Frankie is enmeshed in a messy, deceptive love triangle. When Jo—and then her parents—catch her in bed with Phoenix, Frankie's response is to take flight. She packs a bag and runs off to New York City. At first, she feels the elation of total freedom. But then she finds that being alone in Manhattan at sixteen can be pretty overwhelming. Jo comes to the rescue, but not before telling Frankie how much her betrayal hurt.

Frankie's journey is one of learning and resilience. While she makes mistakes in her personal life, she also advocates fiercely for Bella's story, being the first woman to tell Bella "I believe you" and supporting Bella's journey through finding justice for her assault. In the end, Frankie is still working through the big questions—Where does she belong? Whom should she love? What should she be fighting for?—but she no longer has to face them alone. She has her friends and her family standing behind her, and a bold future ahead.

"Of course they were blondies. Even your brownies are Caucasian."

"Do I stress you out?"

"I'm frustrated by your apathy."

DANGER
RESTRICTED AREA

I'll be post-feminis
in the post-patriarc

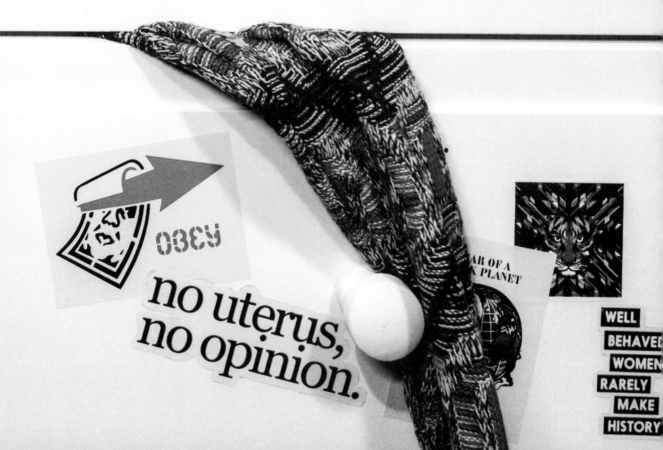

OBEY

no uterus,
no opinion.

AR OF A
K PLANET

WELL
BEHAVED
WOMEN
RARELY
MAKE
HISTORY

NO HUMAN IS ILLEGAL

DOES MY PERIOD SCARE YOU?

#believe survivors because I AM ONE

END THE STIGMA END THE SHAME

Stand with SURVIVORS

NO

ON STOL LAN

SEXUAL ASSAULT IS EVERYONE'S ISSUES

IT TOOK ME 10 YEARS TO STOP BLAMING MYSELF #meToo

OUR IS

STAND UP DON'T STAND BY

Don't ~~Get~~ Rape~~d~~
FUCK FASCISM
DON'T TELL ME HOW TO DRESS. TELL THEM NOT TO RAPE!
ALL
BE A
FOOL
KNOWS
NO
BELIEVE
BLACK
WOMEN
END
RAPE

VIVEK J. TIWARY   ARVIND ETHAN DAVID   EVA PRICE

and

CAIOLA PRODUCTIONS   LEVEL FORWARD & ABIGAIL DISNEY   GEFFEN PLAYHOUSE-TENENBAUM–FEINBERG
JAMES L. NEDERLANDER   DEAN BORELL MORAVIS SILVER   STEPHEN G. JOHNSON   CONCORD THEATRICALS
BARD THEATRICALS   M. KILBURG REEDY   42ND.CLUB   BETSY DOLLINGER   SUNDOWNERS
THE ARACA GROUP   JANA BEZDEK   LEN BLAVATNIK   BSL ENTERPRISES   BURNT UMBER PRODUCTIONS
DARREN DEVERNA & JEREMIAH HARRIS   DARYL ROTH   SUSAN EDELSTEIN
FG PRODUCTIONS   SUE GILAD & LARRY ROGOWSKY   HARMONIA   JOHN GORE THEATRICAL GROUP
MELISSA M. JONES & BARBARA H. FREITAG   STEPHANIE KRAMER
LAMPLIGHTER PROJECTS   CHRISTINA ISALY LICEAGA   DAVID MIRVISH   SPENCER B. ROSS
BELLANCA SMIGEL RUTTER   IRIS SMITH   JASON TAYLOR & SYDNEY SUITER   RACHEL WEINSTEIN
W.I.T. PRODUCTIONS/GABRIEL CREATIVE PARTNERS   INDEPENDENT PRESENTERS NETWORK
UNIVERSAL MUSIC PUBLISHING GROUP   AND   JUJAMCYN THEATERS

CONSULTING PRODUCER: TAMAR CLIMAN

present

the AMERICAN REPERTORY THEATER
production of

- -

jagged little pill

- -

Lyrics by	Music by	Book by
ALANIS MORISSETTE	ALANIS MORISSETTE & GLEN BALLARD	DIABLO CODY

Additional Music by
MICHAEL FARRELL & GUY SIGSWORTH

KATHRYN GALLAGHER   CELIA ROSE GOODING   DEREK KLENA
SEAN ALLAN KRILL   LAUREN PATTEN   ELIZABETH STANLEY

ANNELISE BAKER   YEMAN BROWN   JANE BRUCE   JOHN CARDOZA
ANTONIO CIPRIANO   KEN WULF CLARK   LAUREL HARRIS   LOGAN HART
ZACH HESS   MAX KUMANGAI   HEATHER LANG   EZRA MENAS
KELSEY OREM   YANA PERRAULT   NORA SCHELL
KEI TSURUHARATANI   EBONY WILLIAMS

Scenic Design	Costume Design	Lighting Design	Sound Design
RICCARDO HERNÁNDEZ	EMILY REBHOLZ	JUSTIN TOWNSEND	JONATHAN DEANS

Video Design	Hair, Wig, & Makeup Design	Music Director/Conductor	Music Coordinator
LUCY MACKINNON	J. JARED JANAS	BRYAN PERRI	MICHAEL AARONS

Casting	Marketing Director	Advertising	Interactive Marketing	Press
STEPHEN KOPEL, CSA	VICTORIA CAIRL	RPM	SITUATION INTERACTIVE	VIVACITY MEDIA GROUP

Production Stage Manager	Company Manager	Technical Supervision	General Manager
IRA MONT	ROSEANNA M. SHARROW	HUDSON THEATRICAL ASSOCIATES	RCI THEATRICALS

Music Supervisor, Orchestrator, and Arranger
TOM KITT

Movement Director and Choreographer
SIDI LARBI CHERKAOUI

Director
DIANE PAULUS

Developed and World Premiere produced by the American Repertory Theater at Harvard University. Diane Paulus, Artistic Director; Diane Borger, Producer.
The producers wish to express their appreciation to TDF for its support of this production.

TABLE OF CONTENTS

FOREWORD

It is May 2020 in New York City as I write this, and while I am sitting in a small room in Brooklyn just across the river from the Broadhurst Theatre, I cannot go there right now. Nobody can. On March 12, the theater, along with every other theater on Broadway, closed its doors due to the coronavirus pandemic, leaving only a lone ghost light burning at the center of the stage. The marquee for *Jagged Little Pill* is still up, as are the show's sets and the costume racks in the dressing rooms. Somewhere, in the wings, the Healy family Christmas tree is gathering dust, waiting for the day that the show can go on. Hopefully, by the time you read this, Broadway will have come roaring back—or at least it will have safely tiptoed back at sixty percent capacity—and it will again be possible to hear Lauren Patten sing "You Oughta Know" with such ferocious urgency

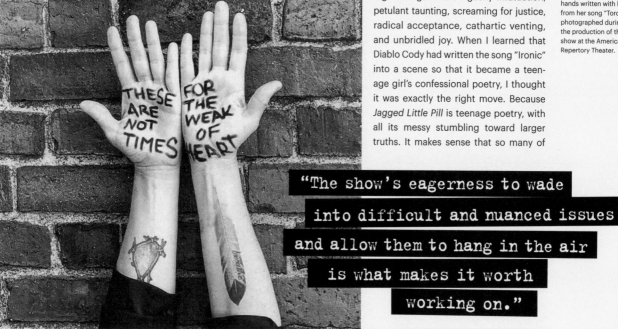

or in "Perfect," which is about sloughing off the expectations of your parents in order to formulate an internal compass of your own. It is always bizarre to me that even twenty-five years after its release, people think of *Jagged Little Pill* as an *angry* record, a shrill yodel from an ex-girlfriend out for revenge. There is anger on the record, to be sure; listen to "Right Through You" and you'll hear Morissette seething at the predatory record executives who took advantage of her when she was a teenage pop star in Canada. Or listen to "Forgiven," a lament about the hypocrisies of the Catholic church and the ways in which Morissette felt that organized religion taught her to keep her mouth shut. But rage is just one of the many emotions that flood the album; if anything, it is a work of emotional maximalism. All the feelings on *Jagged Little Pill* are Big Feelings. There's gushy infatuation, petulant taunting, screaming for justice, radical acceptance, cathartic venting, and unbridled joy. When I learned that Diablo Cody had written the song "Ironic" into a scene so that it became a teenage girl's confessional poetry, I thought it was exactly the right move. Because *Jagged Little Pill* is teenage poetry, with all its messy stumbling toward larger truths. It makes sense that so many of

Left: Alanis Morissette's hands written with lyrics from her song "Torch," photographed during the production of the show at the American Repertory Theater.

> "The show's eagerness to wade into difficult and nuanced issues and allow them to hang in the air is what makes it worth working on."

that it makes you want to stand up in your seat, or to hear Celia Rose Gooding turn "Ironic" into an inside joke about poetic license and grammatical errors. For now, even while separated, the cast is trying to stick together: just this week, the company of *Jagged Little Pill* and Alanis Morissette got together on Zoom to perform several numbers from the show to benefit The Actor's Fund, with Morissette ending the night by singing a slow rendition of "Hand in My Pocket." Watching Morissette perform that song, at such an anxious and unpredictable time, I realized that it had taken on a new resonance. It is hard to say if everything is going to be *fine, fine, fine* right now. But in a way, that has always been the point. Morissette wrote that song at only nineteen years old, speaking to the swirling uncertainty she felt in her own life as part of a generation that had been labeled as listless slackers. "Hand in My Pocket" is a song about feeling everything and nothing at once, and moving through the day anyway. It's about allowing one hand to worry while the other grips the wheel. It feels oddly prescient for this time, when many of us are just trying to find some sense of equilibrium to get through the day.

Equilibrium—finding it, maintaining it—was always a central theme of *Jagged Little Pill*, the album. You hear it in songs like "You Learn," which recommends swerving between risks and mistakes so that you can ultimately find a wiser place to land,

us (myself included) have strong memories associated with belting the album in our bedrooms and cars; Morissette, with her yelping voice that always invites you to sing along at high volume, gave listeners permission to indulge in the overwhelming. The goal was, as Morissette sings in "You Learn," to find grace at the end, but to howl along the way.

The first time I saw *Jagged Little Pill* on Broadway, I wasn't quite sure what to make of it. There was so much going on—it was about sexual assault, transracial adoption, opioid addiction, porn obsession, gender identity, parental pressure, power, privilege, and SoulCycle (and that's just Act 1). But when I met Morissette to discuss it, she told me that it was supposed to feel like a deluge, much in the way that her original album feels like a forceful weather pattern. She described herself at nineteen to me as "a happy little mess, writing songs," and in a way, the Broadway musical is truly reflective of that. As Mary Jane says at the end of the show, it is about "perfectly imperfect" people. In speaking to Diane Paulus, Diablo Cody, and Morissette, I learned that for them, the show's eagerness to wade into difficult and nuanced issues and allow them to hang in the air is what makes it worth working on. It is rare to see issues of consent and abuse discussed on the Broadway stage, let alone in a family-friendly musical, but it was due to Morissette's insistence that the show tackle sexual violence

that Bella's assault became such a crucial part of the show. There is a direct correlation between the "too-muchness" that surrounded Morissette when *Jagged Little Pill* first came out in 1995 (*Rolling Stone* magazine labeled her the "stormy girl du jour" and "Angry White Female") and the Broadway show, but now, Morissette is owning and leaning into that label. The show is too much, but that is no longer something to be feared. In taking on so many issues, it is a show that is reaching out to the audience for connection. It wants those watching to remember the times that they were heartbroken or discounted or isolated and feel less alone watching the characters on stage face these feelings head on. It doesn't offer easy answers. Will Bella find justice? Will Nick ever understand the full consequences of his actions? Will Jo and Frankie ever be friends again?

The show leaves questions dangling when the curtain falls. For Morissette, that's part of the message. Learning isn't always linear. "Reflection and processing are everything," Morissette told me in March, when I called her to discuss the show. At the time, she was quarantining with her family in California. "Even in the most challenging times and the biggest conflicts and the strangest chapters, not unlike the one we're in right now. Ten years from now or two years from now, there's going to be some reflection on what beauty was yielded from it. And in the moment, when hard, challenging, difficult times are happening, it's tough for me to conjure the 'You Learn' energy. But that is what it's all about. Even when it's not fun."

I think often about an taped interview that Morissette gave to MTV right when *Jagged Little Pill* first came out, in 1995. She looks so young, with her wavy brown hair falling into her face. At the end of the interview, the reporter, a young man, asks her about the fury behind "You Oughta Know." "Some people say, well, she's a man-hater," he asks, as Morissette struggles not to roll her eyes. "How do you respond to people who say that?" Morissette juts out her jaw and lets out a deep, world-weary sigh. "I say, 'No I'm not,'" she says. "And I mean, the song was written for the sake of release, and this really dysfunctional subconscious part of myself. It was a way to let go of that certain situation, of which I take part responsibility for what happened. I was the one who put my self-esteem in his hands and basically gave him free rein to do with it what he would." I think about the composure she had at only twenty-one years old, when the media wanted to paint her as a shrill harpy out for blood. And she had equal composure when it

This page: Some favorite moments from the music videos released for Jagged Little Pill. From top: "Hand in My Pocket" (directed by Mark Kohr), "You Learn" (Michele Laurita), "Ironic" (Stéphane Sednaoui), "Head Over Feet" (Michele Laurita).

came to the criticism of her peers, who saw her wild success (*Jagged Little Pill* still remains one of the top-selling albums of all time) and accused her of being a slick studio creation who borrowed from the grunge aesthetic to make pop hits. What I think now that the critics missed was that Morissette was trying to be legible, above all things, and she was trying to be heard. She made music for teenage girls who wanted an accessible way to express their inaccessible feelings, and to process subjects like abuse and betrayal safely within the borders of a radio hit. Morissette's main goal, as she told me many times, is open communication above all things.

I think the Broadway show embodies that spirit—it is about a family who cannot be honest with one another, and about the ripple effect that follows. They hurt themselves and others, all because they are scared to express what they really want around the breakfast table. What Morissette's music brings to this story is a willful, and sometimes complicated, outpouring of what has been bottled up. Frankie has been *waiting* to sing "Unprodigal Daughter" since she was a little girl. Jo has been *waiting* to sing "You Oughta Know," about all the ways that she and other queer people feel unseen and overlooked, since her mother began taking her to oppressive church socials. Mary Jane has been *waiting* to sing "Forgiven," where she can rail against the Catholic church, ever since she was told to keep her mouth shut about her college sexual abuse and remain a good, churchgoing girl. Diablo Cody, Diane Paulus, Tom Kitt, and Sidi Larbi Cherkaoui crafted a show that allows every Morissette song to feel like catharsis, the way it feels when you sing the chorus of "Ironic" at karaoke. These songs are meant to feel a bit melodramatic, a bit overwrought. It's watching characters move through them with their bodies and their throats that gives them a new grounding.

I hope that by the time you read this, *Jagged Little Pill* will be back on stage at the Broadhurst for eight performances a week. Theater is a communal art form, and *JLP* is a show that longs to bring people together, both during the show (the spontaneous standing ovation for Lauren Patten's "You Oughta Know" every night feels electrically interactive) but also afterward. It wants you to go home and ask the Big Questions, feel the Big Feelings. And until the show is back on Broadway, we have Morissette's music to keep us company. It's hard to know if everything is going to be quite alright, but, as *Jagged Little Pill* reminds us, the only way we can face the future is together.

—RACHEL SYME
May 2020

Introduction

STILL REMEMBER THE MOMENT, nine years ago, when I was sitting across from the producer Vivek Tiwary and musical director Tom Kitt in New York, and they ran past me the idea of turning *Jagged Little Pill* into a musical. It was a heady, intriguing, and inspiring invite, to be sure. I remember quietly telling them (and myself) that I would want to be part of this only if it truly moved me, spurred me to grow, and asked something of me on multiple levels—emotionally, psychologically, spiritually, and intellectually.

After I met with Vivek and Tom, I began to really think about how this record could transform from what Glen and I did alone in the studio when I was nineteen years old into a fully realized Broadway production. Could we really take the hyper-autobiographical, stream-of-consciousness style from the album and reconstruct it for the stage? More broadly, how could we not just reimagine it, but truly integrate into it all that has emerged in our hearts and in this world over the last twenty-five years?

I also wanted this new journey to challenge me in terms of activism and giving back. I told Vivek and Tom, as well as lead producers Arvind Ethan David and Eva Price, that my favorite thing in the world is to collaborate with people who are willing to allow a partnership to push us to the next place in our evolution as artists, scribes, and leaders. In my experience, it is in those kinds of partnerships that our expression becomes more than the sum of its individual parts. I told them that I would be very interested only if we took what the record meant to me to a whole other level. There truly would not have been any other reason for me to do it.

I had a sense of how much blood, sweat, and tears would be required. I was aware that all of us would be asked things of our bodies, our minds, our spirits that would potentially take us out of our comfort zones and shift our perceptions of the world. I had the sense that we were poised at the edge of a great adventure. I knew that what we could create together would be worth waiting for, that we had to stand by for whatever amount of time it took to build out a full creative team who would share in the mission.

The task was large and looming—but drool-inducing. I love this record, and fortuitously, today I can still sing (almost) all of the lyrics with aligned consistency. For me it is essentially a record about permission giving—the permission to feel anger, rage, sadness, grief, ambivalence, terror, numbness. It's about permission to fail, stand back up, and fall again—permission to be human. How could we carefully intertwine a story with the music, ideally with both being expanded upon in the process? Fathoming these questions was truly daunting—and gorgeous.

Turning *Jagged Little Pill* into a musical presented a unique challenge: so many parts had to be lined up. Perhaps the most pressing next step was to find someone to write the libretto—the "book" that would connect all the songs. It had to be someone with a deep soulfulness, vision, humor, and emotional sophistication. Someone who could hold the complexities and humor and subtleties of each character's onstage evolution. The search took a few years, during which I had the privilege of meeting some of the most exciting writers around today. For whatever reason, it didn't quite feel like an intuitive fit until I met Diablo Cody. She brought a combination of giddiness, terror, certainty, and a searing focus. She was ready to bravely address all that each character would experience—as a family and as a community in an increasingly awakening world. Diablo foresaw a plan to set each character at a personal, self-defining crossroad. (As she brilliantly put it, she "pulled the characters out of the songs themselves.")

As more of the team began to solidify (Diane Paulus! Sidi Larbi Cherkaoui!), I felt this musical turning into something far beyond myself, far beyond anything I had written in the songs on *Jagged Little Pill*. Diane, Larbi, Tom, Diablo, and I had an incredible brainstorming session at my home where we gathered around a whiteboard and tossed around ideas for characters and songs that might help tell the story. The characters took on a life of their own as we hashed out different songs and storylines. I offered up other songs that the rest of the team didn't know because either they weren't singles or were on different albums. Before we knew it, each character started to inform the others to create a truly interwoven, complex narrative.

It became a collaboration of my dreams, of the pinch-me variety—an embarrassment of artistic riches. Each creative choice was one born from a place of deep care. Everyone around me pulled me higher and higher. We would philosophize together while researching. We leaned on and trusted

> **"I wanted this new journey to challenge me in terms of activism and giving back."**

dances. It was an emboldened interactive dance that birthed this musical from the deep wisdom, empathy, and passion that this whole team lives by.

This experience has been crackling for me. I now feel less alone in my life, in this world. I suppose I never was, but this musical shifted my perception of myself as a lonely artist to a partner in the sweetest of art-crimes. This story is one that touches on many topics—each one treated with deep respect, vulnerability, open-heartedness, and sanctity. Lord knows, we artist-activists want nothing less.

I am deeply grateful to everyone involved in this *Jagged Little Pill* musical. Tears again. I thank you for caring so deeply and for blowing my mind with your performances. I thank you for your quiet whispers to me and for the intense intelligences each of you bring to this project. When things were hard, scary, and overwhelming—with the targets constantly moving—we stayed the course and kept showing up. We have stuck with the original promise to tell a story that would demand everything from us. The whole time, we kept our eye on the north star of "why are we doing this" and "what matters the most." I knew from the start what matters the most, why I signed on to do this heart-spinning musical: service, awareness, movement of energy, feelings, visions, empathy, validation, catharsis, healing, and deepening the inquiry, always.

each other to know when were the right moments to step out, to show up, and to serve. I felt like a kid in a candy store (albeit a candy store laden with a lot of gravitas).

Being a solo artist, whether on tour or otherwise—and as a female working within a patriarchal context—I am used to a somewhat lonely lifestyle. However, thinking back on my brief involvements in theater as a child, I was reminded of the profound sense of community and belonging that being part of a musical can beget. I was not alone in the cockpit anymore.

After the whole team was solidified, workshops and rehearsals began. It was in this period that I began having—for the first time in my life—a visceral experience of objectivity around these songs. In the years prior to starting the musical, I had had the pleasure of soliloquizing, in a sense, onstage, around the world. Night after night, I would move these stories through myself, dancing and singing. While that afforded a great sense of catharsis, there wasn't the kind of healing happening that I now realize can only emerge in relationship with others. This stems from the theory that if we were wounded *in a relationship*, then healing can happen only *in a relationship*—whether that means with just one person or a group. In terms of this musical, this healing opportunity plays out inside the relationships among the Healys and their community.

I'm also talking about the relationships among everyone involved in the building of the show. My appreciation of their respective roles, the ceaseless sharing of their God-given talents, and the experience of having committed to this team touched something deep within me. That's when the floodgates opened and the tears began to flow (they have not stopped since). At one point I remember being at one of the workshops and crying so hard (and so quietly!) that Tom Kitt came up behind me and put his hands on my shoulders to help me ground and contain myself. Watching Diablo, Diane, and Larbi work together with the entire cast and artistic team at large was like watching the greatest of

> **"The one thing I was not anticipating is the way the show would be so deeply healing on a personal level."**

The one thing I was not anticipating is the way the show would be so deeply healing on a personal level. I am not exaggerating when I say that I no longer feel alone. I feel met and catapulted by everyone who worked on this musical. I dreamed of "next level" and you all created "next galaxy." Thank you for growing my awareness, thank you for being willing to blossom our consciousness through this musical and the process itself. May this movement-of-a-musical serve as a balm, a spark, and an out-breath—a harbinger of a shift toward each other in times of difficulty. Laughing and crying, we need each other. Thanks for holding this book in your hands. I love you.

Alanis Morissette

1

OVERTURE

A VOICE: *Swallow it down*

THREE VOICES: *What a jagged little pill*

THREE MORE VOICES: *It feels so good*

THREE VOICES:
*Swimming in your
stomach*

VOICES:
*And what goes
around*

VOICES:
*Around and around
and around*
Around and around
Wake up

Never comes

Around
Wake up
Oh

All I really want

Oh

Is deliverance

Oh

*A way to calm the
angry voice*
These are my words
This is my voice
This is my taste
*Of which you have
no part of*
And I'm here
To remind you

Oh

Ah
Ah
Ah

You you you you
You you you you

ALL: *Of the mess you left / when you went away /
It's not fair to deny me / Of the cross I bear that
you gave to me / You you you you you*

ACT 1 · SCENE 1

THE HEALY HOUSE—NIGHT

MARY JANE HEALY sits with a laptop. She addresses us as she begins to compose a letter.

CHORUS:

MARY JANE/STEVE/NICK/FRANKIE: *La la la la...*
Merry Christmas from the Healys! *La la la...*

MARY JANE: Dear friends and loved ones, old and new: You probably guessed from the signature gold envelope that this is the annual Healy Christmas letter!

I always look forward to sharing the *Ooh...*
events of our year with all of you. I feel particularly cozy this holiday season—or *gezellig* as they say in Amsterdam. (We *Ooh...*
learned that on our tour of Europe this summer!) I can even hear carolers in the neighborhood. *Aah*

We hear CAROLERS singing softly outside; it's haunting and only semi-real. As Mary Jane composes her letter, she switches between "acceptable" anecdotes (the stuff that actually makes it into the letter) and truthful asides that she only shares with herself and us.

MARY JANE: Steve is now in his seventh year at The Pepperwood Group. He's thoroughly enjoying his new role as partner!

We illuminate Steve Healy, 45, at his desk.

MARY JANE: *(to herself)* As for the kids and me, we're enjoying his bonus. L-O-L! Is that refreshingly self-aware or obnoxious? *(thinking better of it)* Delete. Steve bills about 60 hours a week, so he doesn't see much of us these days. But I'll tell you what he does see a lot of— *(again, to herself)* hardcore pornography! I know because I've been secretly monitoring his Internet use. Let's just say it's been educational.

Steve is clicking listlessly away.

MARY JANE: Moving on to the kids! The kids are outstanding. Frankie is 16 now, but she's still our little princess.

Illuminate FRANKIE, 16, black, a rebellious descendent of the original Riot Grrls. She's in her bedroom.

MARY JANE: She's very artistic. Always expressing herself. In fact, right now she's upstairs with her best friend Joanne working on a little craft project.

Jo shows Frankie her finished sign. It says "FUCK FASCISM."

MARY JANE: I've always emphasized the importance of female friendships.

Frankie and Jo start making out.

MARY JANE: I remember those endless conversations about clothes and boys. Fun stuff! *(then, with great affection)* And then there's Nick, ah. My son Nicholas.

We see NICK, 18. He's a teenage god.

MARY JANE: He received the most incredible news today and so happy to share it here: Nick has been accepted early to Harvard!

Mary Jane and Steve explode with joy, hugging Nick, who looks overwhelmed.

STEVE/NICK/FRANKIE: Woo!!!! Boo ya!!!

MARY JANE: Thank you Jesus! Thank you Jesus! THANK YOU JESUS! Harvard has been our dream school *(deleting, quickly)* his dream school since he was ten, and now, that dream is becoming a reality. All those years of cello lessons, Connecticut Debate Society tournaments, Kumon, Mathletes, A.P. everything, and five a.m. swim practices are *finally* paying off!

As for me, it's been an interesting year. I've recovered from my little fender-bender in February—my car may have been totaled, but you can't total Mary Jane Healy! After a couple of surgeries, my body is stronger than ever.

CHORUS: *I see right through you*[1]

MARY JANE: How did I do it? I've turned to natural healing solutions. Pilates, acupuncture, and anti-inflammatory foods like miso and blueberries.

CHORUS: *I know right through you*

MARY JANE: ...Oh! And *lots* of hot yoga. Hot yoga is my favorite.

CHORUS: *I feel right through you*

MARY JANE: It's so good for you. Really gets rid of those toxins! And after all these months of practice, *I don't even notice the heat at all!*

CHORUS: *I walk right through you*

MARY JANE: It's amazing what you can get used to with a little discipline. The mind and body are connected in ways we can't even imagine. *I've gotten to a point where I can't feel anything!*	**CHORUS:** *Mmm...*

CHORUS:

I see right through you

I know right through you

I feel right through you

STEVE/NICK/FRANKIE/ JO/BELLA/ANDREW/ PHOENIX:

We all had our reasons to be there

We all had a thing or two to learn

We all needed something to cling to

I walk right through you[2]
So we did
So we did
So we did
So we—

---

1 Songwriter Alanis Morissette says, "'Right Through You' is a response to some producers and other people I worked with when I first got into the entertainment business. They saw me as being too young to be taken seriously. So this song is basically about how difficult it is to be a young woman in the context of patriarchy in this industry. It's about setting boundaries and saying, 'I won't be snowed, even though I'm young.'"

2 "The original fifth verse after the chorus has the line, 'Now that I'm Miss Thing / Now that I'm a zillionaire.' At the time I wrote that, it was directed toward the record executives from the start of my career and how little respect they gave me. Now, though, whenever I sing those lines, I'm always just slightly cringing."

BEYOND THE FACADE

We open on a pristine living room in the ritzy (and fictional) town of Greenport, Connecticut. It is December. The Healy family—Steve, Mary Jane, Nick, and Frankie—are nestled together on an oversize sofa wearing their winter sweaters. They are perfectly cozy (or *gezellig,* a word they learned on their summer trip to Amsterdam) as Mary Jane recites the family's annual Christmas letter. Her tone lands somewhere between smug and chipper as she types out updates on the family successes: Steve made partner at his law firm (with a giant bonus to boot), Nick was accepted early to Harvard (his—or rather, Mary Jane's—ultimate dream school), and Frankie, ever the rebel, is part of a student-activist group with her very good friend Joanne. (What Mary Jane doesn't know is that the BFFs spend most afternoons making out in Frankie's room.)

> "We know right away that this is a family of veneers... and the seams are starting to show."

We know right away that this is a family of veneers; their privileged bliss is as sparkly and shiny as an icicle, but just as ephemeral. Everything they have is in danger of melting away. Steve, for example, is hiding a porn addiction and hasn't touched his wife in months. Nick is on the verge of a nervous breakdown from the enormous parental pressure to excel in both school and sports. Frankie, who was adopted as a baby, doesn't feel like she fits in anywhere in Greenport —not only as a black queer woman, but as a person who truly yearns to make a difference in the world. While her classmates are raiding their parents' cabinets for expensive scotch, she and Jo (the only members of her social-action group) are fighting for free tampons in the bathrooms at school. And Mary Jane, well, she has been hiding a growing pain-medication addiction since a traumatic car accident last year. She bounced back from the crash right away—or at least she pretended to—but the incident rattled loose a lot of bad memories, including a college sexual assault that she now tries to numb with opiates. The entire Healy household is as brittle as one made of gingerbread; one nudge, and the whole structure could collapse.

And yet Mary Jane glosses over these problems in her perky letter. She insists she has healed her body with miso and blueberries and a daily hot-yoga practice. But inside, she's aching. And the seams are starting to show. As Mary Jane sits on the couch and waxes about the family's "great" year, the *Jagged Little Pill* ensemble, who serve as the Greek chorus throughout the show, begin to swirl around her. The ensemble, as director Diane Paulus and Alanis Morissette conceived of it, would act as a kind of undulating subcon-

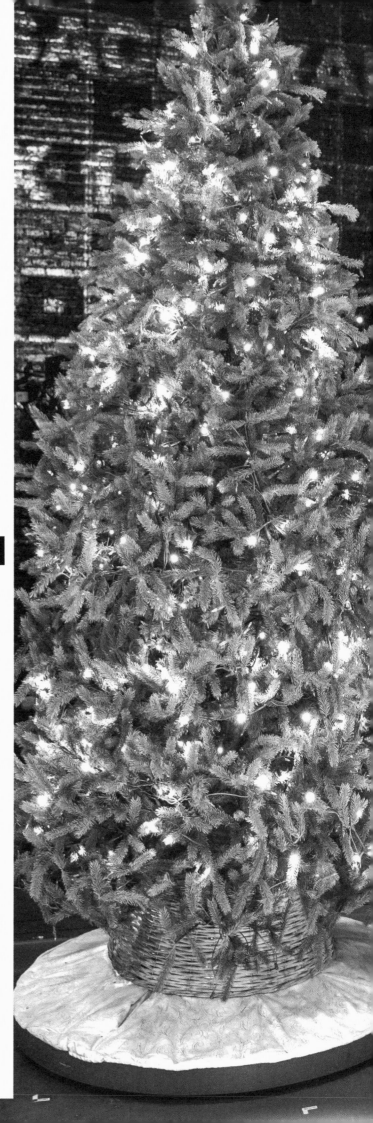

scious for the main characters as they grapple with their day-to-day difficulties. "Alanis was so into this idea of the chorus illuminating all the fractured cells of every character, the psyche of every character," Paulus says. So while Mary Jane claims everything is placid on the surface of her life, the chorus surrounds the sofa and sings the truth: "I see right through you."

"Right Through You," the fifth song on the original *Jagged Little Pill* album, was Morissette's not-so-subtle way of speaking to the predatory, misogynistic music executives she encountered in Canada as a teenage pop star. "You took me for a joke/You took me for a child," she sings. "You took a long, hard look at my ass/And then played golf for a while." It is an openly angry, growling song, as Morissette claims to see right through all of the men who want to infantilize her and capitalize on her talent. In an album full of so many emotions—bliss, humility, vengeance, acceptance, enlightenment, love—"Right Through You" is a song about seething, righteous anger. But it isn't just an angry song; it is deeply *funny* as well (it gave us the phrase "wine, dine, sixty-nine me," after all). Morissette took her exasperation with exploitative men and learned how to laugh in its face, and in doing so, she created an anthem for women everywhere who are fed up with the way they are being treated. "I walk right through you," Morissette wailed. And the rest of us learned how to keep going.

ACT 1 · SCENE 2

THE HEALY HOUSE (KITCHEN), MORNING

Mary Jane is fussing around at the kitchen table. Steve enters, dressed for work.

STEVE: Hey.

MARY JANE: Hi there.

Steve leans in to kiss Mary Jane. She recoils.

MARY JANE: I haven't brushed my teeth yet. You know I'm not a big morning kisser.

STEVE: You're not such a fan at night either. Is there a time slot that works for you?

Frankie enters, wearing denim cutoff shorts and holding a protest sign she made last night.

FRANKIE: Dad, you're home?

STEVE: I'm going in late today so we can celebrate Nick's acceptance.

Mary Jane holds up her phone to take a photo of the breakfast she's made.

MARY JANE: *(lightly)* What filter should I use for these pancakes? Hudson, Valencia...

FRANKIE: Suburban Despair?

Before Mary Jane can complain, Steve cuts her off (purposely) by greeting Nick as he enters the kitchen.

STEVE: *(interrupting)* Here he is! Our future Harvard grad.

NICK: You bought that shirt before you knew I got in?

STEVE: Well, you've never let us down before!

MARY JANE: I made pancakes! Don't worry—they're paleo; you can tell Coach we didn't cheat.

NICK: Thanks, Mom.

MARY JANE: I tried to write "Nick" on them in agave syrup but it looks more like...

FRANKIE: *(loudly reading over her shoulder)* "Dick."

MARY JANE: *(annoyed)* Okay, Frankie. Look, I know it's unseasonably warm for December but those shorts are a bit much.

FRANKIE: The Puritans are alive and well in Connecticut.

MARY JANE: *(to Frankie)* Whether you like it or not, how you present yourself to the world matters.

Nick and Steve realize a fight is brewing. This is a well-worn dynamic in the Healy family.

STEVE: MJ, please don't start. I'm missing work so we can have a nice breakfast.

FRANKIE: *(to Mary Jane)* You're obsessed with my shorts, but you haven't asked one question about the sign I made.

Frankie holds up her sign. It says "DOES MY PERIOD SCARE YOU?" in big letters.

STEVE: Does anyone want some more syrup?

FRANKIE: SMAAC is protesting today because we think the school should provide free tampons and pads for students.

MARY JANE: What's SMAAC?

NICK: The Social Movements and Advocacy Committee. Frankie just started it.

MARY JANE: You don't have to shock people to get attention. When I was in high school, my friends and I wanted to save endangered sea lions. So we made brownies and sold them on the quad! *(thinking)* Actually we made blondies.

FRANKIE: Of course they were blondies. Even your brownies are Caucasian.

MARY JANE: Why are you being so rude to me?

Frankie begins singing "ALL I REALLY WANT."

FRANKIE: *Do I stress you out?*

MARY JANE: Yes.

FRANKIE: *My sweater is on backwards and inside out*[1] */ And you say "how appropriate."*

NICK: She didn't mention your sweater...

MARY JANE: *I don't like to dissect everything today / I don't mean to pick you apart you see / But I can't help it*

STEVE: You said you were gonna try.

FRANKIE: *And there I go jumping before the gunshot has gone off / Slap me with a splintered ruler / And it would knock me to the floor if I wasn't there already / If only I could hunt the hunter*[2]

MARY JANE AND STEVE: *And all I really want is some patience / A way to calm my angry voice*

FRANKIE/CHORUS: *And all I really want is deliverance*

FRANKIE/MARY JANE: *Ah*

CHORUS: *Ah ah*

MARY JANE/CHORUS: *Do I*

FRANKIE/CHORUS: *Do I*

MARY JANE:
*Wear you out
You must wonder why I'm
relentless and all strung out
I'm consumed by the chill
of solitary*

Wear you out

CHORUS:
Ahh...

FRANKIE: *I'm like Estella*[3]
*I like to reel it in
And then spit it out
I'm frustrated by
    your apathy*

*I'm like Estella
I like to reel it in*

*Your apathy,
your apathy
Your apathy,
your apathy...*

*And I am frightened by
the corrupted ways of
this land
If only I could meet the maker
And I am fascinated by the
spiritual woman*

Ooh...

Ooh...

Ooh...

Ooh...

---

1 "I really did wear my sweaters backward and inside-out, but not intentionally or anything. I was just a happy little mess, completely disheveled, writing songs in Canada."

2 "This lyric is about empowerment in a world of sexual, emotional, and financial predation. 'Hunt the hunter' is me turning it around, saying, 'I know what your agenda is. I know your strategy. I know you want money from me. I know these [record] contracts are unconscionable. I wanted to turn the tables and just say, "You know what? I'm after you now."'"

3 "I was reading *Great Expectations* at the time, and I just really related to Estella. And *Wuthering Heights* and Kate Bush—I was just kind of obsessed with that haunted thing. I still am, actually."

All I Really Want

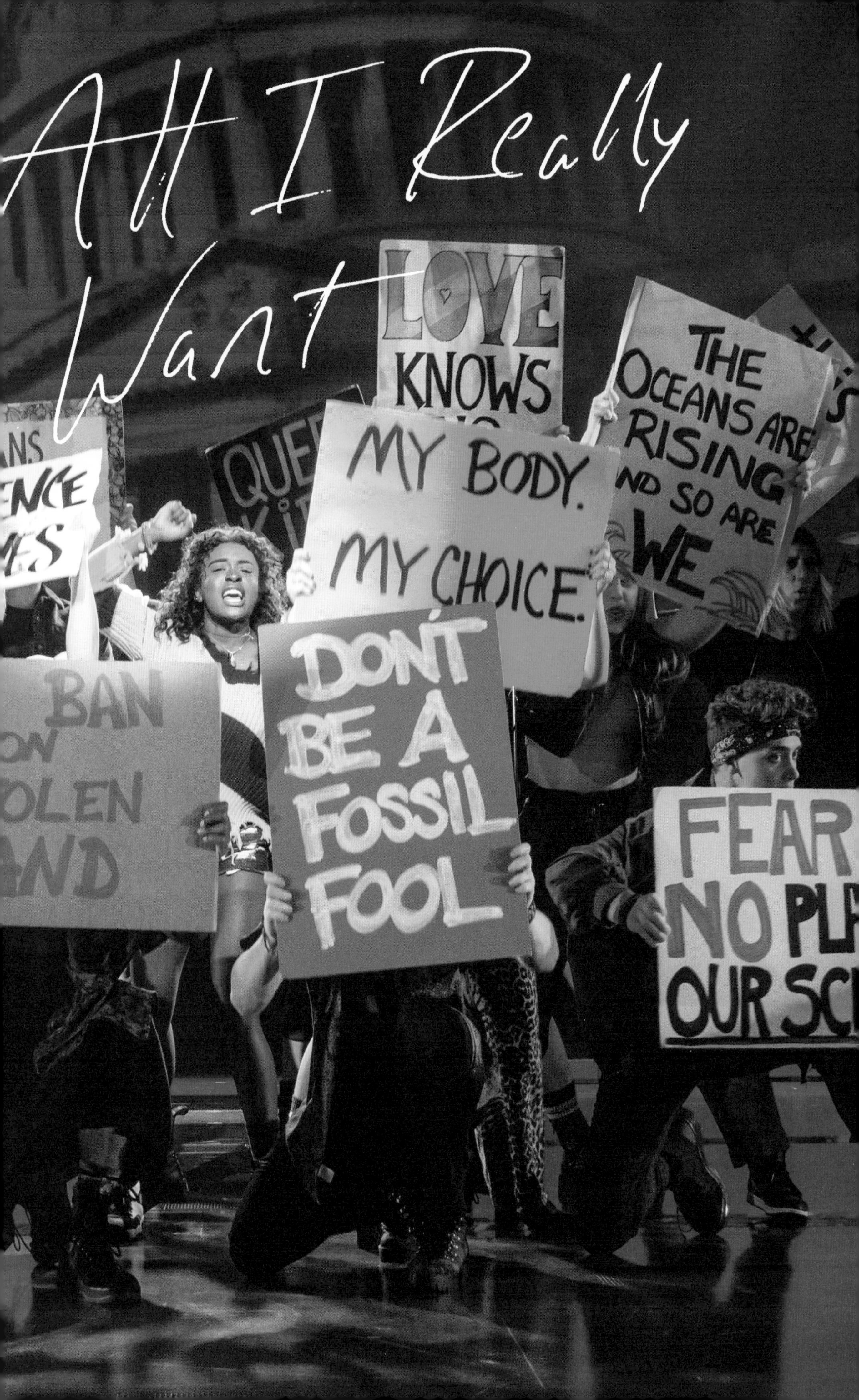

FRANKIE/CHORUS: *I'm humbled by her humble nature, yeah / And what I wouldn't give to find a soul mate / Someone else to catch this drift / And what I wouldn't give to meet a kindred*

MARY JANE/FRANKIE/NICK/STEVE/CHORUS: *Ahh...*

FRANKIE: *Enough about me, let's talk about you for a minute*

MARY JANE: *Enough about you, let's talk about life for a while*

FRANKIE: *The conflicts*

MARY JANE: *The craziness*

FRANKIE/CHORUS: *And the sound of pretenses falling / All around all around*

FRANKIE: *Why are you so petrified of silence*

Here, can you	**CHORUS:**
handle this	*Ahh...*
Did you think about	
Your bills, your pills	*Bills, pills*
Your deadlines	*Deadlines*
Or when you think	
you're gonna die	*You're gonna die*
Or did you long for	
the next distraction	*Mmm...*
And all I need now is	*Di-dip dip...oh...*
Intellectual intercourse	
A soul to dig the hole much deeper	

STEVE: *And I have no concept of time other than it is flying*

CHORUS: *If only I could kill the killer / Ahh...*

NICK: *And all I really want is some peace, man / A place to find some common ground*

FRANKIE: *And all I really want is a wavelength, ah*

MARY JANE:	**CHORUS:**
And all I really want	*Oh*
Is some comfort	*Oh*
A way to get my hands untied	*Oh*

FRANKIE:	*Oh*
And all I really want is some justice, ah	

MARY JANE: *Ahh...* **FRANKIE:** *Ahh...* **CHORUS:** *Oh Oh Oh*

MARY JANE: *Ahh / And all I really want is some patience / A way to calm me down*

During the above, Mary Jane has dropped her pills. Steve retrieves them from the floor and hands them to her.

FRANKIE: *And all I really want is deliverance, a way to find some common ground*

	MARY JANE:
	Common
FRANKIE: *Ground*	*Ground*

Guitar wah wah

June 13, 1995

JAGGED LITTLE PILL - LYRICS

— poetic female rage

— SPIRITUAL LONGING —

— female call to arms

ALL I REALLY WANT

Do I stress you out
My sweater is on backwards and inside out
And you say "how appropriate"
I don't want to dissect everything today
I don't mean to pick you apart you see
But I can't help it

And there I go jumping before the gunshot has gone off
Slap me with a splintered ruler
And it would knock me to the floor if I wasn't there already
If only I could hunt the hunter

And all I really want is some patience
A way to calm the angry voice
And all I really want is deliverance
Ah, aao, aao, aao, aa, aah

Do I wear you out
You must wonder why I'm so relentless and all strung out
I'm consumed by the chill of solitary
I'm like Estella
I like to reel it in and then spit it out
I'm frustrated by your apathy

(Charles Dickens' Great Expectations)

And I am frightened by the corrupted ways of this land
If only I could meet the Maker
And I am fascinated by the spiritual man
I am humbled by his humble nature, yeah

And what I wouldn't give to find a soulmate
Someone else to catch this drift
And what I wouldn't give to meet a kindred
Ah, aao, aao, aao, aa, aah

(harmonica)

Enough about me, let's talk about you for a minute
Enough about you, let's talk about life for a while
The conflicts, the craziness and the sound of pretenses
Falling all around...all around

Why are you so petrified of silence

YEARNINGS EXPRESSED

"All I Really Want" is the first song on *Jagged Little Pill*, but it was the last song that Morissette wrote for the album. She was in the studio writing the song, in fact, when Guy Oseary, a 23-year-old A&R executive with an ear for new talent at Maverick Records, called her and said that he wanted to meet her that afternoon. At first, she told him that she could not go—she was in sweatpants and had dirty hair after spending hours in Glen Ballard's studio. Still, the label told her to come in so she wouldn't miss her window, and the meeting—which she went to in her sweatpants—ended up changing her life. Oseary heard "You Oughta Know," "Perfect," and "Hand in My Pocket," and told Morissette and Ballard that he wanted to sign her on the spot.

where." More than a dozen labels passed on the chance to release *Jagged Little Pill* before Oseary heard the demos.

"All I Really Want" opens with a growling, fierce harmonica riff and sets the tone, both aurally and lyrically, for the rest of the album. It is a song of *yearning* for connection, a song about wanting to be seen, heard, and understood. "There are masculine yearnings and feminine yearnings, righteous yearnings and just really simple yearnings," Morissette says. In 1995, it was revelatory to hear a young woman singing openly and directly about what she wants—and in many ways, it still is. Morissette decided to lead the record with the song because, as she said in one interview in 2015, "It was a tying of the bow, it was an encapsulation and a big summary of everything that had been the experience of writing *Jagged Little Pill*. It was the perfect introduction for what was to come."

For the Healys, the song—the first one they all sing together to kick off the show—serves as a vibrant, jolting illustration of all the tensions and frustrations that run through the family at the start of the show. From the moment Frankie Healy sings "Do I stress you out?" to her mother over a paleo pancake breakfast, the song becomes a flurry of cross talk and competing desires. Mary Jane, who is hiding her addictions and traumatic memories from her husband and children, compensates for her pain by nitpicking at her daughter and overexaggerating the celebration of Nick's Harvard acceptance. Nick, who should be thrilled to be heading to the Ivy League, wakes up feeling numb and exhausted by his family's bickering. He sings, "All I really want is some peace, man/A place to find a common ground." Steve, who cannot even get a kiss from his wife on what should be a happy morning, sings, "All I really want is some patience."

Meanwhile, Frankie and Mary Jane rage at each other throughout the song. Frankie screams for comprehension: she just wants someone to realize that she doesn't fit in and that she is fighting for others like herself. The Greek chorus swirling around her suddenly leaps into her mind and dances out her imaginary visions; she sees a world where she is leading a righteous protest against injustice and can be a "spiritual woman." (On changing the lyric "I am fascinated by the spiritual man" to "spiritual woman" for the show, Morissette says, "I have a lot of different women spiritual teachers. Women are just born connected to spirit. We don't even have to try.")

Mary Jane, on the other hand, is screaming internally for someone, anyone, to understand what she is going through. "All I really want," she belts at the end of the song, "is some comfort." She cannot yet admit what she wants comfort for—to recover from an assault that happened to her years ago, to get help with her addiction—but she knows she needs to reach out for her family and find that she has a soft place to land.

"All I Really Want" cleverly serves as the musical's "I Want" song—a trope in which the lead characters lay out their hopes and dreams at the start of the show—and also as a broader mission

This page and opposite: These are excerpts taken from director Diane Paulus's pre-production notebook. Similar notes appear later in this book.

Jagged Little Pill went on to be one of the best-selling albums of all time, but that success was not a given when Oseary agreed to release the record. He was taking a huge chance on an untested artist (at least outside of Canada's niche pop-music scene)—and was one of the only producers in Los Angeles to do so. About halfway through the writing process, Morissette and Ballard started shopping the record, and, according to Morissette, "It was just rejected every-

statement for Morissette's music in general. She *wants* to say the things that usually remain unsaid, she *wants* everyone to speak their mind, she *wants* everyone to hear others and feel truly heard. When she sings, "Here, can you handle this?" and the music drops out, she's really asking universal questions: Can you sit with your wants and needs? Can you communicate them to others? And if you did, could it, ever so slightly, shift the world?

AT HOME WITH THE HEALYS

In February 2019, the Healy family—Frankie (Celia Rose Gooding), Nick (Derek Klena), Steve (Sean Allan Krill), and Mary Jane (Elizabeth Stanley)—met in the velvet seats of the Broadhurst Theatre to discuss "All I Really Want" and what it meant to them to become a family throughout the making of *Jagged Little Pill*.

with. Putting her energy into these other three people is kind of a distraction.

CELIA ROSE GOODING: I think that Frankie is aware that she is just living her truth, but it rubs her entire family the wrong way. I think she is at this point where she's sort of just like, "If it's going to bother you, fine. I'm going to do what I want because I am an independent, grown woman, and I can do what I want at the age of sixteen." And even though the Healy life for Frankie has always been very Nick-centered, with Nick getting into this incredible school, it is just another thing that makes Frankie feel isolated—and when she feels isolated, she lashes out. So Frankie is constantly working in the place of, "See me as who I am and not as what you want me to be."

DEREK KLENA: The first time we really see Nick, he's having the experience that his entire family and he has worked for his entire life. So you're kind of seeing him at the peak. And then from that peak, he's at that crossroads between

"All I Really Want" is the first song you all sing together as a family in the show, as you are sitting down at a celebratory breakfast for Nick getting into Harvard. What do you think your characters are feeling at the start of the show, during this scene?

ELIZABETH STANLEY: Mary Jane is very much in survival mode, but she is high functioning. She's still fooling herself that everything is just fine and really perfect and totally great. I think Frankie is behaving in a way that is usual and which she finds frustrating, but it's not anything new. And she really wants to celebrate Nick and this big, exciting accomplishment of getting accepted into Harvard. Steve, well, she just finds it kind of annoying that at breakfast he brings up their sex life.... I think every day, Mary Jane is quite consumed with her addiction, and so that's kind of the over-riding thing that she's actually thinking about and dealing

adolescence and young adulthood and finding out, "This is the person that I was built to be and conditioned to be. Is this somebody that I want to continue being for the rest of my life, and am I satisfied with the product?" And as Nick starts to see his family and his friends and the world around them celebrate this supposed prize, there's that feeling of emptiness that he's starting to realize comes with that success.

SEAN ALLAN KRILL: You meet this family in crisis. Almost a year earlier, there was Mary Jane's car accident. And I think what's happened is that Steve's in a little bit of a renaissance, like he's woken up a little bit because he was shaken awake by that. He's looking at his family going, "Wow, this isn't right. Something's wrong. What is it?" So he's reaching out.

You have to show this family at its optimal state before we start to see the slow and steady decline, and then the inevitable destruction, and then rebuilding at the end of the show. So it's kind of a tricky tightrope walk we all go on at the beginning of this show before giving too much too soon.

You all get to sing different lines about what you "really want" during the number. What do those lyrics mean to you?

KLENA: My line, Nick's line, in "All I Really Want" is, "All I really want is some peace, man/A place to find a common ground," and it's kind of Nick in a nutshell. I mean, his first instinct is to be the peacekeeper and the Mr. Fix It and to put other people's needs and wants over his own. He kind of acts like the go-to person while Steve is at work most days, and he becomes a surrogate parent in that way. Nick has the answer. Nick will figure it out.

KRILL: Mine is, "All I really want is some patience, a way to calm my angry voice," and then later I say, "I have no concept of time other than it is flying." Steve is reaching out, he's saying, "Can we go to this counselor? What's wrong?" I've always thought it was so interesting that that's what Diablo Cody wrote, is that Steve's the one who's always saying, "Can we try to communicate?"

STANLEY: I sing a few different "I want" lines, but the one that I love probably the best is, "All I really want is some comfort, a way to get my hands untied." For so many of us in the world, our biggest flaw is that when we're comfortable, we're just not motivated to do things to help other people or to help ourselves or to change. And so there's something that's kind of gross about that line. "All I really want is to be

> ## "See me as who I am and not as what you want me to be."
> ### —CELIA ROSE GOODING

comfortable," basically. But then there's also the other side of it, which is, "All I really want is some comfort, a way to get my hands untied." She needs these pills to make her feel functional and OK and fine, and her hands are kind of tied because she can't get out of the situation she's in.

GOODING: My favorite line I sing is, "All I really want is some justice," because for Frankie, justice means so many things. But I think the one that hits hardest for her is justice for herself. Frankie feels that she's being treated unjustly in this community and this family, in this town that she's living in. And all she really wants is justice and fairness and to be delivered to another place in which she can be herself, really.

You have to become a family quickly in the show. After this scene, your story lines all burst apart and you don't all come back together until the end. What discussions did you have throughout the show's development to help you bond as the Healy family unit? What did you discuss about your backstories?

GOODING: We talked a lot about Frankie's adoption, about it being a closed adoption. We decided that when she was really young, MJ and Frankie were super close. She was very much mommy's little girl. And then Frankie became aware of her place in this world, and things started to crumble and fall apart, because there are clear differences between the two of them, and Frankie doesn't have anyone she can go to and say, "What does it mean to be a black woman in

Connecticut?" And so there's angst that builds up with that. Frankie's always looked up to Nick, but in a way, well for Frankie, she's looking up to Nick because she desperately wants to be looked at the same way. Everything that's great with Nick is everything that's wrong with Frankie.

KLENA: I do feel like Frankie and Nick have a closeness. We're buds.

KRILL: Yeah, we talked a little bit about how Frankie would be daddy's little girl and Nick would be mama's boy. But then, ultimately, Steve becomes more and more absent. So anything to do with the kids falls on Mary Jane.

STANLEY: And we talked about how MJ and Steve would have met in our later college years. And I think it was a good relationship when it began. And I think it was very picture-perfect, Barbie and Ken.

How has this song, which is so much about communication, helped you learn how to communicate better in your own lives?

GOODING: For me, I have learned to ask the uncomfortable questions, especially with my family. And I think a lot of what I've learned is speaking on what you feel and not speaking on what someone else has done to you and saying, "You have done this, and that was wrong." It's saying, "I feel this way, please act accordingly." And so yeah, *Jagged Little Pill* has been super helpful with speaking from the "I" instead of labeling what others have done and then saying, "That's why I feel that way, because you did this." No, it's action, response, reaction.

KLENA: I think that's kind of been a fun thing when you have family and friends that come to see your show. Usually people are so congratulatory and are just so excited to be seeing someone they know on Broadway and on this epic stage. But it hasn't really been that celebratory experience after the show. People are dazed and confused, in a state of constant thought and processing that lets me know that our show is impacting people on a deep level. And having a way of encouraging that self-reflection and communication that we hope for.

STANLEY: This is not about my family, but one friend said after she saw the show, "You know, I've talked to my daughter, who's a teenager, about sex, but I haven't talked to her about my past sexual experiences. And I wonder if I should do that." And my first reaction was, "Well, no." And then I was like, "Actually, maybe that's helpful because not every single one of them was a perfectly positive experience." Of course, as you're figuring it out!

KLENA: I love that, because I think it also kind of instills a sense of trust between parent and child, saying, "I'm entrusting you with this information, and I'm setting this kind of open playing field of open discussion between you and I" by a parent initiating that.

KRILL: One true thing about me is that I've never, ever had a problem communicating my feelings. I wear my heart on my sleeve and I'm an open book, but I think the thing that the show has taught me is, really thinking about it, that I'm not always a good *listener*, and listening is such an important part of communication. It isn't just two people talking at each other, and that's what I'm trying to work on now.

ACT 1 · SCENE 3

HIGH SCHOOL CLASSROOM

As Frankie walks into the classroom, Nick is joined by his friend BELLA.

BELLA: That is the world's most depressing bell.

NICK: Sounds like an Amber Alert.

BELLA: Hey—congrats on Harvard!

NICK: Thanks, Bella.

BELLA: At least one of us is going places...

NICK: What are you talking about? You're getting into that art school.

Nick's best friend ANDREW walks up to them...

ANDREW: Healy, your mom must be losing her mind! Are you gonna celebrate at Lancer's party tonight?

BELLA: *(to Nick)* I get off my shift at nine, but I'm coming right after.

NICK: *(to Andrew)* We have practice in the morning. You want to swim 200s with a hangover?

ANDREW: It's at 5 AM. We'll still be drunk!

Nick, Bella, and Andrew exit. Frankie is in a high school classroom.

FRANKIE: Anyone want to stay for the meeting? All are welcome!

DAVID/KELSEY: *(ad-libs)* Definitely. / I gotta go.

LANCER: *(exiting)* I have church.

Students exit. Frankie is greeted by Jo, who also carries a POSTER. It says "Let My People Flow."

JO: Packed house today.

FRANKIE: We'll get some members eventually.

JO: You look like the beginning of a Zoloft commercial.

FRANKIE: I got in yet another fight with Mary Jane. She's the literal worst.

JO: No way, your mom is iconic! She's one salad away from a psychotic break. I live for it.

FRANKIE: It's funny to you, because you don't have to cohabit with the woman. The second I came down to breakfast she's started complaining about my shorts. It's 68 degrees in December. Might as well enjoy the climate emergency!

JO: Look, it could be worse. Your mom just yells at you. Mine prays for me:

(imitating) "Dear Jesus, please don't let my only child be a gay. Especially not one of those obvious gays who wears performance fleece and utility sandals. In the name of Fox News, Amen."

FRANKIE: She's still giving you shit about your clothes?

JO: Oh yeah, the queer panic is at an all-time high. She's like "Why would you choose to look like a boy?" And I'm like "Why would *you* choose to look like the Talbot's catalog threw up on you?"

FRANKIE: I'm sorry you're dealing with that, Jo.

JO: I don't care. I've been out of fucks to give since the early two-thousands.

Jo begins singing "HAND IN MY POCKET."

Hand in My Pocket

JO: *I'm broke but I'm happy, I'm poor but I'm kind / I'm short but I'm healthy, yeah / I'm high but I'm grounded, I'm sane but I'm overwhelmed / I'm lost but I'm hopeful, baby / And what it all comes down to / Is that everything's gonna be fine, fine, fine / 'Cause I've got one hand in my pocket*[1] */ And the other one is giving a high five*

They high five. Popular girl LILY FISHER passes through and casually touches Frankie's hair.

LILY FISHER: Oh, is this new?

FRANKIE: *Really?*

JO: *Don't touch her hair?*

LILY FISHER: I was being nice, G.I. Jo.

JO: That's funny, Legally Bland.

JO: *I feel drunk but I'm sober, I'm young and mis-understood / I'm tired but I'm working, yeah / I care but I'm restless, I'm here but I'm really gone / I'm right and I'm sorry, baby / And what it all comes down to / Is that everything's gonna be quite alright / 'Cause I've got one hand in my pocket / And the other one is flicking a cigarette / And what it all comes down to / Is that I haven't got it all figured out just yet / But I've got one hand in my pocket / And the other one is giving a peace sign*

FRANKIE: A peace sign? What year is this?

JO: We need it now more than ever, baby.

JO: *I'm free but I'm focused, I'm green but I'm wise / I'm hard but I'm friendly, baby / I'm sad but I'm laughing, I'm brave but I'm chicken shit / I'm sick but I'm pretty, baby*[2]

Frankie joins in as they harmonize.

FRANKIE AND JO: *And what it all boils down to / Is that no one's really got it figured out just yet*[3]

JO:	**FRANKIE:**
But I've got one hand in my pocket	*One hand in my pocket*
And the other one is playing the piano	*Piano*

FRANKIE AND JO: *And what it all comes down to, my friends, yeah / Is that everything is just fine, fine, fine / 'Cause I've got one hand in my pocket / And the other one is hailing—*[4]

They're interrupted by the bell. They groan:

FRANKIE AND JO: Shit...

JO: The bell can blow me.

They hurry off to class.

---

2 "Something's unfinished if it's just one part of the duality. If I say that I'm a cranky, hormonal bitch, it's unfinished until I also say that I am a warrior who's transcending hormonal, chemical challenges, and I'm really showing up."

3 Says music arranger Tom Kitt, "The song's duality is enhanced and intensified with the switch to a duet between the characters." Kitt refers to the vocal arrangement as a "car harmony," saying it's a rather simple layer, like one you might add to a song on the radio when you're singing along while driving your car.

4 "I wrote all the lyrics for 'Hand in My Pocket' in sixty seconds. Glen and I wrote the entire song in ten minutes. Sometimes people ask me how long it takes to write a song. And I'll say, 'Well, forty-five years to live it, and then ten minutes to write it.'"

---

1 "Before the Maverick producers signed me to a contract to make *Jagged Little Pill*, they wanted to make sure I could perform live. I sang this song for a group of them in a tiny four-hundred-square-foot studio. It was really awkward! But at the end of the meeting, they were like, 'OK, she can sing live, we're good,' and signed me."

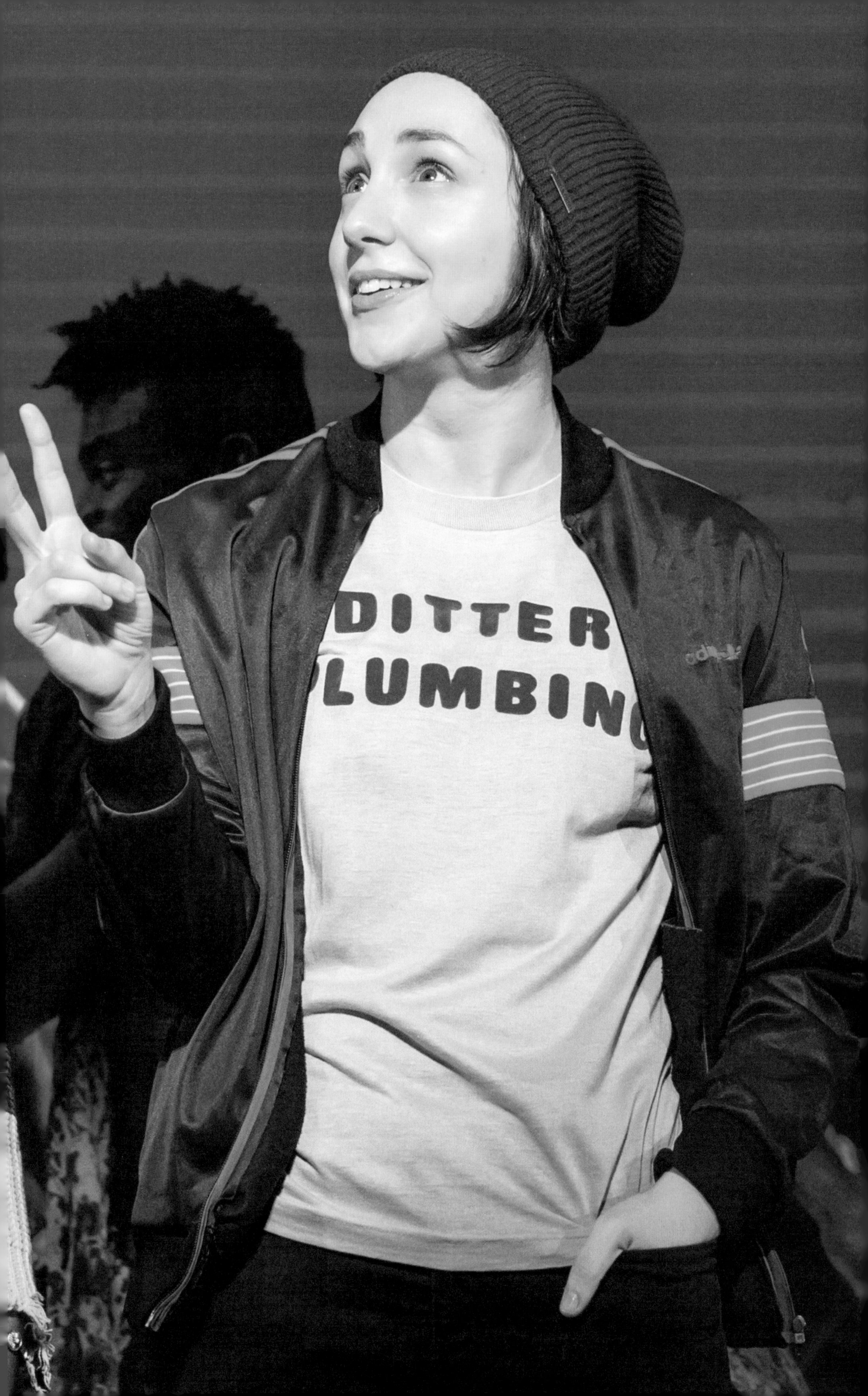
DITTER
LUMBIN

"I'm broke
but I'm happy."

"I'm poor
but I'm kind."

"I'm high
but I'm grounded."

"HAND IN MY POCKET":

DUALITY

"Hand in My Pocket," the fourth song on *Jagged Little Pill* and the second single to be released from the album, is a song about opposing forces. "I'm broke but I'm happy," Morissette sings. "I'm poor but I'm kind/I'm short but I'm healthy, yeah." Morissette, who was only nineteen at the time she wrote those lyrics in 1994, wanted to write an anthem for the youth of Generation X, who were labeled from the outside as "slackers" and "burnouts" by their elders, who saw a sea of flannel and ennui and decided that the kids were simply not alright. But what Morissette wanted to stress about her peers was that they contain multitudes and unknown depths; even if they seemed to be floating through life, they were roiling underneath the surface. People are kaleidoscopic and unpredictable. They can be sane but overwhelmed, lost but hopeful. They can use one hand to play a piano and the other to hold themselves steady. "Hand in My Pocket," from that first trademark harmonica lick, is a hopeful song; it says that it is OK to feel conflicted or torn apart or even exhausted. It's OK to not have it all figured out just yet. It says everything is going to be fine, even when the world is confusing and unpredictable. All we have to get through it are our own two hands, and they are capable of doing so much.

In the Broadway show, "Hand in My Pocket" comes early in the first act, as Frankie (Celia Rose Gooding) and her girlfriend, Jo (Lauren Patten), hold a meeting for their activist club at school between classes (as it turns out, they are the only two members). Frankie laments her mother's controlling, nitpicking ways and says she fears that as a black queer woman, she will never fit in easily with her clean-cut, white-as-milk family. Jo feels similarly displaced. "It could be worse," she tells Frankie. "Your mom just yells at you. Mine prays for me." Her Fox News–watching, pearl-clutching mother insists that Jo go to church socials to try to "pray the gay away." She makes Jo, who prefers to wear track jackets and slouchy beanies, wriggle into a scratchy hot-pink cardigan that makes Jo feel so uncomfortable in her own body, she begins to shake. Both Frankie and Jo have real problems, real conflicts.

And even though they are still young, they already know what it is like to feel isolated and anxious, out of step with the world around them. But they do have each other. And through each other, they have access to joy.

In the context of the show, "Hand in My Pocket," takes on a new resonance; the struggles that Morissette felt as a member of Gen X still apply to the young people of Gen Z. Young people still feel misunderstood and yet optimistic, terrified and yet attuned and alive. If anything, the song feels deeply prescient for this time, like a message in a bottle sent from twenty-five years ago to remind us that we are not alone in feeling adrift. Lyrics like "I'm young and I'm underpaid," and "I'm tired but I'm working," apply more than ever in a world where young people like Frankie and Jo will graduate into one of the most extreme recessions the country has ever seen. No one knows the future now, and all we have to hold on to is the knowledge that those before us had no clue what was to come and kept going anyway. When Jo grabs Frankie's hand and starts singing, it feels like an invitation to let go, to cut each other a little bit of slack. They both begin to dance, first in an imaginary rock concert and then, with the full chorus, in a rousing step number—Sidi Larbi Cherkaoui, the choreographer, said he put in stepping because he wanted a style that would allow the dancers to make noise with claps and slaps, emphasizing the theme of hands running throughout the song. There is a newfound exuberance to the number in the show. Whereas the original music video for the song was understated, as Morissette stood on a crowded Brooklyn street in black and white and let the world pass her by while she sang calmly about all the different aspects of her complex and ever-changing self, now Frankie and Jo turn their complexity into the street party itself.

"I think it's one of the most joyful moments of the show," says Patten. "It's sort of Jo's philosophy. I think that everybody is this or that. And I think that perhaps in our generation, we might just be more open about it and more accepting. Our joy is complicated. It is a joy that doesn't come wrapped up in a bow."

> "Young people still feel misunderstood and yet optimistic, terrified and yet attuned and alive."

FACING THE FACTS

LGBTQ IDENTITY

LGBTQ stands for lesbian, gay, bisexual, transgender, and queer or questioning. Many other identities fall under the LGBTQ umbrella that are not specifically referenced in the acronym, including nonbinary, asexual, genderqueer, intersex, and more.

"Over the past two decades, Americans have experienced a significant evolution in their understanding and cultural acceptance of LGBTQ people" according to media-monitoring organization GLAAD. Marriage equality has become the law of the land, and media portrayals of LGBTQ people have gone from running jokes to fully formed characters on scripted and reality series.

Unfortunately, many LGBTQ people, especially LGBTQ youth, still experience considerable levels of both overt and covert discrimination, which can lead to much higher rates of depression, anxiety, alcohol and drug use, and lower self-esteem compared to their non-LGBTQ peers, according to the Human Rights Campaign (HRC).

In June 2019, the world marked the fiftieth anniversary of the Stonewall Riots, which took place in New York City's Greenwich Village in 1969. All across the country, people celebrated in parades and marches and gathered in greater numbers than ever before to show their pride. Sadly, during this period there was a spike in violence against LGBTQ people, according to a report by the National Coalition of Anti-Violence Programs (NCAVP). In the two months around the Stonewall anniversary, there were 10 hate-related murders of LGBTQ people and the majority of those were Black trans women.

LGBTQ youth living with homophobic and transphobic relatives have even higher rates of stress and depression, leaving them at greater risk for substance abuse. In many cases, "their fear of rejection is compounded by the negative comments they hear about the LGBTQ community from their parents or family members," says HRC.

LGBTQ youth of color can face an extraordinary amount of bullying, harassment, and bias because, in addition to homophobia or transphobia, they may also experience racism. Studies show that this compounds their feelings of isolation and lack of belonging.

Additionally, LGBTQ youth are more likely to be homeless, in foster care, and in the juvenile justice system. According to True Colors United, 40 percent of the 1.6 million youth experiencing homelessness identify as LGBTQ. Accepting families, however, can lead to greater self-esteem, well-being, and resilience among LGBTQ youth, lowering their risk of adverse health effects.

SINGING WITH THE BODY

Sidi Larbi Cherkaoui served as the movement director and choreographer on *Jagged Little Pill*. Cherkaoui creates dances for companies and artists including Beyoncé, Cirque du Soleil, Joe Wright, Cedar Lake Contemporary Ballet, Pilobolus, Benjamin Millepied's L.A. Dance Project, and Martha Graham Dance Company. He has received ballet commissions from Paris Opera Ballet, Les Ballets de Monte-Carlo, and the Royal Ballet in London. Cherkaoui is the artistic director of the Royal Ballet of Flanders and his own company, Eastman.

Was Jagged Little Pill **an important album in your youth?**
Yes, it was. Alanis is two or three years older than I am. It was something none of us had heard before. I was living in Hoboken in Belgium, a suburb of Antwerp. And I was impressed by the power and the range of her voice. She was wild, but she also knew exactly what she was doing. And if it was angry, it was relatable. I had just come out of a personal situation with a boyfriend, and I could really relate to "You Oughta Know," which is a love song, in a way.

Tell me a bit about your background in dance.
I was always influenced by pop artists, like Kate Bush or Madonna, Janet Jackson, Michael Jackson, anything where there was choreography involved. I used to learn every single choreography on television. I would tape it on VHS and then just keep practicing. I only started formal training at seventeen.

For my parents, it was just not in their cards to be thinking that their youngest son would go into the arts. People are very good at discouraging, by saying, "Yeah, you started too late, you're not going to make it. You're not that special." But then at the same time, there was something very small, a little deeper that just knew like, I don't give a fuck. I'm going to do what I do. And I knew deep down that I wanted to be an artist. I felt like I wanted to express myself, I wanted to liberate myself. I knew I was gay since I was eight. It took me up until I was seventeen to dare to come out.

I did one very important contest, which was the Best Belgian Dance Solo. It's like winning *So You Think You Can Dance,* but in Belgium. So that opened a lot of doors. I went to study in P.A.R.T.S., which is a contemporary dance school in Brussels. That's when I decided to make a career in contemporary dance.

There is so much contemporary dance in this show—a lot of free-form, experimental movement. It's different from what a lot of Broadway actors are used to. How did you get the actors to be comfortable with your style of dance?
I remember Lauren Patten got quite emotional about it, because she said, "I've done the dance classes and stuff," but she never felt like it was actually allowing her to tap into a place where she felt really at ease with the choreography. On the contrary, it always felt a little bit oppressive. And I realized, it is kind of paradoxical when you think about how free they are when they're singing. They have found their voice, and when they sing it's not constrained. It's free. And I was like, your movement can be like your singing. You can literally just listen to your body react. Let it happen. It sounds so corny and easy, but it's the hardest thing because you don't know what's going to come out so you're not in control.

I love that the choreography for "Hand in My Pocket" feels so free—it veers from a rock concert to stepping to a full-on party.
It's kind of like a queer fantasy in a very, very straight world.

I know you, Diane Paulus, and Alanis worked hard to develop this idea of "doubles"—every main character has a dancer that acts as a kind of id. This is especially powerful in the song "Uninvited," when Elizabeth Stanley dances on a couch with her double Heather Lang, who represents her alter ego as she is experiencing an opioid overdose.

> ## "It's kind of like a queer fantasy in a very, very straight world."

We discovered that in the room. It just appeared to us, it demanded itself. Right away, I had that idea of a person fighting herself. It's like a conversation with yourself that you always lose. She's seeing herself on the sofa, but she's having an out-of-body experience. So she's trying to pretend it's just her mind playing tricks on her. And then slowly she's praying, let's hope this goes away. Then it's still there, and she's trying to reach it, but it's like a mirror. She's reaching; she sees it coming back to herself. I said to Heather always, "You are the real one, and you are not her demon. She's yours. Actually, you think she's the one who's not real."

During the dance for "Predator," you have Lang also serve as Bella's double and show Bella's sexual assault happening during a very intense dance sequence. How did you approach showing something traumatic like that through the medium of dance?

As a kid I saw a lot of physical realities, people with each other in places that were comfortable or uncomfortable, where it felt like a form of psychological abuse. So there's a lot in my personal life that I can tap into. It wasn't like I was dabbling. It was in my body. Abuse was something that had happened in my own family. But if Diablo Cody doesn't shy away from speaking about it, I shouldn't shy away from choreographing it.

You came up with a truly creepy, reptilian movement for Andrew, the rapist, to have during the assault scene.

I imagined a cockroach coming from the wall onto your bed. The idea that there is something that you don't want, like a spider in a web. There's a spider coming at you to eat you alive. That was the image I had, and having him crawl to her rather than just walk to her, felt right.

Did you consult with Alanis about movement? She has such a specific way of moving her own body.

When she describes movement, she has a million words for it. There's so much imagery in her. Words just keep pouring out. And she has a very open mind. There's no boundaries there. She likes to dance, it's clear. You'll see it in those videos. She really threw her whole body into the singing.

ACT 1 · SCENE 4

Mary Jane, in her signature "athleisure" garb, walks up to a pharmacy counter. The PHARMACIST knows her well.

MARY JANE: *(cheerful)* Hello! Refill for Healy?

PHARMACIST: Yes. I know. Good afternoon, Mrs. Healy.

MARY JANE: How are you? You know, I just love coming in here. I'm so glad I switched to a family-owned pharmacy. So much of small town America is disappearing and being replaced by big box stores and impersonal service. That's why I stopped going to Care-Rite; they just—

PHARMACIST: I can't give you a refill.

MARY JANE: Excuse me? I called earlier.

PHARMACIST: *(sighing)* We can't refill a Schedule II drug. We need a new prescription each time.

MARY JANE: Right, I know. Well, I have a different doctor since last time. Did you call Dr. Choudry or Dr. Maspeth? I stopped going to Dr. Choudry but the number might still be—

PHARMACIST: *(interrupting)* I spoke to your new doctor.

MARY JANE: Oh, wow, well, there's definitely a mix-up there. I'll call her ASAP. In the meantime, you can just do the one refill. That'll be fine.

PHARMACIST: As I said, you need a new prescription. I'm sorry. It's the law.

MARY JANE: I know this has become a big problem for you guys. I get it. But I'm just a mom recovering from a car accident. I'm in pain. Can you try my doctor again? *(She stares at the pharmacist in desperation. It's not going to work.)* I'm taking my business back to Care-Rite.

She storms out of the store. As she walks down the street, pulling her phone out of her bag, she passes a COFFEE SHOP. In the coffee shop, JILL, COURTNEY, and DENISE—three of Mary Jane's mom "frenemies"—chat.

JILL: ...so she's boasting that her kids are bilingual and I'm like, okay, they learned Spanish from your *nanny*...

COURTNEY: ...It's kind of not something to brag about?

DENISE: God, this warm weather is so amazing. It almost makes me want to open the pool.

They notice Mary Jane approaching. Jill smirks.

JILL: *(to the other moms)* There's Little Miss Sunshine. *(hails her, waving)* MJ! Hey! Come in!

MARY JANE: I'm in a rush...

JILL: Just for a sec! We have to talk about your superstar son!

Mary Jane reluctantly enters the coffee shop. Courtney greets her in a sing-song.

COURTNEY: We didn't get a chance to talk, you ran right out of Soul Cycle!

MARY JANE: How are you, Courtney? *(acknowledging)* Jill. Denise.

BARISTA: Can I start a drink for somebody?

JILL: *(brusque)* I'll have a skinny flat white.

BARISTA: *(to herself)* How appropriate.

COURTNEY: We all saw your post about Nick's acceptance! Congrats!

JILL: You'll have to tell me your secret—we start the whole college thing with Jace next year.

MARY JANE: Well, you'd have to ask my son. He did it all himself.

DENISE: MJ, you have to give yourself some credit. We all know you're "Super Mom."

COURTNEY: Nick didn't drive himself to those cello lessons...

DENISE: Or pay for the S.A.T. tutor...

MARY JANE: He didn't need a tutor. He just took a class.

JILL: *(tiger mom)* What class? What was the name of the class?!

COURTNEY: *(to Mary Jane)* Are you okay, hon? Your eyes look glassy.

MARY JANE: I'm fine. It was just a tough workout.

DENISE: Hip Hop Friday is a killer!

DENISE/JILL/COURTNEY: I feel so fat. / Totally. / Tough ride!

BARISTA: Would anyone like a pastry?

ALL THREE MOMS: *(in unison)* NO.

DENISE: Is Frankie looking at colleges yet? You know, she'll have a real advantage when she applies.

MARY JANE: *(knowing full well)* Oh, are you referring to the poetry award she won? Her hundreds of hours of volunteer work?

DENISE: And that's all great, but you know, she also has the *diversity* edge? My cousin's daughter is only half Mexican and she got into Brown. So someone like *Frankie,* she could get into...

MARY JANE: Extra Brown?

DENISE: *(laughing uncomfortably)* You're so funny, MJ.

MARY JANE: I live to entertain you, Denise. So, Jill, where is Jace planning to apply?

JILL: Well, his top choice is Princeton, but—

MARY JANE: *(interrupting)* Oh, that's a nice school. That was Nick's safety! See you guys later.

Mary Jane won that round. She exits as quickly as possible. Finally free, she walks away.

MARY JANE: *(to herself)* This isn't a big deal. I'll just shoot him a text. *(texting)* "Are you in town?"

She waits for a torturous beat or two. Blessedly, her text is returned.

MARY JANE: *(relieved, to herself)* ...Oh. There he is. *(texting)* "I'll be in the alley behind Connecticut Muffin."

Another beat as she reads the response.

MARY JANE: *(relieved)* He's coming. I'll get just enough. *(cheerful)* I'm tapering. A little less every day.

We hear the opening of "SMILING." Throughout the song, we move backwards through time, re-tracing Mary Jane's morning.

MARY JANE: *This is a life of extremes / Both sides are slippery and enticing / These are my places off the rails / This loose recollection of a falling / Barely remember who I failed*

MARY JANE AND ONE VOICE: *I was just trying to keep it together*

MARY JANE:	CHORUS:
This is the first wave of my white flag[1]	*Ahh...*
This is the sound of me hitting bottom	
This my surrender if that's	
what you call it	*Ahh...*
And the anatomy of my crash	*Ooh...*
And I keep on smiling	
Keep on moving	
Can't stand still	
Me the ceilingless great achiever[2]	
Me the notorious perfect mother	
Lured to the ends of overwhelm	
This is the first wave of my white flag	*Ahh...*
This is the sound of me hitting bottom[3]	
This my surrender if that's	
what you call it	*Ahh...*
And the anatomy of my crash	*Ooh...*
And I keep on smiling	*Ooh...*
Keep on moving	
Can't stand still	*Can't stand still*
Such pretty forks in the road	*Ooh...*
On this continuum	*Ooh...*
	Ahh...
I've been bouncing	
Life flashing promise before my eyes	*Ahh Ahh Ahh Ooh*
This is the first wave of my white flag[4]	*Oh...*
This is the sound of me hitting bottom	*Ahh...*
This my surrender if that's	
what you call it	*Ahh...*

MARY JANE AND CHORUS: *And the anatomy of my crash*

MARY JANE: *And I keep on smiling / Keep on moving / Can't stand still / Can't stand still Can't stand still*

---

1   "For a long time, I had all these survival strategies, and—you know—fight, flight, or freeze? A lot of mine was fight, survivalism, showing up no matter what. Just show up, just get through it."

2   "I changed the lyrics for my version of it on the *Such Pretty Forks in the Road* album to 'Me, the notorious bottom dweller / Me, the ceilingless brave explorer.'"

3   "To write this, I drew from my experiences with depression, addiction, disordered eating, being a parent—just everything."

4   Composer Tom Kitt says, "I added a backing choir so it felt like MJ was praying. The arrangement gives the character's pain and defense mechanisms a bit of a holy place. The sound of a gated snare drum here matches the lyric. The tight, boomy quality makes it feel very substantial."

"This is a life
of extremes.

This is the sound
of me hitting bottom."

GOING THROUGH THE MOTIONS

Mary Jane Healy is trying desperately to keep her life together, but it is falling apart at the seams. Not that anybody around her would know it. She looks calm and effortless as she glides through the motions of her day—wake up, make a pancake breakfast, sweat out the carbohydrates at SoulCycle, grab a nonfat latte at Connecticut Muffin, stock up on groceries at Trader Joe's, clean the house, rinse, and repeat—but underneath the surface, she is a wreck. For one thing, she's got the shakes and she is running low on pain pills. She visits the local pharmacy, but like many drugstores that have put new systems in place to respond to the opioid crisis, she cannot get a refill without a prescription. This is how Mary Jane finds herself in the back alley behind Connecticut Muffin, in her Lululemon leggings and pristine white goose-down vest, buying illegal black-market painkillers from a scruffy drug dealer who rides a skateboard. Privately, she's spiraling completely out of control. Publicly, she knows how to hide the chaos. She knows how to keep smiling.

"Smiling" is one of two brand-new Alanis Morissette songs that appear in the musical (the other, "Predator," comes in Act 2), and it was the first single off of Morissette's 2020 album, *Such Pretty Forks in the Road.* Morissette says that she wrote "Smiling," which is about the struggle to maintain external perfection while roiling within, shortly before the *Jagged Little Pill* creative team (director Diane Paulus, musical director Tom Kitt, and librettist Diablo Cody) had one of

their first "whiteboard meetings," in which they would sit together inside Morissette's house in Los Angeles and scribble out ideas for the musical on a large erasable surface. "It was so fun," Morissette says of those early brainstorming days. "It was like a candy store. I was sitting in front of my laptop and we'd be talking about the story, and then I was like, 'Oh, I have a song for that.' Tom [Kitt]'s running joke with me was, 'Oh, I have a song for that.'"

In the case of "Smiling," when Morissette played it for the room, "They went, 'Ooh, MJ.'" The team instinctively felt that this would be the perfect song for Mary Jane to sing in order to introduce the audience to her internal turmoil while also showing the banal isolation of her suburban life. Mary Jane cannot, as the song says, "stand still." If she does, her boredom, loneliness, and trauma come rushing back. So she scampers around like a posh Catholic rabbit, making sure every surface in her life is gleaming and spotless.

The song's central theme—of keeping up appearances despite feeling deep pain within—has appeared often in Morissette's work over the last twenty-five years. You hear it in "Perfect," off of *Jagged Little Pill,* or in "Hands Clean," on *Under Rug Swept,* in which Morissette sings about keeping an abusive relationship secret in order to preserve a man's sterling reputation. Morissette is constantly exploring the lies that people tell themselves, both in order to submerge traumatic memories and also to simply keep moving from one day to the next.

> **"My friends can't read me because I have a tendency to present as smiling."**

"Smiling" came out of Morissette's own experiences with postpartum depression and the way she saw the people around her would assume that she was doing fine just because she was outwardly cheerful. "My friends can't read me because I have a tendency to present as smiling," she says. "But for me, that's just because I want to get the job done. It's very masculine too. It's not just because of the patriarchy, it's also because I'm super androgynous and I love to get stuff done. It's a mature muscle, I think."

Morissette says that her ability to stay positive has been a survival mechanism. "It's kept me alive, it's kept me going," she says. "But it can be confusing in relationships because people are like, 'I had no idea.' And I'm like, 'Really? I was saying it.' And they're like, 'I know, but your whole self was so happy.' And I'm like, 'Well, they were both happening.' I was happy and struggling."

Mary Jane is happy *and* struggling. She's got a lovely home, an accomplished husband, two healthy children, and she outbikes every other uptight WASP at SoulCycle. She also has a drug addiction, unprocessed sexual trauma from college, a communication gap with her daughter, unhealthy boundaries with her son, and a marriage that is hanging by a thread. "Smiling" is about that tension—between joy and sorrow, taking charge and breaking down—that so many of us feel. This is, as MJ sings, the first wave of her white flag, her surrender. She's ready to hit rock bottom so that she can start her journey back to herself.

"Her ability to stay positive has been a survival mechanism."

ELIZABETH STANLEY (Mary Jane Healy)

previously appeared on Broadway in the revival of *On the Town* (which received a Drama Desk nomination), *Million Dollar Quartet*, *Cry-Baby*, and the Tony Award–winning revival of *Company*, as well as the first national tours of *The Bridges of Madison County* and *Xanadu*. On television, Stanley can be seen in *NOS4A2*, *FBI*, *The Get Down*, *The Affair*, *Black Box*, *Made in Jersey*, *Fringe*, *The Chappelle Show*, and *PBS Great Performances: Company*.

What is your first memory of hearing Jagged Little Pill, the album?

My history with the album goes back to my teenage years, and I always think of it in conjunction with learning to drive, because that must've been what was happening in my life around the time. I remember being in the car without parents, which felt new, and really cranking up the hits whenever they would be played, because her music is...it's like you have to sing along at the top of your lungs. We moved a couple of times, but at that point in time I was living in a town of a thousand people called Camp Point, which is in rural Illinois.

Did you connect to the lyrics at the time?

I think I was a little bit sheltered, just being where I was. It's been such a treat to circle back to the album now as a woman in her forties and be like, "Oh, I did not understand those lyrics at the time." It's amazing to me that Alanis had that maturity and that depth at that age. It's like, "Wow." Way beyond where I was, that's for sure.

How did you get the role of Mary Jane?

I got the appointment for the audition a couple of years ago. I remember it was a self-tape, which is unusual for theater to have that be the first step. I was like, "Why?" They said, "The creative team is all very fancy, and so it's hard to coordinate their schedules." I was like, "OK."

But I was going out of town the next day. My brother and sister-in-law were having a baby shower, and so I was like, "I have to do it today." The audition was singing the song "Forgiven." And "Forgiven" was one of the songs that I didn't know because that one didn't get a lot of radio play at the time. I really spent the whole day studying, and then in the last hours of sunlight, put myself on my iPhone and then got it.

Did you feel any pressure at first to sing in the style of Alanis? Because she has such a distinctive voice.

No. They always asked us to make it our own. Even in the first audition, I remember seeing the breakdown saying, "Please do not imitate Alanis Morissette. Make it your own," which is such a relief, because who could be her?

I guess I feel like I was always just sounding like me, and not really trying to be anything else. Our music team has great ears, so any time something starts to sound not quite appropriate in style, they would rein us in. Sometimes, for me, I know because of where I grew up and just the way that I learned to sing, every now and then they'll be like, "That's starting to sound a little country, so that's maybe not the right style."

Alanis and I both have a big voice, and we both have the capability to flip it around. I feel like there are some moments where I was like, "Oh, I can sing this almost yodel-esque," which I think is a little bit of an homage to her.

Your character has an opioid addiction, an issue that affects so many American families. How did you prepare to take on such a serious subject?

I did and continue to do a lot of research on that because I just feel like it's so delicate, and I want to be absolutely as truthful as I can be in telling this story, which is such a real story for so many people in our world. I watched a lot of documentaries. One that really comes to mind was *Heroin: Cape Cod, USA*. One of the great books I read was *Dopesick*, by Beth Macy. It's really just so angering about the epidemic itself.

The show was able to connect us with this man, Dr. Peter Grinspoon, who wrote a book called *Free Refills*, which is

day are you taking? How much is that costing you? Where are you getting them from? What is your behavior like if you don't have them? How do you feel if you have them? How do you feel if you don't have them? Then, also, what is the emotional side of that, but then also what does that look like in a relationship? How is that perceived by those who love you? Because all those questions are useful information as an actor in wanting to really give the scenes authenticity.

You get to sing a brand-new Alanis Morissette song in the show, "Smiling."

Yeah, it feels really special to be singing a brand-new song that Alanis wrote. Because Alanis is so iconic in her style, I actually had never heard her sing "Smiling" until she did an unplugged concert in December just before we opened. When we were in rehearsals for the first lab, our music director said, "Do you want to hear the demo that Alanis

about his own experience as a doctor becoming addicted to opioids and then losing everything and then working back to get his license again. Now he really works with patients who are dealing with recovery and addiction. He has been a great resource, both his book and then also he just made himself available for phone calls. And there's another woman, Joanne Peterson, with a nonprofit called Learn to Cope, which is a support group, really, for families and individuals who are dealing with the epidemic of it all. I attended some Narcotics Anonymous meetings. People have been really generous with sharing their personal information about it.

How important was it to you to depict Mary Jane's descent into pill dependency accurately?

So important. I wanted to educate myself from all angles like, factually, what are we talking about? How many pills a

made?" I said, "I really don't, because I just don't want to be tempted to copy her in any way." Because she's so iconic, I know that if I hear it, it'll be in there somehow, and it'll come out.

Lyrically, "Smiling" is such a great shorthand for who this character is. We see this monotony in some ways that I think is easy for people to fall into. MJ makes breakfast for her kids, she's celebrating them, and then she's going to SoulCycle and she's going to Trader Joe's and she's seeing people in the coffee shop. It's seemingly benign, but peppered with all of her feelings, which include going to the pharmacy to get a refill for a prescription that she's denied and then resorting to buying drugs on the street. It's "I have this really great, privileged life," undercut with true desperation and self-loathing. It is a wild juxtaposition, and as an actor, it is a great challenge.

FACING THE FACTS

OPIOID ADDICTION

Opioids, sometimes called narcotics, are a class of drugs that act on the nervous system to produce feelings of pleasure and pain relief. This simple description belies the heartbreak, tragedy, and ruin that opioid addiction can cause.

Addiction—which occurs when someone feels a powerful physical or psychological need for a drug despite the potential for negative consequences—can lead to major health problems, including overdose and death. In fact, according to the Centers for Disease Control and Prevention (CDC), drug overdose is one of the top causes of death in the U.S., leading to more deaths among 25- to 64-year-olds than car accidents.

Some opioids (for example, oxycodone, hydrocodone, fentanyl, and tramadol) are prescribed legally by healthcare providers to manage severe and/or chronic pain, and some opioids, such as heroin, are illegal.

We don't definitively know why some people are more likely to become addicted than others, but we do know that opioids are one of the most addictive drugs available because they trigger the brain's dopamine receptors, causing extreme euphoria. The brain tells the body it wants more of these good feelings, leading to addiction—sometimes even when the medications are prescribed appropriately and taken as directed. According to the CDC, "opioids change the chemistry of the brain and lead to drug tolerance, which means that over time the dose needs to be increased to achieve the same effect." This can lead to a greater risk that the user will take an unsafe amount and potentially overdose. In an overdose, breathing slows or stops, leading to unconsciousness and, in some cases, coma, permanent brain damage, or death.

Many people, including drug users themselves, have mistaken beliefs about drug addiction and recovery, according to Learn to Cope, a nonprofit addiction support network. "Two of the most pervasive myths are that a person can get off drugs alone and that most addicts can become permanently drug-free. These ideas stem in part from notions that continued drug use is voluntary and that a person's inability to overcome addiction stems solely from character flaws or a lack of willpower," says Learn to Cope.

Addiction recovery is a long-term process that requires commitment and caution. "Many of the same temptations will exist if the recovering addict returns to the environment in which the addiction started," says Learn to Cope.

"SMILING":

LIFE IN REVERSE

One of choreographer Sidi Larbi Cherkaoui's big innovations in *Jagged Little Pill* is his intricate staging of "Smiling" as Mary Jane's day lived *in reverse*. Everyone in the ensemble is moving backward, as if being rewound in slow motion. This number was incredibly intricate to choreograph—every movement has to be razor-sharp and exact (try jump-roping backward in a straight line!). Here is a brief oral history of how "the backward dance" came to be.

DIANE PAULUS (DIRECTOR): I will never forget the day we were in my house, it was Larbi and I think Tom Kitt [the music director] was there, and we were just again listening to the songs. We asked, if this is a song about how MJ lives her life, how would we physicalize it? And Larbi said, "Well, what if we saw her day in backward motion? What if she were reliving her whole journey?" I think I looked at Tom, and we were like, "Genius. Done. Yes."

CHERKAOUI: I proposed to Diane that I wanted to see a day in the life of MJ. She needs to go buy groceries, she needs to cook. The song is about, like, she's crashing, but she's pretending she's OK. So she's like, I just go with the flow. But inside, she's dying. There's something wrong. And she knows, but she's avoiding the subject, the addiction, the problem with the drug that's starting, a trauma she had that's reemerging. I wanted to show the thing that the book kind of reveals about her, but visually. Diane was helping me be very specific and precise about the order of things.

PAULUS: Oh my God, the hours on that song in rehearsal. Hours.

ELIZABETH STANLEY (MARY JANE): Ah, the backward dance. "Smiling" is the most-rehearsed number in the whole show. When it would be on the rehearsal schedule, we'd be like, "Oh, we're working on 'Smiling,'" and everyone would be like, "Great, I'll see you next week!" It's a brain twist to figure out, "Wait, is that forward? Is that backward? Well, what would this look like in real time?" The constant figuring out of the storytelling, but then also to figure out, "What does that movement look like in reverse?"

PAULUS: It was so hard to do. We would write out, "She woke up. She did this. First she went to the pharmacy, then she couldn't get the pills. So she went to the coffee shop..." We would then analyze how we would stage it backward, how it would land in the song, which lyrics would be hitting when. The whole backward life of her day, really rigorous.

CHERKAOUI: Elizabeth, bless her, she's so intelligent. And I was thinking that here, she has to stand still, and all of this is happening around her. Here, she's the one who's moving backward, and then things stand still. It was like trying to find a surreal way of seeing that song.

ELIZABETH: I think it's all Larbi's brainchild. It's his pretty genius interpretation of what it *feels* like when you are going through the motions of your life.

ACT 1 · SCENE 5

········· A CLASSROOM AT FRANKIE'S HIGH SCHOOL ·········

Kids take their seats. The TEACHER is a sarcastic, officious type, burnt out on life.

TEACHER: Okay, okay. Everyone. Quiet down. It's our last class before Winter Break, so I know you're all a bunch of library books: Checked out. But, we have Writers' Workshop today. We're going to be workshopping Frankie Healy. Frankie will read her piece and we will then use constructive criticism to help her shape it into something brilliant-ish. Frankie what have you prepared for us today? More poetry?

FRANKIE: Kind of. It's like an essay-poem-story-type thi...

TEACHER: *(interrupting)* A hideous mutant! I see. Well, please, unleash the chimera.

Frankie walks up to the front of the classroom. Deep breath.

FRANKIE: Wow. Okay...

FRANKIE: *An old man turned 98 / He won the lottery and died the next day / It's a black fly in your chardonnay / It's a death row pardon two*

minutes too late / And isn't it ironic, don't you think...[1]

CLASSMATE #1 interrupts.

CLASSMATE #1 (DAVID): Hold up, wait a second, that's actually *not* ironic?

CLASSMATE #2 (LANCER): Right? If we're using irony as defined in Greek tragedy, I don't see how, like, a fly in your beverage applies...

DAVID: That's not irony, that's just, like, shitty.

TEACHER: David! *(beat)* He's right, though.

FRANKIE: Can I please finish my piece?

FRANKIE: *Mr. "Play It Safe" was afraid to fly / He packed his suitcase and kissed his kids goodbye*

---

1 "I get it when people mock these lyrics. The real irony of all time for me is that I'm usually the grammar police. I'm usually the one going, 'Ah, that's not the King's English.'"

He waited his whole damn life to take that flight / And as the plane crashed down, he thought / "Well, isn't this nice!" / And isn't it ironic—[2]

CLASSMATE #3 (CHARLIE): *(interrupting)* It's not, though?

CLASSMATE #4 (LILY): It would be irony if the guy in the crash was, like, a airplane mechanic...

PHOENIX, a good-looking and yet offbeat/mysterious teenage boy, stands up.

PHOENIX: What is this, a literary inquisition?

CLASSMATE #5 (PHOEBE): Big word, new kid!

PHOENIX: How about you guys let her finish?

FRANKIE: *(embarrassed)* No. I'm done.

PHOENIX: *(matter-of-fact)* Look, they're projecting their insecurity on you. You're obviously a great writer and their only defense is to be hyperliteral.

FRANKIE: *(stunned)* Do I know you?

TEACHER: That's enough, Frankie, Phoenix.

FRANKIE: Your name is Phoenix?

PHOENIX: Yep. Like the mythical bird of flame. Or the third-rate city. Your choice. Now are you going to shut these fuckers down or should I?

Frankie's confidence is renewed.

FRANKIE: *It's like rain on your wedding day / It's a free ride when you've already paid / It's the*

good advice that you just didn't take / And who would have thought, it figures / Well, life has a funny way

PHOENIX: *Of sneaking up on you / When you think everything's okay and everything's going right*

FRANKIE: *And life has a funny way*

PHOENIX: *Of helping you out when you think everything's gone wrong and / Everything blows up in your face...*

FRANKIE: *A traffic jam when you're already late*

TEACHER: *A no-smoking sign on your cigarette break...*

PHOENIX: *It's like ten thousand spoons when all you need is a knife*

FRANKIE: *It's like meeting the boy of my dreams, and then meeting his...[3]*

PHOENIX: *...I'm not seeing anyone.*

FRANKIE: *And isn't it ironic, don't you think*

FRANKIE/PHOENIX: *A little too ironic*

PHOENIX: *Yeah, I really do think*

FRANKIE/PHOENIX: *It's like rain on your wedding day / It's a free ride when you've already paid / It's the good advice that you just didn't take / And who would've thought it figures...*

---

2 "For me to write a song that is, top to bottom, completely wrong just tells you how happy I was working with Glen on that album—because I couldn't have given a shit."

3 "For the last eight years or so, whenever I perform it in concert, I sing, 'Meeting the man of my dreams / And then meeting his beautiful husband.' Which is true. I have fallen in love with a lot of gay men."

Ironic

TEACHER: Does anyone else have feedback on that?

CLASSMATE #4 (PHOEBE): *(pointing to Frankie and Phoenix)* You guys should do it!

TEACHER: Thank you, Phoebe. Class dismissed. Enjoy Winter Break—I know I will!

As everyone rises to file out...

PHOENIX: I think you forgot something.

FRANKIE: *(to Phoenix)* Oh. Hey, thanks for that. I want to be a writer someday, so I actually care what people say about my stuff.

PHOENIX: I understood your piece.

FRANKIE: Who are you, and why are you being so strangely nice to me?

PHOENIX: I'm a casual fan. *(then)* Hey, are you going to that party tonight?

FRANKIE: *(chuckling)* Lancer's? Nah, I don't really do those red cup parties.

PHOENIX: I might go.

FRANKIE: Yeah, me too.

FRANKIE: *Well, life has a funny way*

PHOENIX: *Of sneaking up on you*

FRANKIE: *Yeah life has a funny, funny way / Of helping you out*

FRANKIE/PHOENIX: *Helping you out*

They look into each other's eyes. Frankie is flustered by this intense attention from a kindred spirit. They walk off as if in a daze. Jo watches them depart, curious, maybe a little jealous...

COMEDY OF ERRORS

"Ironic," the third single off of *Jagged Little Pill*, came out in February of 1996 and was an immediate, polarizing hit. The chorus is undeniable—who can hear the hook without wanting to belt "It's like raiiiiiiin on your wedding day" at the top of their lungs?—but almost as soon as the song came out, Morissette's critics began questioning whether or not her lyrics were grammatically correct. Is a "black fly in your Chardonnay" an example of dramatic irony or just plain, old-fashioned bad luck? Is "ten thousand spoons when all you need is a knife" ironic or just a deeply inconvenient cutlery error? In *Reality Bites*, a film about ennui-laden Gen Xers that came out in 1994, when Morissette was writing the songs for *Jagged Little Pill*, Winona Ryder says, "I can't really define irony, but I know it when I see it." Perhaps Morissette's definition worked much the same way; she was pointing out bizarre coincidences and odd twists of fate in order to try to get closer to an overriding absurdity she saw in the world. Later, in an interview, she would say that she never expected listeners to take the song so literally. "Although there are times where I'm grammatically very intense and very perfectionistic, there are other times where clearly I don't care," she said. "I make up words, and I play with words linguistically like they're paint."

Despite her critics, Morissette has a playful sense of humor around the song and its malapropisms. You can even see her poking fun at herself in the original music video, in which she plays four different versions of herself sitting in the same car, in four different colored sweaters. One of her characters is thoughtful and serious, but another makes mischief throughout the ride, sticking her head out the window to sing, her long brown hair flapping in the breeze like a dog's ears. Over the years, Morissette has come to love the controversy around "Ironic" and believes that the song is all the more lovable for its linguistic foibles. She says the arguments around the lyrics have led her to feel more humble about her own mistakes. "A lot of people are afraid of not being intelligent," she says. "But I am clearly really, really intelligent, and also not intelligent, and it depends on where you catch me."

When it came to putting "Ironic" in the context of a Broadway musical, Diablo Cody, who wrote the book, knew right away that she wanted to address the elephant in the room head-on. "I mean, there is such a discourse around the inaccuracy of that song," Cody says. From the draft of the script, she knew she wanted to set the song inside a high school English class, with Frankie reading the lyrics out loud as part of a poetry workshop. "I would not have taken that meta approach unless I had felt that the song demanded it," Cody adds. As Frankie recites her lines about "a traffic jam when you're already late," her classmates rag on her for not quite deploying the correct grammar. Instead of feeling humiliated, Frankie stands up boldly for her artistic decisions. She also has backup: the new kid in school, Phoenix, tells her to ignore the haters. Frankie and Phoenix end up singing the song's rousing chorus in harmony, falling for each other a little bit in the process.

Cody insists that this comedic approach is a valentine to Morissette's hit rather than an indictment of it. "I think the song's amazing," Cody says. "It wasn't at all like, 'We're ashamed of "Ironic." Let's make fun of it.' That was never the intent. It was more like, 'Let's make fun of the song's critics.'"

For her part, Celia Rose Gooding, who plays Frankie, says "I love the way [Diablo] put 'Ironic' in the show. I think it's so perfect, Frankie being this writer sharing this, what

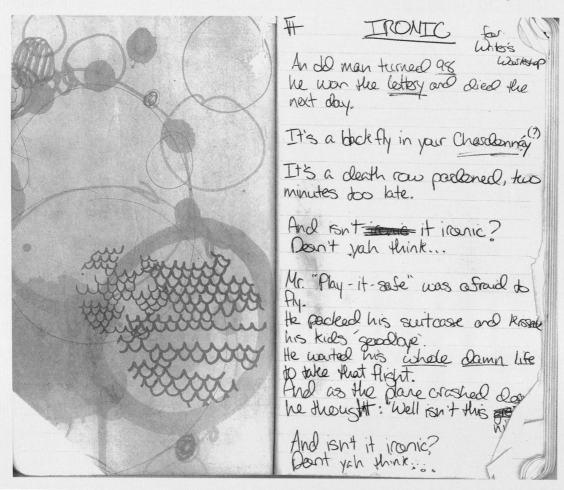

"There is a deeper, more serious undertone to the way Frankie's classmates pick on her."

she believes to be an incredibly deep piece about irony and then it being thrown in her face." But she also adds that there is a deeper, more serious undertone to the way Frankie's classmates pick on her and call out her use of language. Just as Morissette's critics undermined her status as a powerful woman in rock by questioning her grammatical decisions in the nineties, Gooding feels that Frankie's classmates are doing the same to her as a black queer poet trying to be heard. "People don't like when women speak

their truth and aren't honest about things," Gooding says. "And when you can find a little piece of something almost fractionally incorrect, it's so easy to just say, "You're wrong. You're stupid. You don't know what you're talking about, girl." And that's not fair. Frankie is again looking out to this predominantly white space and being rejected yet again." Gooding adds that Frankie is attracted to Phoenix's decision to act as an ally to her in a vulnerable moment. "He's this guy who didn't have to stand up for her. He could have just let the tide wash over her and swallow her whole."

By now, Morissette is at peace with "Ironic" and the decades of late-night dorm-room debates that it has sparked. Cody said that from the beginning, Morissette gave the show's team her full blessing to poke gentle, yet loving, fun at the song. "Alanis was open to it," she said. "She was like, 'I think sometimes the best thing in the world is to be really dumb and really smart at the same time.'"

ANTONIO CIPRIANO (Phoenix)

has starred in productions at La Jolla Playhouse, York Theatre Company, Second Stage Theatre, New York Stage and Film, and Michigan Opera Theatre. He won the 2017 Sutton Foster Ovation Award for Best High School Theater Actor and has performed in multiple concerts at Feinstein's 54 Below. His television credits include *God Friended Me* and *City on a Hill*.

What is your first memory of Jagged Little Pill, *the album?*
I was not born until five years after the album came out, which is crazy. I try not to say it too much! I grew up listening to songs like "Ironic" and "Head Over Feet" and "You Learn" and "You Oughta Know," but ever since I listened to "Hand in My Pocket," I was like, "Oh, my God, this is my jam. It's my feel-good song. It's the best." My parents would play it. My mom loved Alanis Morissette. Alanis wrote the songs when she was nineteen. I'm nineteen right now. She was feeling these things in 1995, and they're still so relevant to today's world.

How did you get involved in the Broadway production? You are so young!
I did the Jimmy Awards (aka the National High School Musical Theater Awards). I was a finalist there. A few months later, an industry professional saw my performance on YouTube, and he Facebook-messaged me to send in a video for *Jagged Little Pill*. When I first got the message, I was like, "This is sketchy, isn't it? He's Facebook-messaging me." But once I read about the creative team, my mom freaked out. She was like, "Oh, my God. Alanis Morissette! This is amazing!" And I was like, "Who is that?"

I sent in a video to audition and made it to the final callback; I flew to New York and booked it about a week later. I was only guaranteed the workshop—every step of this process was an audition for me. I had to prove myself with the workshop to get to the out-of-town tryout, then was offered the out-of-town tryout, proved myself there, and then, the offer came out for Broadway. Little did I know I'd still have to wait about a year and a half before we actually made it to Broadway, but it's all been worth it.

One of your big songs in the show as Phoenix is "That I Would Be Good," which you sing with Celia Rose Gooding

and Lauren Patten. It's a trio of teenagers singing through how hard it can be to live up to expectations.
"That I Would Be Good" is actually one of my favorite moments of the show. For me personally, I think it's a moment of connection—well, not really a love connection between Frankie and Phoenix. It's more like, "Oh, I empathize with what you're going through, because I'm going through something at home as well." A lot of the kids in that town may not really be able to relate to what they're going through. I think that's where the connection between Frankie and Phoenix comes together. It becomes romantic because of their connection through empathy. We get to be really vulnerable with each other. We're going through these situations in our heads, but the fact that we're able to share

> "A majority of this cast has been together since the first workshop. We have just grown as a family."

our personal stories with each other is such an intimate moment in the show. Celia is also such a great scene partner. Then also when Lauren comes in, it's just heartbreaking. That's where the love triangle is introduced as well.

I heard that when "That I Would Be Good" was added to the show, you had to record a tape of the three of you singing it for Morissette to listen to so that she could approve of you singing it.
Yes, that was crazy. Because at that point, we had already fallen in love with the song. We were like, "Oh, my God, we need to make Alanis like it..." It was the first time Alanis was hearing anyone else sing it as well—which is another thing that is so awesome about this show and being a part of it, that Alanis can receive the songs in a different way than how she intended for them to be out in the world. I remember that rehearsal day when we recorded it. I think we redid it a few times because we were like, "OK, we need to make it perfect because this is my favorite song in the show now." That was a big nerve-racking moment, but it was incredible. [Alanis] is one of the most gracious human beings on the

You have an intimate scene with Celia—where Jo walks in on the two of you in bed together. I love that line where she says you were wearing a "dog tag, like a douche."

We were going over that scene in the first workshop, and they were like, "OK, take your shirt off!" And I didn't know I was going to be doing that, and I had my dog tag on, because I wear a dog tag that my grandma got me. And Lauren comes into the room and sees me with my dog tag on and no shirt, and she laughs her ass off. She's like, "Oh, my God," and then all of a sudden when we were running through it again, Lauren literally said the line that's in the show, "He was wearing dog tags with no shirt like a douche." She said that unscripted, and the room went wild! They immediately wrote it into the show. It's one of my favorite moments. It's like a trademark. For my opening-night gift, I got everyone a dog tag. It just says, "*Jagged Little Pill* opening—Love your casual fan, Phoenix."

You are one of the youngest cast members in the show, along with Celia Rose Gooding. What was that like?

We were both still in high school when we were cast, so we did tutoring together every day for three hours. It was awful, but it was good bonding. Celia saw me with my little lunch box just sitting on the ground, and she was like, "Yup, that's going to be my best friend."

We have been so close. A majority of this cast has been together since the first workshop. We have just grown as a family. When we were in Boston, my family rented out a little Airbnb on the beach for the Fourth of July. The whole cast came, and it was just this big family. It was one of the best Fourth of Julys I've ever had.

planet. I love her to death. She's like my mom. She's like my other mom.

Speaking of nerve-racking, when you sing "Head Over Feet," you have to hold onto a rapidly spinning swing set...

Yes, I get to do dance moves on the swing set while it is spinning furiously. The number one comment that I get at the stage door is where people are like, "I was so nervous watching you on the swing set!" And I'm like, "Yeah, don't try it at home. It is not an easy situation." We have never fallen. Larbi is a brilliant choreographer. We spent whole rehearsal days working that number out because he wanted us to be very safe, but he also wanted it to look good. We don't change it because if you did, it could get dangerous. We all have a very set formation that we do. It is very safe.

One of your biggest moments in the show is when—after sneaking out of Frankie's house—you get to crawl across the front row with your shirt off.

Yeah! There was one time when I had a cough drop in, and I giggled a little bit and spit it. I saw the people at the stage door, and they were like, "You spit your cough drop on us!" It's always fun to talk to people at the stage door who sat in the front row. There's a guy on Twitter, actually, who started a GoFundMe page to be able to buy a ticket front-row center to experience that.

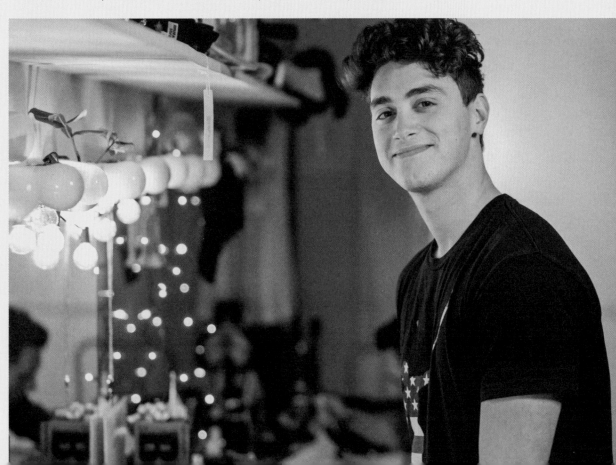

ACT 1 · SCENE 6

········ THE HEALY HOUSE ········

We hear the instrumental opening to "SO UNSEXY" as Mary Jane's phone buzzes on the arm of the couch. She picks up.

We illuminate Steve at his desk, still at work.

MARY JANE: Hey.

STEVE: *(on phone)* Hey...I'm underwater on the Kleinfeld case. I'm going to be...

MARY JANE: *(on phone)* ...Really late. Fine. I mean, I figured. It's fine, I'm just decorating the tree.

STEVE: Right, the tree. There's nothing I can do about it, the deal is closing tomorrow. I'm just checking in, like you asked.

MARY JANE: There's no need to get defensive. I said it's fine. I like decorating by myself. You know I'm a total "control freak"—your words! I'm fine.

STEVE: You know what; I'm gonna go.

MARY JANE: If you're going to be that late, you might as well spend the night in the city.

STEVE: *(loaded)* I guess it doesn't matter where I sleep. I'll just be sleeping anyway, right?

MARY JANE: Right.

Mary Jane hangs up. Steve looks at his phone handset like what the hell just happened?

Steve sings "SO UNSEXY."

STEVE: *All these little rejections / How they add up quickly / One offhanded word and I feel so ungood[1] / And somewhere along the way / I think I gave you the power to make / Me feel the way I thought only my mother could*

---

1 "The lyrics are based on my dating experiences. I basically interpreted men who were not interested in me to mean that I wasn't interesting. It was a whole downward shame spiral."

I can feel so unsexy to
someone so beautiful
So unloved, like I'm
not on your mind
I can feel so boring,
feel so uninteresting
So lonely
But I say that
I'm just fine

CHORUS:
Ahh...

Not on your mind

so lonely
but I say that
I'm just fine

Steve calls Mary Jane back.

MARY JANE: Yes?

STEVE: Look, I'm really sorry about tonight. I just called to keep you in the loop and you—

MARY JANE: Yes. Thank you. I am *in the loop.* It just keeps going in a circle. That's what loops do. They don't change.

STEVE: Honey...would you please just consider seeing that couples' counselor with me? The one I told you about?

MARY JANE: So we can pay someone to tell us you're a workaholic?

STEVE: Okay. I'm glad I called. (*Steve hangs up.*)

MARY JANE: *Oh these little protections*
How they fail to serve me
One last minute phone
call and I'm deflated

CHORUS:
Ahh

STEVE: *How these little abandonments / Seem to sting so easily / Your hand pulling away and I'm devastated*

CHORUS:
I'm devastated

STEVE:
I can feel so unsexy
To someone so beautiful

CHORUS:
So—
Someone so

MARY JANE: *So unloved,*
Like I'm not on
your mind

So unloved,
Like I'm not on your
mind

STEVE/MARY JANE:
I can feel so boring,
Feel so
uninteresting
So lonely
But I say that

I'm just fine

So—
Feel so
uninteresting
So lonely
But I say
that

I'm just
fine

CHORUS 2:
Feel so

So lonely
But I say
that

I'm just
fine

MARY JANE: *When will you*
stop leaving me baby

Ahh...

STEVE: *When will you*
stop deserting me baby

Ahh...

MARY JANE/STEVE:
Am I just living
with myself[2]

CHORUS:
Am I just living
with myself

MARY JANE: *Oh these little rejections how they disappear quickly / The moment I decide not to abandon me*

---

2 "This is basically a super-low-self-esteem song."

INTIMACY

Alanis Morissette did not release the song "So Unsexy" until 2002, when the song appeared on her fifth studio album, *Under Rug Swept*. By that time, Morissette was twenty-eight years old and had begun to write songs not only about yearning for justice and exorcising her anger, but about the subtle, tender dynamics of long-term relationships and the struggle—and also joy—of maintaining and nurturing a committed romance. "So Unsexy" is, more than anything, a song about how difficult it can be to give your love to another person when you still have not learned how to offer it to yourself. "Oh, these little rejections, how they add up quickly," Morissette sings. "One small sideways look and I feel so ungood." She explores just how easy it is to sink into insecurity in a relationship when you are still holding on to trauma and doubt from your past.

In the musical, the song takes place after a tense phone call between Steve and Mary Jane. Steve calls from Manhattan; it's going to be another late night at the office. Mary Jane reminds him that they were supposed to decorate the Christmas tree, but not to bother coming home. She feels abandoned; he feels rejected. They are not communicating—they are simply talking past each other, isolated in their bubbles of hurt and silence. This song signifies a low point in their marriage: they've stopped being intimate, they've even stopped kissing. They both feel so unsexy to someone they find so beautiful. This is a moment in the show to dive into the alienation that can happen in adult relationships when either person is not being honest—about their past, their secrets, their needs. Mary Jane doesn't want to be intimate because her car accident triggered her past sexual trauma. Steve has become over-involved in his work—and in porn—because he doesn't know how to stop moving and

truly notice the disturbances in his family life. Both of them want to reach out, but they can't quite cross the divide. They are left feeling lonely on either side of a bad phone call, longing for the closeness they once had.

Though the emotional range on *Jagged Little Pill*, the album, is vast, it doesn't quite address the simmering resentment of a long-married couple unable to find the words to be open with one another. As the team was searching for a ballad for Steve and Mary Jane to sing past each other to show their disconnection, they realized they might need to look to Morissette's greater body of work. One afternoon at a meeting at her house, the singer suggested "So Unsexy," and according to Diablo Cody, the idea just clicked. "I had heard the song before, but it had never occurred to me," Cody says. "It was kind of perfect, because we had been talking about how we thought it would be powerful and relatable for Mary Jane and Steve to have this sexual dysfunction because of the long-term impact of rape and assault on survivors."

Cody said she felt it was powerful to hear the song, which had previously only been sung by a woman, to be shared by a husband and wife. "I would've never imagined it sung from the male perspective because I hear a song called 'So Unsexy,' and I relate to it on a level of society expecting me to be sexy all the time," Cody says. "Which is a pressure that we think of as being specific to women. But then to hear it sung from the perspective of a man who's being sexually rejected by someone that he truly loves and is longing to be intimate with, it just broke my heart."

> "They are simply talking past each other, isolated in their bubbles of hurt and silence."

"They are left feeling lonely
on either side of a bad phone call."

SEAN ALLAN KRILL (Steve Healy)

has performed on Broadway in *Honeymoon in Vegas*, *On A Clear Day You Can See Forever*, and *Mamma Mia!* His off-Broadway credits include roles in *Joan of Arc: Into the Fire*, *Brother/Sister Plays* (Public), *Hit the Wall* (Barrow Street), and *A Civil War Christmas* (NYTW). Sean has also played in the touring productions of *Thoroughly Modern Millie* and *Mamma Mia!* Among his regional theater appearances are *Chess* (Kennedy Center), *Sense and Sensibility* (for which he received a Craig Noel Award), *Hamlet*, *The Comedy of Errors* (Chicago Shakespeare), *Sideways* (La Jolla), and *Hot L Baltimore* (Steppenwolf). Sean has appeared on television as well in *Search Party*, *Godfather of Harlem*, and *Mr. Robot*.

What was your first memory of hearing Jagged Little Pill**?**
Well, Alanis and I are similar in age. I'm a couple of years older, so *Jagged Little Pill* came out when I was in my early twenties. It was such a formative album. I was in Chicago. I had just moved, just out of college, and I was doing a musical called *Forever Plaid*. And that album just really held my hand and ushered me through so many important things in my life. So it means a lot to me.

What did you connect to in the record?
What she was writing about was so universal. It wasn't just an angry young woman. She was writing a formative piece of art. It's like a tapestry. It's one of those albums that stays with people because it taps into something that's so beautifully, so fundamentally human that it's timeless.

How did you get the role of Steve Healy?
Well, it was out of the blue. I was rehearsing a new version of *Chess* that we did at the Kennedy Center at the time. And I remember I got an email saying, "If you are available and interested in this, Diane Paulus is a very busy woman. She has one hour to see four people on Monday." I think it was Thursday night. I have to admit, my first gut instinct was, oh no, I don't want them to mess with this beautiful album. But I was five pages in and just blown away by how good it was. And my other favorite song of Alanis's has always been "So Unsexy." So when I got to "So Unsexy," I kind of couldn't believe how beautiful it was as this duet between these two people.

How did you approach the role at first?
They needed someone who can kind of look like this guy, this sort of Connecticut lawyer dad, but is emotionally unavailable. I just tried to do that, and in this case, that's what they wanted. I don't think Steve has always been emotionally unavailable, obviously. But I think at this point in his story, his mind is being cracked open and he's struggling to express himself in a way he never has before.

Yes, Steve is *trying* to reach out to Mary Jane, as you can tell listening to "So Unsexy," but they just cannot connect. And he is also suppressing a lot of his feelings.

I think ultimately everyone, including Steve, is dealing with a lack of communication. I really do believe that the bedrock of the problems this show speaks to is this sort of toxic masculinity in our culture that tells everyone, men and women and children, to just shut up and deal with it—that it is wrong to express your emotions. Or that it's wrong to reach out and say, "I need help." And the show is saying exactly the opposite. This is Alanis's mantra! She says no, this is how we *heal*. We reach out. It's relational therapy. You reach out to someone else, another human being, and say, "I'm lost, I'm confused. Can you help me?"

And do you think that Steve's fear of saying "I need help" leads to his distancing from the family?

I think the real issue with Steve is workaholism. It is a very modern condition, and certainly not just for men. I mean, it's just for anyone who has to go to earn the money to maintain the life that they have created. And then you wake up twenty years later, and you realize, I don't know my family as well as I'd like to. But Steve can't *not* go to work. So it's a real struggle for so many people. And also then you throw in, as I mentioned before, those resentments that are living in those wedges in the relationship. And you kind of look at it and you go, OK, well when was the time where you started choosing to go to work because it was too awkward at home, because it's easier to focus on the work than to focus on this sort of systemic problem in a relationship?

How did the "So Unsexy" scene evolve over time?

So in the beginning, in the Boston run, the "So Unsexy" scene took place in our closet, with Steve getting ready to

"I think ultimately everyone, including Steve, is dealing with a lack of communication."

go to work. And he attempted to touch MJ, and she withdrew a little bit. It was really kind of about Steve putting on his armor and leaving. But it became clear after that it was more important to show in Act One, especially, Steve's absent quality in the family. So that was why we chose here to have it be a split screen—where she's at home and he is at work and can't come home. I do think that that's very important, just because certainly what I've learned is that it forces MJ to deal with everything on her own. Steve is not there to deal with all of the things that are going on with Frankie and Nick. It's a large contributing factor to MJ's real downfall, or her spiral, that she does not have her partner with her to help her deal with all of these things.

Yes, and it's not just about their sex life. It's about what they cannot say.

We were all very interested in "So Unsexy" being about so much more than just, "I feel like you don't want to have sex with me." It's a metaphor for their relationship in the larger sense of, what has happened to us? Why don't you crave me anymore as a human being?

Have you had a big reaction to that song from men who see the show?

I've had dads with tears in their eyes come up to me and say, "I lived that life for twenty years, and you nailed it. That show nailed it." It is a struggle that so many people, so many parents, face.

As Steve disappears into darkness, Nick enters and sees that Mary Jane is distressed.

NICK: Mom, is everything okay?

MARY JANE: It's just—your father...Oh, look the nativity scene! You always loved the little lamb, remember? *Baaa!*

She holds up the lamb from the nativity scene.

NICK: Yeah, I guess...

MARY JANE: So how was school today? People must have treated you like a rock star.

NICK: *(embarrassed)* I mean, we don't really talk about college that much. People get in where they get in.

MARY JANE: Nick, you've got to own your accomplishment.

NICK: Yeah.

(then) You know, I thought I'd feel more excited about it, but I kind of don't feel anything.

MARY JANE: You're just in shock. It's so new. You are going to have the most amazing life ever and all the opportunities I always wished I'd had!

NICK: What if I hadn't gotten in?

A pause. Then Mary Jane laughs at the absurdity of this idea.

MARY JANE: You were always going to get in. I didn't doubt it for *one second.* I'm so proud of you, Nick. Sometimes I feel like you're the only thing I've done right.

(then) How about we do one of our movie nights tonight? It's Christmas, let's watch *Die Hard!*

NICK: I was thinking of going to this party.

MARY JANE: Is it like a swim team thing?

NICK: No, just the general student population.

MARY JANE: *(surprised)* Oh.

NICK: I don't have to go. I mean, even Frankie's going, but—

MARY JANE: No, you should.

(then) I mean, generally you don't like parties like that. Remember that time you called me to pick you up because kids were drinking? I—

NICK: *(interrupting)* Yeah I was 13, Mom. I've been to parties since then.

MARY JANE: I'm just saying. It's not really your scene.

NICK: I don't know what my scene is.

MARY JANE: Well, you'll figure it out at college. You'll make some friends that are on your level.

NICK: You know what, I'll stay home. *Die Hard?*

MARY JANE: No, no, don't just do it for me. You have to make decisions for yourself.

Somehow, this seems worse than doing it for her. Nick hangs an ornament on the tree and Mary Jane adjusts it.

MARY JANE: Not there. I'm going to go get some more ornaments from the garage.

She tosses him an ornament and exits. Nick is alone with Mary Jane's perfect tree. Nick reflects on the situation with "PERFECT."

NICK: *Sometimes is never quite enough / If you're flawless, then you'll win my love / Don't forget to win first place / Don't forget to keep that smile on your face / How long before you screw it up / How many times do I have to tell you to hurry up / With everything I do for you / The least you can do is keep quiet*[1]

Nick has a decision to make—seemingly minor, but meaningful.

NICK: *Be a good boy / You've got to try a little harder / That simply wasn't good enough / To make us proud*[2]

Nick changes his shirt, smooths his hair. He's going to that party.

NICK: *I'll live through you / I'll make you what I never was / If you're the best, then maybe so am I / Compared to him, compared to her / I'm doing this for your own damn good / You'll make up for what I blew / What's the problem, why are you crying / Be a good boy / Push a little farther now / That wasn't fast enough / To make us happy / We'll love you just the way you are / If you're perfect*[3]

Nick heads from the Healy house to the PARTY, as night falls. We transition into an illicit, energetic high school party...

---

1 "'Perfect' is my way of writing about the pain of trying to be the hero child, in terms of archetypes in the family."
2 "There's not a lot written about the child who's got the straight As, but they suffer too, from neglect or from projection or from just expectation."
3 "Tons of kids who are planning to go to college have parents who are making concerted efforts to help them get in. There's all this pressure to be erudite and perfect and academically flawless. As opposed to how I teach my kids now, which is, 'Let's just see what your particular intelligences are.'"

PRESSURE

"Perfect" is the third song on *Jagged Little Pill*, and for Morissette, it came from a deeply personal place. She was a child star in her native Canada—in junior high school, she appeared on the children's television program *You Can't Do That on Television* (famous for dumping green slime over its cast members' heads). She recorded her first demo at only thirteen years old, and by the time she was seventeen, she released her debut pop record, *Alanis*, on MCA Records Canada. That record, full of synths and perky, danceable beats, went platinum, and soon Morissette was touring across Canada's shopping centers and stadiums, with curly hair and denim jackets in the style of American teen stars like Debbie Gibson and Tiffany. As a result, she felt a great deal of pressure, even as a child, to perform, to put on a show—and to be "perfect." Morissette talks a lot l now about "parentization"—the need for the child to become their own parent—and how she suffered, growing up, from being expected to mature quickly and navigate a career before she was even out of high school.

Still, "Perfect" is not a strictly autobiographical song. Instead, Morissette says she wrote the song "dialogically," as a conversation between imaginary characters in her head. In this case, it was a set of strict, demanding parents speaking to their child, asking them to live up to an impossible standard of excellence. "For me, 'Perfect' is the plight of the over-achiever," Morissette said in an interview in 2015. "I had straight As as a kid. I was that end of the continuum, which to me is equally as traumatizing as the other end. We either underfunction or over-function, depending on what we think we can do best to survive."

As to why she thought the song might work for Nick, Morissette said that she felt that he was the child with the heaviest burdens laid on his shoulders. Not only was he expected to play varsity and be valedictorian as an arbitrary exten-

sion of his parents' success, but he also came to stand as a kind of surrogate husband for his mother, Mary Jane, who is often alone in the house while Steve is stuck in the city at work. In the scene just before Nick sings "Perfect," Mary Jane asks him to stay home from a high school party to decorate the Christmas tree with her and watch a movie. Nick is torn about what to do—comfort his anxious mother or live a normal teenage life? When he does decide to go to the party, he dashes off a note and runs out, almost in tears. The crushing pressure he feels has started to feel like an anvil sitting on his chest.

"And that is covert child abuse," Morissette said recently of Nick's role in Mary Jane's life. "And it really fucks with young men when their mom's primary person is their son and they don't have that connection with the husband or the partner. Because you constantly feel like if you're honoring yourself first, you're betraying your mom."

According to Diablo Cody, "Perfect" was Nick's song from the earliest iterations of developing *Jagged Little Pill*. Even though the original version was sung by a nineteen-year-old woman dealing with her very particular situation, Cody felt that the song could expand to include the struggles of any young person feeling the squeeze of parental expectations—even a clean-cut Connecticut jock. "I do think of Alanis as such a specifically feminine artist," Cody says. "She's such a goddess. But I think the material translates."

"We either underfunction or overfunction,
depending on what we think we can do
best to survive."

DEREK KLENA (Nick Healy)

has performed in the Broadway productions of *Anastasia* (as Dmitry, Original Broadway Cast), *The Bridges of Madison County* (Original Broadway Cast), and *Wicked* (as Fiyero, Tenth Anniversary Company). His off-Broadway credits include *Dogfight* (Second Stage) and *Carrie* (MCC). Derek has also appeared on television in *The Code*, *Unbreakable Kimmy Schmidt*, *Quantico*, *Last Week Tonight with John Oliver*, *Blue Bloods*, and *Law & Order: SVU*.

How did you first hear Jagged Little Pill, the album?

Well, I am an early nineties baby. I was born in 1991, so when this album came out, I was a wee one. But I did grow up in Southern California, so I spent a lot of time in the car with my mom, and I do have very specific fond memories of driving around, whether it be by the beach or through L.A., listening to "Hand in My Pocket," "Ironic," and "You Oughta Know." I think those were the three that kind of stuck out to me at that time. And it wasn't really until getting involved with this project that I realized that they're all on the same album, which was shocking to me because they're such staples!

How did you get involved with the Broadway show?

I've been a part of the show now since its first reading in New York. So it'll be three years come summer 2020. It's been quite the labor of love over the years. When I first got involved with this project, I was working on *Anastasia* on Broadway. It doesn't happen often, but I didn't have to audi-

tion for this. The casting director, Stephen Kopel, thought that I was right for the role.

In an early version of the show, Nick was a college student dealing with the fallout from a death during a fraternity hazing. It seems like your character underwent many changes!

Yeah, the original plotline was much different—it involved a frat incident where a pledge had been hazed to death, and Nick was involved in that, in the night that led to this kid's death. When we sang "You Learn" at the end, Nick was in jail! It was not a direction I think any of us wanted to go in. But, part of the process is you see what you have, and you take the pieces that work and you take the pieces that don't. You reconfigure them, and then you do it again. So when we came back about six months later, that's when we had the version that more closely resembles what you see today involving the sexual assault with Bella Fox and my witnessing that.

What do you think Nick is going through when he sings "Perfect"?

Nick is this kid who seemingly has everything going for him, who's smart, athletic, the picture-perfect citizen. I think especially in today's climate, with how competitive college applications are and the type of extracurriculars that adolescent kids and young adults are forced to add to their résumé to bolster themself up these days, that is intimidating. And I think everybody can relate to those stresses. So that's what sends Nick into this spiral. He spent his entire life living up to the expectation that his parents have set for him and the expectation that those around him have of him.

But doesn't he have everything he wants? Acceptance to Harvard! Friends! He's an athletic star!
Sure, he's finally accomplished basically his life goal of getting into the top school with the top grades, being the top of everything that he's worked for his entire life. And what is he left with? This overwhelming sense of emptiness. And it's then that he realizes that he had been doing it for all the wrong reasons and starts to doubt everything he stands for. And so going back to "Perfect," this song actually used to be placed later in the show. It used to be Mary Jane and Nick have an argument in Act Two, and the song came after that. But it didn't feel quite right.

How did "Perfect" end up in Act One?
That was part of the reworking process on the path to Broadway. We did a lab last December, and we experimented with moving "Perfect" up, and then Diablo wrote this beautiful scene between Nick and his mom before going to this party. Nick is yearning for that social environment that he missed out on because of his commitment to his schooling and his athletics and everything. But Mary Jane has leaned a lot on Nick. So this scene portrays her reliance on him, and his yearning to be there for her and the overwhelming guilt that has consumed him by sticking by his mother and taking on that leadership role within the family. So having this dynamic triggers something in Nick, telling him that this is not who he wants to be. He is his own person.

He's now contemplating all these different choices. Do I stay in what's comfortable for me and be there for my mom and be in a safe place and be that savior, or do I do something for myself for once? Do I go to this party? Do I have the experience that I've yearned for? Do I share this love with the people that I've grown up with, the people that I'm going to continue to grow with, and find myself as an adult?

For you, why do you think Jagged Little Pill *is still connecting to people after twenty-five years?*
I think this album is still speaking to people because of Alanis's understanding of human connection and the relationship between the individual and the masses. These are universal, timeless topics. The way that Alanis has addressed those themes and those ideas is so direct and raw. And I think that's why it initially garnered the attention that it did. The ups and downs of a relationship, conflict, healing, injustice, self-reflection, self-expression—I think all of those things, all of those major things that Alanis has so thoughtfully portrayed through her music, are things that will never go away. It's why we can still sing those same lyrics twenty-five years later, and they still have the same kind of effect on people. And I think they will continue to have that effect on people, because we're always going to be a work in progress.

ACT 1 · SCENE 7

.... LANCER'S PARTY ....

Frankie and Nick arrive at the party. We hear the upbeat instrumental that begins "SO PURE."

CHORUS: *I love you when you dance*
When you freestyle in trance
So pure, such
an expression
I love you when
you dance
When you freestyle in trance
So pure, such an expression

CHORUS 2:
Ahh...
So pure, such
an expression

FRANKIE: I'm kinda surprised you wanted to come to this.

NICK: Uh, I'm kinda surprised you wanted to come to this.

Frankie isn't quite ready to disclose the reason she came.

FRANKIE: Maybe we've both been missing out on an essential part of the high school experience.

A shirtless kid walks by wearing a bear mask and carrying a bong. Frankie and Nick exchange glances. Maybe not.

NICK: Where's Jo?

FRANKIE: Her mom dragged her to some church thing.

They're interrupted by Bella Fox, who—like everyone—wasn't expecting to see Nick here.

BELLA: Holy shit, you came! 'Sup, Frankie?

FRANKIE: Hey.

The youthful excitement builds. Partygoers drink from red Solo cups, sing and dance...Someone arrives with a bottle and passes out shots. Andrew walks up to them.

ANDREW: "Saint Nick" is here! It's a Christmas miracle!

CHARLIE: Healy! The last party I remember seeing you at was when Andrew turned 8, and his parents rented all those ponies.

BELLA: *(remembering)* Oh, yeah. Wasn't there a Ferris wheel too? You were a spoiled little shit!

ANDREW: Guilty as charged. *(to Bella)* You want a Fireball shot?

LILY: *(holding up a flask)* I brought a roadie. *(mispronouncing)* It's Don Julio.

We can see Nick is pleased to be in on the trashy fun.

NICK: Where'd you get that?

LILY: Same place I get my weed and my Adderall. (fondly) I love my dad.

CHORUS: *I love you when you dance / When you freestyle in trance / So pure, such an expression*

Frankie turns and sees Phoenix.

PHOENIX: You came!

FRANKIE: I did! (looking around) Not sure I'm feeling this party.

PHOENIX: Yeah, I just saw someone mixing DayQuil and rum. (beat) That won't end well. (then) You want to get out of here?

Frankie nods gratefully and they begin walking.

CHORUS: *Let's grease the wheel and be free / Let's discuss things in confidence / Let's be outspoken, let's be ridiculous[1] / Let's solve the world's problems*

They've arrived at a playground.

PHOENIX: So when are you going to let me read some more of your writing?

---

1 "I love working with and being in partnership with other alpha women. When two people are fighting for who's going to give more, that's my definition of love."

FRANKIE: (secretly delighted) I mean...whenever. I just—I get self-conscious sharing it. The only person I ever really show my stuff to is my brother Nick.

PHOENIX: Are you close with your whole family?

FRANKIE: (weighing her response) Well. It's complicated. (decisive) I'm adopted. And people act like my parents are heroes or something just for wanting me. My mom always says she "doesn't see color." But sometimes I wish she did. Is that weird? It's kind of hard to explain.

PHOENIX: Is your brother adopted too?

FRANKIE: Oh, have you not seen Captain America? (chuckling) No. Nick is the homegrown hero. But after my mom had him she couldn't get pregnant again so my parents went to Catholic Family Services and I've been fucking up their lives ever since!

PHOENIX: Good times. Well, I have this theory that happy families only exist in orange juice commercials and Utah.

FRANKIE: (chuckling) What's your situation?

PHOENIX: I live with my mom. Haven't seen my dad in a minute. And I have one sister. She has a lot of medical issues, so that kind of sets the tone for everything else. I help my mom take care of her most of the time.

FRANKIE: That's definitely not an orange juice commercial.

PHOENIX: Nope.

FRANKIE: Do you wish you had a different family?

PHOENIX: No. I love them. It's more like I wish *I* was a different person.

FRANKIE: Yeah! I know exactly what you mean.

PHOENIX: Like if I was a better kid I'd have it all figured out. I could fix things at home... *(bittersweet)* My dad might still call me...

FRANKIE: *(musing)* ...My mom might still love me.

Phoenix and Frankie sing "THAT I WOULD BE GOOD."

PHOENIX: *That I would be good even if I did nothing*[2]

FRANKIE: *That I would be good even if I got the thumbs down*

PHOENIX: *That I would be good even if I got resentful*

FRANKIE: *That I would be good even if I gained ten pounds*

Jo appears with her mother, ANGIE. Jo is unbuttoning a feminine shirt.

JO: There. I wore it. Are you happy?

ANGIE: You don't even try, Joanne. I don't know why I bother.

As Angie exits, Jo is left alone.

PHOENIX: *That I would be fine, even if I act like a child*

JO: *Why won't you accept who I need to be*

FRANKIE: *That I would be good, even if my hair stays wild*

JO: *Does anyone hear me?*

PHOENIX: *That I would be great if I just stopped standing by*

JO: *Everything is fucked / When you're not here*[3]

FRANKIE: *That I would be grand if I was not all knowing*

JO: *I need to know / That I would be loved, even when I am my true self*

FRANKIE/PHOENIX: *It has to get better*

JO: *That I would be good, even when I am overwhelmed*

FRANKIE/PHOENIX: *I pray it will*

PHOENIX: *That I would be loved*

JO: *Am I loved?*

PHOENIX: *Even when I was fuming*

JO/FRANKIE: *I need to hear that / That I would be good, even if I was clingy*[4]

FRANKIE/PHOENIX/JO: *That I would be good, even if I lost sanity / That I would be good / Whether with or without you / Hi hi hi nnno aye nnn loh aye ho hi*[5]

PHOENIX: Do you have a boyfriend?

FRANKIE: A boyfriend? No.

---

2 "Every single line of this song is a deep prayer for me."

3 "I get easily overstimulated, so I used to hide in a closet or a bathroom to get a little peace. For this song, I hid in a closet and lit a candle, and it just poured forth in about ten minutes."

4 "The idea of 'being clingy' is so ridiculous. The sweetest part of my marriage is when we're both clingy with each other."

5 "This song gets to people's root fears. This musical, and almost every song I write, is a prayer for the allowance to be human."

A MESSY TRIANGLE

One of the most tender moments in *Jagged Little Pill* comes close to the end of the first act, when three of the youngest cast members come together in delicate three-part harmony to sing Morissette's song "That I Would Be Good." The song brings together Frankie and Phoenix, who have run off together after Lancer's party, and Jo, who is unable to reach Frankie to process her own dramatic night—her mother made her attend church bingo, where the minister chastised her for being queer. All three teenagers are at an inflection point: Frankie is considering starting a new romance with Phoenix, Phoenix opens up about his own difficult family issues, and Jo feels completely alone (and cannot wait to take off the itchy pink cardigan her mother made her wear). They find release in singing "That I Would Be Good," a song about sloughing off the expectations of others and finding the strength internally to just be enough. We spoke with Lauren Patten (Jo), Celia Rose Gooding (Frankie), and Antonio Cipriano (Phoenix) about the story behind the song.

> ## "I'm a sucker for a three-part harmony."
> —CELIA ROSE GOODING

Let's talk about how you three have developed a relationship over time, maybe as actors and then the characters.

CELIA ROSE GOODING: I know that I met Antonio briefly before the first day of rehearsal. Since we were young, we'd have to go to tutoring every day, and I think that's how a lot of our bonding started—sitting in the tiniest room on the planet and doing schoolwork, which we had no intention of actually *doing*, but it was a legal requirement.

ANTONIO CIPRIANO: Yeah, we kind of became best friends through that process, which was really cool.

GOODING: I was very ready to be the only young kid in the show, and then this dude shows up and saves me from that idea of being like the only baby. And a lot of what happens onstage I draw from this feeling of gratitude that I have for Antonio. And the same thing with Lauren. Our relationship started at the reading, and we've been really, really close, and a lot of the trust that Celia has for Lauren, Frankie also has for Jo.

LAUREN PATTEN: Luckily, Celia has not broken Lauren's trust as Frankie has broken Jo's. [*Laughs*]

"That I Would Be Good" actually started out as a solo for Frankie, right?

GOODING: Yeah! It was originally before "All I Really Want." Frankie sang the whole thing by herself in bed—and then Jo arises from the bed that Frankie is singing this song in.

CIPRIANO: What? I did not know this!

PATTEN: Yeah, in the original script, I was going down on Frankie for the entirety of "That I Would Be Good." It was a hookup. Because the first line in the old script when I popped out was, "I'm really glad you got all that off your chest, but this has been a pretty intense hookup or a pretty maudlin hookup, even by lesbian standards."

GOODING: I didn't know that! I never put two and two together, maybe because I was seventeen, and I probably didn't think it was possible.

But then the song dropped out of the show for the first workshop.

PATTEN: It wasn't in the workshop at all. But I think they missed that song, and they missed that reflective moment for the young people in the show. Then it was Tom [Kitt]'s idea to put it together as a trio and to see where these three young people are connecting and disconnecting. It was a stressful day where we had to learn it, and then record it perfectly for Alanis to listen to it so we could have approval.

CIPRIANO: We were very picky on ourselves. We were like, "This needs to be perfect."

PATTEN: We hadn't actually met Alanis yet...

CIPRIANO: She was like this God to us.

PATTEN: Still is!

The three-part harmony came together so beautifully!

GOODING: I'm a sucker for a three-part harmony. Onstage every night it's always something I look forward to, because it blends so nicely. I love that that song is a trio now.

CIPRIANO: I remember the first time that we hit that "sanity" chord, we were freaking out. We're like, "Oh my God, this is gorgeous."

PATTEN: There's so much requirement for blending in this show as far as all the voices together and how the ensemble functions, but I think that this is sort of a special moment. Of not being a larger choral ensemble, but just the three of us. It's not really about who is outsinging each other. It's actually just about really listening to each other. I think the song has challenged us to do that.

> "It's actually just about really listening to each other. I think the song has challenged us to do that."
> —LAUREN PATTEN

How did you all personally connect to the themes running through the song?

PATTEN: I mean, I think it's probably the central human fear. I know it's certainly my central fear and is just, "Am I good enough? Am I enough as a person?"

CIPRIANO: Especially as young people in this business. I mean, we came in, Celia and I were both seventeen. And we were like, "Are we good enough for this?" I mean, we're still so young trying to prove ourselves in this business.

> "We kind of became best friends through that process, which was really cool."
> —ANTONIO CIPRIANO

GOODING: I don't think there's ever a moment where you can look and say, "I went to sleep feeling like not enough, and I woke up the next day feeling enough." I don't think that will ever happen as a person. And it's the falling into that truth, and it's the realizing of that that is a constant struggle.

PATTEN: I think something that's interesting to you about when you're young, though, and I think we really see this super clearly with all three of these characters, is that you're in this place in your life where you're starting to become independent and to understand things about yourself that aren't necessarily based on what you see modeled for you. That's a really heightened experience and a really confusing experience.

This song is technically about a "love triangle," though you are all struggling in your own ways. It is hard to say who is in the right and wrong in the situation.

PATTEN: I think something that I love about the development of the triangle is that it's not about somebody being a bad person and somebody else being the good person in the situation. It's just three flawed people.

GOODING: Trying to function.

PATTEN: Yeah, who are not necessarily the best at communicating. I think it would have been very easy for the show to go into the direction of Phoenix being this kind of jerk who's just sleeping around and not really connecting with anybody. And I think it's awesome that the show really avoids that scenario.

CIPRIANO: And that's almost where it was in the workshop—because this scene went right into "Head Over Feet." It went right into them kissing. There was no connection there before they jumped into this. So I think obviously it's grown from the workshop.

PATTEN: "That I Would Be Good" is a big part of that because you get to see where Phoenix is coming from too, and you get to see the connection between Phoenix and Frankie.

GOODING: And I think that's such an important takeaway from the show—as one of the characters who's easy to pinpoint as the person "in the wrong" or "the bad guy," because Frankie wasn't faithful to her friend. I think a really awesome, a really important takeaway from this is that she's sixteen, and a kid, and just trying to figure it out. She has no idea who she is when she's placed in this community that is constantly telling her whoever she is is wrong.

PATTEN: Oftentimes, I feel like there's this weird disparity between what young people actually go through in their real life versus what is portrayed in the media for young people as what they're dealing with. But I think this really resonates with young people, because it isn't afraid to get really complicated and messy and deep and deal with really intense issues. And that's obviously taken from the depth of Alanis's lyrics, which she wrote when she was eighteen and nineteen.

ACT 1 · SCENE 8

We flow from the playground into the next morning, with Frankie and Jo.

JO: So. How was the party?

FRANKIE: *(dismissive)* Typical teenage ratfuck.

JO: I'm sure I would have preferred it to the church social I attended with my mother. Did you know that God forgives "gay feelings" as long as you don't act on them? Thanks for the life hack, Father Tim! *(beat)* Did you see that guy?

FRANKIE: What guy?

JO: *(semi-playful)* That new kid who's clearly into you? I saw you two in the hallway. I think he had drool on his shoes.

FRANKIE: *(vague)* Oh. Ha. Yeah, he was there. I don't know...I left early.

JO: Well, if you left early I guess you missed the drama. There's these pictures going around. I guess Bella Fox was really drunk and she passed out, and her shirt was pulled up? It's all over people's Stories. *(pulling out her phone)* Nice caption, huh? People are such assholes.

Frankie looks at the pic.

FRANKIE: This isn't okay. We should do something about this. Call people out. *(realizing)* And we should check on Bella... *(thinking out loud)* and, like, tell her we have her back...

JO: Like...right now?

FRANKIE: Remember our mission statement for SMAAC?: "We will endeavor to protect the voiceless and be proactive about reaching out."

JO: We're the only ones in the club, Frankie.

FRANKIE: Yeah, because *no one else cares.*

JO: You're right. You're amazing, you know that?

CHORUS: *Ooh this could get messy*

ANDREW: Bella was all over me last night.

NICK: You were all over her too.

CHORUS: *But you don't seem to mind*

ANDREW: She always goes too hard at those things.

NICK: I guess. It was an insane night.

CHORUS: *Ooh don't go telling everybody*

ANDREW: I can't believe I'm witnessing your first hangover. Another friendship milestone.

CHORUS 1:
And overlook this supposed—

CHORUS 2:
This could get messy...

Don't overlook this supposed—

This could get messy...

Don't overlook this supposed crime

We transition to BELLA'S HOUSE.

BELLA: I'll sign your petition or whatever; it's just not a good time.

FRANKIE: No, it's not anything like that.

JO: *(fumbling)* We just—we saw something that we wanted you...to be aware of...

BELLA: *(dry)* Yeah. I know about the pictures. So why are you here? You want me to autograph one?

FRANKIE: If you want to talk about it—

BELLA: Why would I talk to you guys?

JO: That's fair.

An awkward beat as Jo shrugs and looks at Frankie as if to say: Well, let's go. But Frankie continues.

FRANKIE: We just want to let you know we're here for you. *(activist mode)* It's not okay that people did that without your consent.

BELLA: Did Nick say something to you about what happened?

FRANKIE: Nick?

BELLA: Well, I was doing shots with him and Andrew, and then I guess I blacked out...That must be when the photoshoot happened.

FRANKIE: Who took those pictures?

BELLA: I don't know. I can't remember.

A VOICE: *Ooh...*

JO: Are you okay?

FRANKIE: Do you remember anything after that? How did you get home?

BELLA: I didn't.

A VOICE: *Ooh...*

BELLA: I think I was in Lancer's little sister's room or something, 'cause there were dolls by my head—

JO: Creepy.

BELLA: I puked in a garbage can by a desk. And then I passed out again, and I woke up for like a second and...Andrew was on top of me...

A VOICE: *Ooh...*

JO: What?

BELLA: But I couldn't even talk, I was just, like, trapped. And when I woke up again, it was really late. Or early. Just like, gray outside. Birds chirping. And I could see my underwear was on the floor. And like, I don't even think he used a condom...

Frankie and Jo exchange glances, as if trying to make sense of this.

FRANKIE: That's rape.

JO: Yeah.

BELLA: What? I'm just a fucking idiot.

The reality of the situation hits Bella.

FRANKIE: No, you're not. *(then)* Did you tell your mom?

BELLA: She's the last person I want to tell.

JO: Maybe you should report this to the police?

BELLA: Are you kidding me?! Like, I'm really going to say *Andrew Montefiore...*? Everyone worships his whole family. There's literally like a statue of his grandpa downtown... Plus, they never believe anyone anyway...

JO: We believe you.

BELLA: Why do you even care what happened to me?

FRANKIE: Because it could happen to any of us.

ACT 1 · SCENE 9

CHORUS: *What if down the line, a few years later / No one knows except the both of us? / Must I honor your request for silence / Will you wash your hands clean of this?*

Frankie heads to Nick's room.

FRANKIE: Did you get my text?

A heavy sigh from Nick. He has. But it's the last thing he wants to discuss right now.

NICK: I can't deal with this right now. I'm sick.

FRANKIE: *(scornful)* Hungover. *(frustrated)* Don't you have anything to say about what I texted you?

Nick sighs.

NICK: Shh. Mom's mutant hearing. *(quietly)* Why did you even go over there?

FRANKIE: Did you see what happened, Nick?

NICK: Everyone was drunk, Frankie. Including Bella.

FRANKIE: But she was passed out. Right?

NICK: I've known Bella since the third grade. She's always been dramatic.

FRANKIE: Are you saying you don't believe her? Is this some kind of bro code shit?

NICK: You shouldn't get involved with this.

FRANKIE: *You like snow but only if it's warm / You like rain but only if it's dry / There's no sentimental value to the rose / That fell on your floor / There's no fundamental excuse / For the granted it's taken for / 'Cause it's easy not to / So much easier not to / And what goes around / Never comes around / To you*

NICK: This has nothing to do with me. Or you.

FRANKIE: She wasn't able to say yes. Why didn't you look out for her?

NICK: Why am I expected to look out for everyone? You, Mom, Bella—I'm fucking sick of it!

Mary Jane enters.

MARY JANE: *(alarmed)* What is going on in here?

NICK: *(to Frankie)* Don't say anything.

FRANKIE: Mom. You know Bella? She—

Nick interrupts with the sanitized account.

NICK: She's claiming that Andrew...assaulted her.

MARY JANE: *(dubious)* Andrew *Montefiore?* What do you mean, assaulted?

FRANKIE: She was *raped.* Andrew forced himself on her while she was unconscious. Bella says Nick was hanging out them at the party. He saw how drunk she was. Nick needs to go to the police!

MARY JANE: Frankie, you can't just go calling the police because a girl got drunk and there's some he-said-she-said. If someone drinks themselves into oblivion, these things can happen. We're all responsible for our own actions.

FRANKIE: What?!

MARY JANE: A girl got drunk and someone took advantage of her. It's a shame but it happens all the time. I wouldn't make this your cause of the week.

FRANKIE: Cause of the week? Why did I think you would understand?

Frankie storms out of the room. Mary Jane is clearly shaken and hurt.

MARY JANE: *(to Nick)* Were you drinking, Nick?

NICK: Is that even pertinent?

MARY JANE: I told you that party was a bad idea. There is no reason for you to get involved in this. Don't borrow...

Nick has a weary familiarity with this phrase.

NICK: ...borrow trouble.

Mary Jane leaves as "WAKE UP" continues.

NICK: *I like pain*[1]
But only if it doesn't hurt too much

CHORUS:
Too much

NICK:
Should I sit, should I wait,
to receive?

CHORUS:
Sit, wait,
To receive

CHORUS:
There's an obvious attraction / To the path of least resistance / In your life

NICK:
Well there's an obvious aversion
No amount of your insistence
Could make me try tonight

CHORUS:
Ooh...
Oh...
Try tonight

---

1 "The point of view changes from 'you' to 'I' throughout the song, switching between accusation and self-examination."

NICK:
'Cause it's easy not to
So much easier not to
And what goes around never
comes around
To you

To you...

To you...

CHORUS:
Easy not to...
Easier not to...
Ahh...

To you

CHORUS:
To you to you to
you to you to you
to you to you

To you to you to
you to you oh...
to you

We see Bella going to the police station accompanied by Frankie and Jo.

ANDREW: There's an apprehensive / Naked little trembling boy

With his head in
his hands[2]

CHORUS:
Hands in
his hands
In his hands

CHORUS 2:
Hands

BELLA: And there's an
underestimated
And impatient little girl
Raising her hand[3]

FRANKIE/JO/CHORUS:
Hand

STEVE enters, home from work, as Mary Jane puts her coat on and prepares to head out.

STEVE: (to Mary Jane) Um, hi? You're leaving? I just got home.

MARY JANE: I need air.

STEVE: Are you okay?

MARY JANE: Yes, why does everyone keep asking me that?!

STEVE: Because you've been acting crazy lately...Can you put your phone away and look at me? Why won't you talk to me about anything anymore? (frustrated, as she grabs her coat) Are you going on one of your walks?

MARY JANE: It's easy not to

MARY JANE/STEVE: So much easier not to

MARY JANE/STEVE/NICK:
And what goes around never

Comes around

To you

CHORUS:
Around and
around and
around
Around and
around
To you

---

2 Says Tom Kitt, "This song checks in on how the effects of Bella's rape accusation are playing out among the different characters. It really becomes a company number where we're trying to track everyone's emotions as Bella's story comes to light."
3 "The little girl here is me. The song is about the patriarchy and being on the receiving end of narcissism. The level of patronizing behavior I've received from men is ridiculous."

MJ/NICK:	STEVE/FRANKIE/CHORUS:	BELLA/CHORUS:
To you	*Ooh this could get messy*	*To you*
To you	*But you don't seem to mind*	*To you*

NICK:		
Get up	**ANDREW:**	**CHORUS:**
Get up	*It's easy not to*	*Get up*
Get up	*So much easier*	**BELLA/ FRANKIE/ STEVE/ CHORUS:**
Off of it	*Not to*	*Get up off of it*

NICK/STEVE/MJ/ FRANKIE/CHORUS:		
Get up,	**BELLA:**	
	And what goes	
Get up	*Around*	
	Never comes	

NICK:	
Get up off of it	*Around to*

STEVE/FRANKIE/ CHORUS:	
Get up off of it	*You*[4]

NICK/STEVE/MJ/FRANKIE/BELLA/CHORUS: *Get out!*

NICK/MARY JANE:	CHORUS 1:	STEVE/BELLA/ FRANKIE/ CHORUS 2:
It's easy not to	*To you...*	*Get outta here*
So much easier not to	*To you...*	*Enough already*

+FRANKIE/BELLA:		STEVE/ CHORUS 2:
And what goes around	*Get up!*	*Get up,*
	To you	*Get up,*
Never comes around	*Around*	*Get up off of it*
To you	*To you*	*You*

ALL: *Wake up! / Wake up / Wake up*[5]

4 "Though I was only nineteen at the time I wrote this, I was speaking to all the men in my life."

5 Kitt says, "This complex number is doing what theater wants to do—it's having something that grows and tracks and involves a number of characters who are able to express internal thoughts."

ACT 1 · SCENE 10

.... CHURCH—NIGHT ....

Mary Jane is outside church. She checks her cell phone. Looks around. No one here...yet. She walks into church.

MARY JANE: Dear God.

CHORUS:
Ooh ooh

I'm sorry I haven't been here in a while. *(sniffing)* Smells the same. Frankincense and Murphy's oil soap. And all the votive candles. Just twenty-five cents to light one and make a wish. That's all prayers are, aren't they?

She puts a quarter in the box. She puts a couple more quarters in the box.

MARY JANE: I have a few if that's okay. My marriage isn't working. I don't know if Steve loves me anymore. In fact, I'm not even sure he likes me. Not sure you can fix *that* one.

She kneels down, trying to pray.

MARY JANE:
Please bless my daughter Frankie. I named her Mary Frances after the Blessed Mother. That has to count for something. I love her so much, but I never know what to say to her. And please bless my Nick. He's the only thing I've done correctly.

CHORUS:
Ooh...
Ooh...
Ooh...
Ooh...
Ooh...
Ooh...
Ooh...

She sits down in a pew.

One more thing...I don't ask you for much. The last time I asked you for something was...well, you remember, back in college—

A VOICE:
Ooh...

even after that night, well, that was my fault— I trusted that—somehow—it was your will.

Ooh...

I remember thinking to myself: really? Is this what God wants for me? But I held it together. I powered through. Now I need your help.

We hear the drum beat of "FORGIVEN" beginning.

MARY JANE: My medicine stopped working. It got so I needed more and more. I'm sure you saw how bad it was getting. *(hopeful)* So I've started tapering! I've been taking a little less every day. But it's really hard. And I'm not myself. I need you to help me get through this. It'll be over soon. I'll be back to normal. And no one will know. *(desperate)* Please—it's Christmas. I've come back home.

Mary Jane sings "FORGIVEN."

MARY JANE: *You know how us Catholic girls can be / Aye yi aye yi yi yi / We make up for so much time a little too late / I never forgot it, confusing as it was / No fun with no guilt feelings / The sinners, the saviors, the lover-less priests / I'll see you next Sunday / I sang alleluia in the choir*

	CHORUS:
Al, alleluia-luia luia	*Al, alleluia-luia luia*
I confessed my darkest deeds	
To an envious man	*To an envious man*
My brothers they never went blind	*No! No!*
For what they did[1]	
But I may as well have	*Ahh*
In the name of the father, the skeptic	*Oh, oh*
And the son	
I had one more	*One more*
Stupid question	*Sinner!*
I have my reason to be here	*Witch!*
I still have a thing or two to learn	*Whore!*
I still needed something to cling to	
So I will[2]	*Ooh you will*
What I learned	*What I learned*
I rejected	*I rejected*
But I believe again	
I will suffer the consequence	*I will suffer the consequence*

---

1 "Within religion, men could be these powerful sexual beings, and if women even think about it, they're judged as whores and dirty, damaged goods."

2 Says Kitt, "Compared to the original version, the chorus comes late—by design. I wanted to avoid having MJ land in the catharsis of the chorus right away, so she could explode after the second verse. I suggested it early in the development process, and it seemed to work on a number of levels."

Of this inquisition
If I jump in this   *If I jump in this*
fountain,   *fountain*
Will I be forgiven...   *Forgiven*

Mary Jane rises and walks out of the church. Her drug dealer walks up to her, palming the goods into her outstretched hand.

CHORUS: *Ooh...*

MARY JANE: What is this? Why don't you have my usual? *(then)* Well if this is all you have. It's just a little stronger? *(then, breaking)* Crazy weather, right?

A light snow falls. As the dealer departs, Mary Jane sings once more.

MARY JANE:
We all have our
reasons to be there

                   CHORUS:
We all have a thing   *Ooh...*
or two to learn
We all needed   **CHORUS 1:**   **CHORUS 2:**
something to cling to   *So we did*   *So we did*
So we did[3]

STEVE/ALL: *We all have delusions in our heads*

NICK/ALL: *We all have our minds made up for us*

FRANKIE/ALL: *We have to believe in something*[4]

FRANKIE: *So I will.*

CHORUS: *So I will*

ANDREW:	CHORUS/STEVE/ FRANKIE/NICK:
We all had our reasons to be there[5]	*Ave Maria*

ANDREW/BELLA:	
We all had a thing to learn	*Ave Maria*

ANDREW/BELLA/JO/PHOENIX:	
We all needed something to cling to, So we did	*Ave Maria, Jesus* *Jesus, sanctus*

MJ+:	CHORUS 1:	CHORUS 2:
So we did	*We all had our reasons to be there*	*Ave Maria*
So we did	*We all had a thing or two to learn*	*Ave Maria*
Ooh ahh yi yi	*We all needed something to cling to*	*Ave Maria*
So we did	*So we did*	*Oh so we did*
Amen!	*Amen!*	*Amen!*

E n d   o f   A c t   1

---

3 "So much about Catholicism is quite gorgeous, right down to the sensuality of frankincense burning and the images in art and architecture. But then there are things about it that are divisive, disconnected, combative, and conflictual. There's so much within the beauty of religion that just loses the plot. So for me, I had to just completely walk away from Catholicism. However, I would describe myself as a little obsessed with religion. There's a thread of continuity that permeates through all religions. There's always something about connectivity, humility, prayer, and ritual."

4 "I love this arrangement and these characters. Mary Jane is trying to get solace. She's trying to get some respite from her intense life. She goes to a church. She's funny. There's so much going on in this song."

5 Says Kitt, "I added these passages from 'Ave Maria' at the suggestion of my wife, actor Rita Pietropinto. I really wanted to bring some sacred music into the end of this, something that spoke to the moment, and she recommended that song."

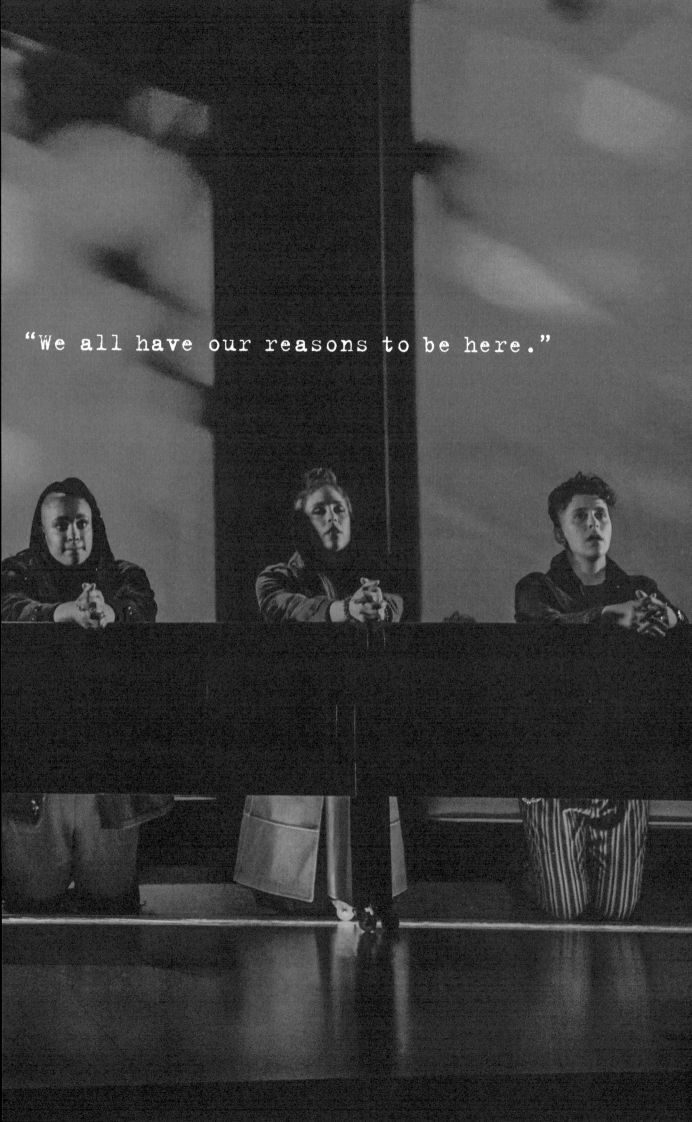

"We all have our reasons to be here."

GRACE

In his 1999 film *Dogma*, director Kevin Smith cast Alanis Morissette as God. It was a small role—she appears at the end of the film, dressed in white satin, to silently stare into an actor's eyes before flashing a huge, beatific smile and skipping away—but one that Morissette had been preparing for throughout her life. Ever since childhood, when she was raised in the Catholic Church in Ottawa, Morissette has been in an ongoing and ever-seeking conversation with the divine. She rejected organized religion when she was young ("At twelve years old, I thought, I'm coming up with some disparities here," she said of her Catholic upbringing in one interview) but never stopped exploring and investigating her own spirituality. In an interview with *Rolling Stone* in 1995, Morissette said that while she no longer subscribes to the strictures of Catholicism, she still felt a kind of communion with audiences when she was performing. "When I'm onstage, it's very spiritual," she said. "I feel very close to God when I'm up there."

"Forgiven," the sixth track on *Jagged Little Pill*, was Morissette's attempt to grapple with Catholicism and its tendencies to repress female desire. "There was one side of me that was crazy and deviant, doing things ahead of my time," she told *Rolling Stone* of the song, "and another side that was very held back, wanting to remain virginal for the sake of being the good white Catholic girl." *Jagged Little Pill* is an album about embracing big, oceanic feelings—rage, infatuation, jealousy, elation, yearning—and "Forgiven," which sits right at the center of the record, is a kind of poignant moment of suspension. It raises more questions than it answers. Morissette wonders aloud if her religious upbringing was different because she was a girl: "I confessed my darkest deeds to an envious man," she sings. "My brothers, they never went blind for what they did, but I may as well have." There is righteous anger here for the double standard that strict religions hold women to, casting them as either the virgin or the whore with little gray area in between. But by the end of the song, she allows her frustrations to melt into acceptance. "We all had to believe in something," she admits. "So we did."

In the Broadway show, "Forgiven" is the finale of the first act—and it marks the first moment that Mary Jane can admit to herself, and by extension to the audience, that she was sexually assaulted in college. Director Diane Paulus knew she wanted Mary Jane to have this revelation inside a church, but she and Diablo Cody struggled at first

with how she should confess the secret. "We didn't want it to be explicit," Paulus said. "I was struggling. So I was asking my sound designer, I was like, 'Could you create a soundscape that's almost like a disturbed memory soundscape?'" It was out of this discussion that Paulus decided to add another motif to the show—a haunting series of falsetto notes that Morissette originally wrote as the opening to the song "Predator"—which the chorus member Jane Bruce sings first during Bella's graphic retelling of her own rape, and then sings again when Mary Jane sits in a pew at the church.

This theme connects the two women across time and experience; they may be from completely different generations, but they have both suffered severe trauma. What separates them is their resources for confronting their pain. While Bella, with the support of her friends and community, ultimately decides to stand up for herself and take her abuser to court, Mary Jane never had that option. As a "good Catholic girl," she internalized the guilt and shame of her assault and buried it deep; it took the jolt of the car accident to bring it back up again like bile. Hud-

> "They have not yet realized that they are all connected—not by religion, but by something more universal. Call it grace or forgiveness."

dled up in her puffy parka, Mary Jane has a raw conversation with God. "Even after that night, well, that was my fault—I trusted that—somehow—it was your will," she says. "I remember thinking to myself, Really? Is this what God wants for me? But I held it together. I powered through. Now I need your help."

Mary Jane confesses that her pain medication is no longer working. She's started to buy fentanyl on the street. Her life is spiraling out of her control. And yet, somehow, she has wandered back into the hallways of the church, which still smell like "frankincense and Murphy's oil soap," looking for absolution. "I think Alanis feels very particular that this monologue doesn't feel too comfy with God," says Elizabeth Stanley, who plays Mary Jane. "Alanis has said that one misstep Mary Jane took after her sexual assault was going to church for help because they were like, "Oh, just do ten Hail Marys and move on," when really she needed help in a much greater sense than that, with people who were specialized to actually assist and hear her story truthfully." Stanley, who herself admits that she "feels an anger with organized religion" after being raised in the church, says that singing "Forgiven" every night has helped her examine her own beliefs. "I've been so interested in exploring where the feminine is in religion, because I do think it's so patriarchal," she says. "I think there is such an underbelly of women being the temptress, being the whore; if you're powerful and you're a spiritual woman, you're a witch."

As Mary Jane sings about finding forgiveness within herself, the rest of the cast appears behind her in their winter coats, singing along with her as the snow falls. As the curtain comes down on Act One, each character is dealing with his or her own demons out in the cold, alone. They have not yet realized that they are all connected—not by religion, but by something more universal. Call it grace or forgiveness. "We all had a thing or two to learn," the chorus sings. "We all needed something to cling to."

"FORGIVEN":

DARE NOT TO KNOW

DIANE PAULUS serves as the director of *Jagged Little Pill*. Paulus is the Terrie and Bradley Bloom Artistic Director of the American Repertory Theater (A.R.T.) and Professor of the Practice of Theater at Harvard University. On Broadway she has directed *Waitress*, *Pippin* (Tony Award, Best Revival and Best Director); *The Gershwins' Porgy and Bess* (Tony Award, Best Revival; NAACP Award, Best Direction), and *Hair* (Tony Award, Best Revival). Her many other credits include *Waitress* (West End); *Gloria: A Life; In the Body of the World* (Drama League nomination) at Manhattan Theatre Club; *Invisible Thread* at Second Stage; and more than seven productions at A.R.T. Paulus was selected for the 2014 Time 100, *Time* magazine's annual list of the 100 most influential people in the world.

You have directed many shows—you directed a Broadway revival of Hair *and brought* Waitress *to the New York stage. Will the experience of working on* Jagged Little Pill *stick with you?*
I poured so much of my life and soul into this; it's not going away. Every night I climb in bed and I think, OK, 10:45. Show's done, the report will be in. I still get a report every night from the stage manager! It's my treat before I go to bed. Our stage manager writes so many wonderful things. He'll say, "Therapy played quite well today. The jokes landed nicely. The emotions were charged."

Do you still stop in to see the show every now and then?
I actually went to see the cast this past week, and we had this amazing conversation. Lauren Patten texted me after that session. She wrote down everything we discussed, and one of those things was "Dare not to know." I told them to

be on the edge—no complacency that the audience loves the show. Listen to them and don't anticipate. Dare not to know. Because it's not about denying the audience. It's actually about riding the audience.

How does this feel different than any other show you have worked on?
You know, with *Hair,* we had this feeling and mission among the cast, even though these are all young people who were not alive in the 1960s. With *Jagged Little Pill,* I always felt like, this feels like a *Hair* for our times. It's dealing with the culture, the politics, the issues of our time. This feels like it's all about life right now. And I found that, as an artist living *right now*, the effort and desire to make work that is an immediate conversation about the times we're living in is more and more necessary.

I know that you and Alanis were both very adamant that Jagged Little Pill *should not feel like the typical jukebox musical.*
We have this guiding philosophy from Alanis. And in that sense it was like a revival, because as a director I'm thinking, There's this cultural phenomenon that I need to deliver. Everybody who loved *Jagged Little Pill*, the album, has an expectation of what they're going to experience. And I like having that challenge as a director. So I'm thinking, OK. I know what I want the room to feel like. It's got to feel like an Alanis Morissette musical that I would dream about experiencing.

But the fact that we were able to go original—we weren't doing the typical jukebox model. We were making this original story that allowed us to put in the kind of issues that we wanted to live inside, that came from Alanis. I would say the album is sort of like the urtext, it was the Bible or the Holy Grail. It was always going back to the album, deciphering the lyrics and analyzing. And of course, we have Alanis to go to and ask, "What did you mean by this? Talk to me about this song. What are the themes?"

So how did you start thinking about what the musical could be early on?
One of the producers, Vivek Tiwary, is an old friend. And he took me to breakfast and said, "I'm very close to getting the rights to *Jagged Little Pill*." And he asked, "When and if I do, would you be interested?" And it took me all of thirty seconds to say, "I'm in." There are just certain projects—as a director, I choose my shows based on this sense of potential. It's never about knowing how to do it. It's just an intuitive response, like, "This—I know this is going to be necessary. I know what I want this to feel like." And that was the case with the album. So it was that breakfast, and then I went home and the first thing I did was listen to the music again because I actually hadn't listened to it in a long time.

I know one of the first things you started thinking about was the movement, the way you wanted the show to feel in the actors' bodies.
I remember not knowing what the story was going to be. I knew it had to be visceral and ritual. And that's why I was thinking a lot about Greek theater and a Greek chorus. And then someone showed me the work of Sidi Larbi Cherkaoui, I didn't know him. I started watching video after video, and I just thought, this is it. That's the kind of physical, emotional life that we have to put in the show. Alanis was so into this idea of the chorus illuminating all the fractured cells of every character, the psyche of every character.

Let's go back and talk about the album itself. Why was it such a totemic text for you?
It was this groundbreaking, earth-shattering moment. I was

shattered by Alanis's Dionysian energy. She just felt so free and unselfconscious as a performer. She was literally shattering the code of what it means to be a woman performer. I listened to the album nonstop. I never got to see her live. So it's kind of crazy to think that all these years later, I would be creating a show with her. It was seminal, I think, to every woman who was coming of age and thinking about voice, agency, power—even though by the nineties, we had the women's movement. Somehow the eighties derailed us, and we needed Alanis to come back and say, "This lives inside us. And if it's not let out, what's going to happen?"

The first version of the musical featured a totally different plot about a frat house.
Well, the first initial idea of the story was to deal with sexual violence. And I think there was concern from our producers that it would be a whole other musical if we went that way. So we were toying with different themes, and Diablo had an idea about this family being torn apart by something traumatic and an inciting incident. In the first reading it was a frat-house kind of toxicity.

All the characters were there. It was MJ, Steve, Nick, Frankie—but there was no Bella. We went through that reading, and it was Alanis who said, "That doesn't really resonate with me." And it was so right of her to say it, that she just felt like that theme of frat-house toxicity didn't really exist in her music. She asked why weren't we going into the sexual violence, which is so much a part of, openly, her life, in her music, in her songs. So we went back and we said, we want to change it. That was one of those critical moments of sticking to your initial impulse and riding that developmental path. You know that you're in the right zone with something when it's just getting deeper and deeper.

> "We're in this dynamic living relationship with everything that Alanis has channeled and learned and is living today."

Did you bring in a lot of outside voices and dramaturgs to deal with the issues this show raises? I know they are very serious issues.
Yeah, because we started up at A.R.T., we had this incredible engine. How does a musical get to Broadway that is breaking a boundary and that is dealing with tough topics? It needs a chance to incubate. It needs a chance to flesh itself out and have that kind of rigorous research behind it. A.R.T. was that kind of hothouse for the show. So we were talking with professors from Harvard Medical School about opioid addiction. We were speaking with all sorts of folks up in Boston about sexual violence. We brought down youth from the Boston Alliance of Gay, Lesbian, Bisexual and Transgender Youth. They sat and watched the show, and gave feedback that impacted the development. That led to the line where Frankie says, "Why did you always make everything a joke?" And Jo says, "It's called a defense mechanism." That wasn't in the show until we had gotten that feedback from these teens.

Then going to Broadway, I said to our producers, "We really need to have training. These issues are all so deep in the show. I don't want any cast member to feel burdened with representing an issue or having to be the expert." So we did trainings on all the major topics. I remember getting a call from one of our producers saying, "You really want to give up ten hours of rehearsal for this?" I was like, "Yes. The investment in this is so necessary." We did workshops for the

actors, but I also said, open them up to the marketing team, to the press people, to the producers. Because it's not just *us.* All the stage managers, all the crew—everyone around the show should understand nuances of the language.

A big part of your show development is deciding how the shows look. *One example of a vibrant visual choice are the protest signs that the chorus holds up during "All I Really Want."*
Alanis said early on, "Do you think we could keep changing those signs?" I said, "Definitely. Those signs are handmade." I told our interns, "Here, take these poster boards and make protest signs." And they were doing research on the web, picking favorite signs. We changed the signs going to Broadway, and we will swap them out as needed. The reality is a lot of those issues are not going away.

Speaking of "All I Really Want," Alanis changed one of her iconic lyrics in that song to fit the show.
Alanis said to me, "You might want to say, 'I am fascinated by the spiritual woman,'" because in the original lyric it's 'I am fascinated by the spiritual man.' I said to Tom Kitt, the musical director, "We can't switch that lyric, the fans will go crazy!" And then I remember Alanis saying, "Oh no, no, no, Diane. I sing *woman* now on tour all the time. And people go crazy and they cheer when I say *woman!*" So she was the one who was living these kinds of changes within her lyrics. Now that idea of spiritual woman is sort of at the core of the whole show.

The show tackles such weighty issues—it's not your standard happy, shiny Broadway fare.
It's not accidental that we're making this show now, when we're more in touch with Alanis who has lived a life. We're not frozen in time when Alanis was nineteen. We're in this dynamic living relationship with everything that Alanis has channeled and learned and is living today. Diablo was asking, "Is it too many issues?" But we just kept working on it and feeling it was interesting, and all the issues that were coming felt like they were threaded and relevant. Sexual violence is really at the core. It's kind of the secret cause, and then all these issues surround it, so you understand that this is not just a pastiche of issues. They're all related. Which is, I think, the way the world feels today—that we can try to silo these issues, but we understand that sexual violence, that sexism, is related to racism and gun violence. These are all connected. And that's the way the world feels, especially to a younger generation.

And every young person I talked to said, "This is what we're navigating. These are all the issues that are present concurrently in our lives." So that kind of gave me early encouragement that we weren't going to simplify the show.

I love that moment at the end of the show, where MJ stands behind Frankie and holds her hand.
Oh my God, that was such a thing—how do I end the show? And I thought, They could be looking at each other, they could be holding hands. But I was like, no, Frankie has to be in *front* of MJ, but she's got to reach back and hold her mother's hand. Because her mother is there, and that is their history. That history is never going to go away. But the truth of the narrative is that young people need to live their own lives. And you may not be able to follow.

Lastly, why do you think that Jagged Little Pill *has stood the test of time?*
Alanis was way ahead of her time. I think she was a prophetess, truly. She was tapping into something in herself that transcends time, something so primal about who we are as human beings. That's why these songs feel like they are speaking to the human condition today.

LOST BUT HOPEFUL

JO TAYLOR
Played by LAUREN PATTEN

WRY JOKESTER, TRACK JACKET ENTHUSIAST, BEANIE WEARER, SARDONIC REALIST, QUEER ACTIVIST, THE "ONLY INTERESTING PERSON" IN GREENPORT

First things first: her name is "Jo," not Joanne. She's not a fabric store. The only people who call Jo by her full name anymore are her mother, who binge-watches Fox News, and Father Tim, the homophobic priest at her mother's church who tells Jo that she can "pray the gay away." But Jo has no intention of denying her sexuality—she is 100% queer, and proud of it. She feels best in slouchy beanies and sporty track jackets; the scratchy pink cardigans her mother makes her wear to church socials make her feel like crawling out of her skin. In Frankie, she has found the one person in Greenport she can really talk to; they bond over being outsiders, being queer, being political radicals, and being really good kissers.

When Jo sings "Hand in my Pocket," she is singing for her entire generation, most of which were born after *Jagged Little Pill*, the album, came out. Even though they didn't inspire the original song, Jo and her peers see themselves in the lyrics, which suggest a playful duality, and a confused internal logic. A person can be high and grounded, sick and pretty. Jo feels like she contains multitudes. She wants to subvert the binary, to undo all of the rigid boxes that we feel the need to shove ourselves into. She sees gender as a construct, and feels that labels only hold people back. Still, she believes in loyalty. Which is why, when she catches Frankie in bed with Phoenix, she feels so betrayed. How could Frankie abandon her for the safety and security of a heterosexual relationship? Has Jo's need to laugh off her insecurities led to Frankie not taking her seriously as a romantic partner?

Jo's "You Oughta Know" is a howl—not just for herself, but for all queer people who feel invisible. She wants the world to know that "I'm here" and that she isn't going away. She gets a cathartic moment between herself and the audience, and through her release, she allows the audience to process their own hurt and pain and emerge feeling cleansed and ready to hope again. At the end of the show, Jo may still be working through her pain, but, as she tells Frankie, "I'm figuring it out." She has a new girlfriend, a new sharp style. She's still turning everything into a joke ("it's called a defense mechanism," she says), but now she is able to control the laughs—and to feel a new lightness in her heart.

> "I've been out of fucks to give since the early two-thousands."

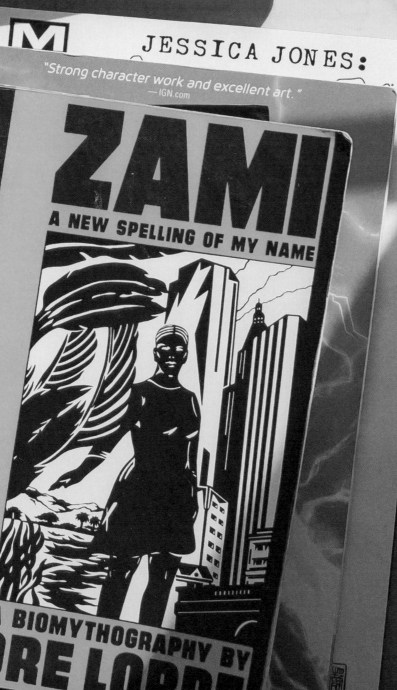

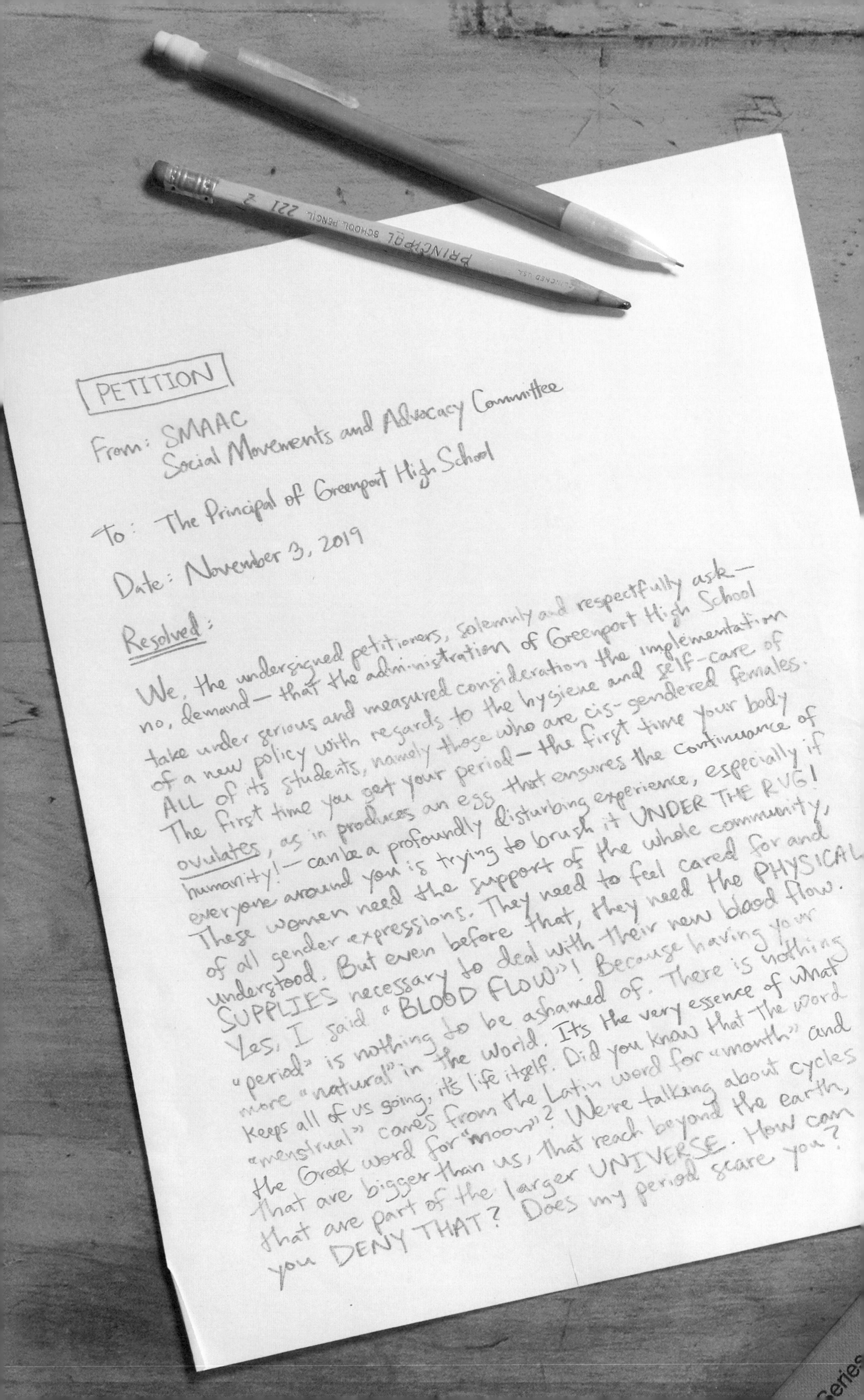

PETITION

From: SMAAC
Social Movements and Advocacy Committee

To: The Principal of Greenport High School

Date: November 3, 2019

Resolved:

We, the undersigned petitioners, solemnly and respectfully ask—
no, demand— that the administration of Greenport High School
take under serious and measured consideration the implementation
of a new policy with regards to the hygiene and self-care of
ALL of its students, namely those who are cis-gendered females.
The first time you get your period— the first time your body
ovulates, as in produces an egg that ensures the continuance of
humanity!— can be a profoundly disturbing experience, especially if
everyone around you is trying to brush it UNDER THE RUG!
These women need the support of the whole community,
of all gender expressions. They need to feel cared for and
understood. But even before that, they need the PHYSICAL
SUPPLIES necessary to deal with their new blood flow.
Yes, I said "BLOOD FLOW"! Because having your
"period" is nothing to be ashamed of. There is nothing
more "natural" in the world. It's the very essence of what
keeps all of us going; it's life itself. Did you know that the word
"menstrual" comes from the Latin word for "month" and
the Greek word for "moon"? We're talking about cycles
that are bigger than us, that reach beyond the earth,
that are part of the larger UNIVERSE. How can
you DENY THAT? Does my period scare you?

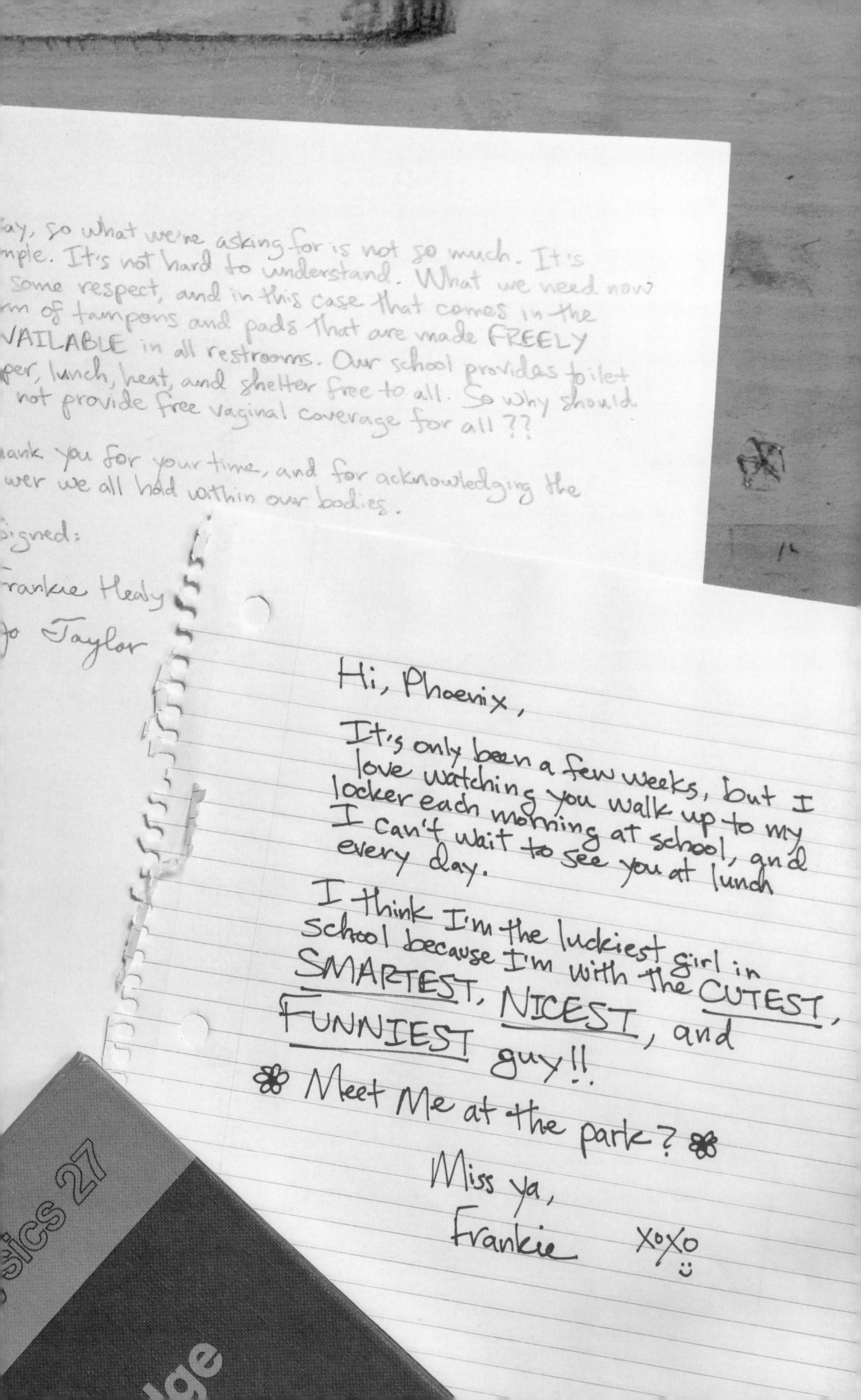

...ay, so what we're asking for is not so much. It's ...mple. It's not hard to understand. What we need now ...some respect, and in this case that comes in the ...rm of tampons and pads that are made FREELY ...VAILABLE in all restrooms. Our school provides toilet ...per, lunch, heat, and shelter free to all. So why should ...not provide free vaginal coverage for all ??

...ank you for your time, and for acknowledging the ...wer we all hold within our bodies.

...igned:

...rankie Healy

...o Taylor

Hi, Phoenix,

It's only been a few weeks, but I love watching you walk up to my locker each morning at school, and I can't wait to see you at lunch every day.

I think I'm the luckiest girl in school because I'm with the CUTEST, SMARTEST, NICEST, and FUNNIEST guy!!

❀ Meet Me at the park? ❀

Miss ya,

Frankie   xoxo ☺

THE BEST LISTENER

PHOENIX

Played by ANTONIO CIPRIANO

POETRY ENTHUSIAST, DOG TAG WEARER, HIGH SCHOOL HEARTTHROB, SIBLING CARETAKER, WINDOW ESCAPE ARTIST

Phoenix—whose name, he says, comes from "the mythical bird of flame or the third-rate city"—is the soft-spoken new kid at school. He has kind, gentle eyes, floppy hair, a skateboard, and an aesthete's appreciation for poetry. During English class, he stands up for Frankie while she reads aloud to her peers, and quickly a mutual crush starts to bloom. Phoenix admits that he is a "casual fan" of Frankie's writing and outspoken, fierce activism. Frankie, who already has a girlfriend, finds herself suddenly confused. Why does she want Phoenix so badly? What does it mean that she is starting to fall for him, head over feet?

The two meet up at Lancer's party, and decide to ditch the beer-fest in order to have a quiet conversation in an empty playground. It is there that Phoenix confesses that while he is so cool and calm at school, his life at home is far from perfect. He cares for his sick sister, while his single mother struggles to support her two children. Phoenix and Frankie connect on a deeper level; they both see through the picket fence Connecticut facades. Their conversation turns to romance, and their romance turns to lust. Unfortunately, Frankie neglects to tell Phoenix that she has a girlfriend. When Jo walks in on the two of them having sex, Phoenix has to quickly leap out of the window (wearing only his dog tag) and slink into the night. The experience is traumatic, and his relationship with Frankie is never the same. They stay good friends, but he realizes he cannot be there to love her the way she needs when he has so much to handle at home. Phoenix is the one who got away—but he is also the one who helps Frankie open up to new possibilities, and in the end, to discover what she really wants.

"I have this theory that happy families only exist in orange juice commercials and Utah."

UNDER RUG SWEPT

BELLA FOX
Played by KATHRYN GALLAGHER

LITERARY MAGAZINE EDITOR, FAST FOOD SERVER, SEXUAL ASSAULT SURVIVOR, WOMEN'S RIGHTS ACTIVIST, VOICE OF A MOVEMENT

"Tell me when I'm going to feel normal again."

Bella is many things. She is a good student. A loyal friend. An editor of the school literary magazine. An after-school employee of a local fast-food joint. A helpful daughter. A girl who can hang with the boys. She never expected to add "rape survivor" to the list, but the night of Lancer's kegger, she was assaulted in the bedroom of the most popular boy in school. None of this was Bella's fault—not how much she had to drink, not what she was wearing, nothing she said or did—but at first she wants to sweep the whole incident under the rug. She knows how vicious her classmates can be, and how little women are believed about what happens to them. And besides she wants to be more than just her worst moments—she knows that sexual assault has a way of following a person around throughout their life. But also, she cannot just stand by and see a person who committed a crime and took away her sense of self go unpunished. With the help and support of Frankie and Jo, she is ready to tell her story. She is ready to stop blaming herself, and start seeing herself as a strong survivor with a valuable voice.

It is important to recognize that Bella does not have an easy road to walk—she doesn't just speak her truth and walk away victorious. She will deal with trauma, shame, hurt, and confusion for many years. Recovery is a life-long process—but so is survival. Bella is so much more than any label, any one night of her life. But she also wants to make sure that girls like her never have to endure a night like she did. She will keep fighting for justice, keep shouting out her right to say "no," and keep advocating for a better world.

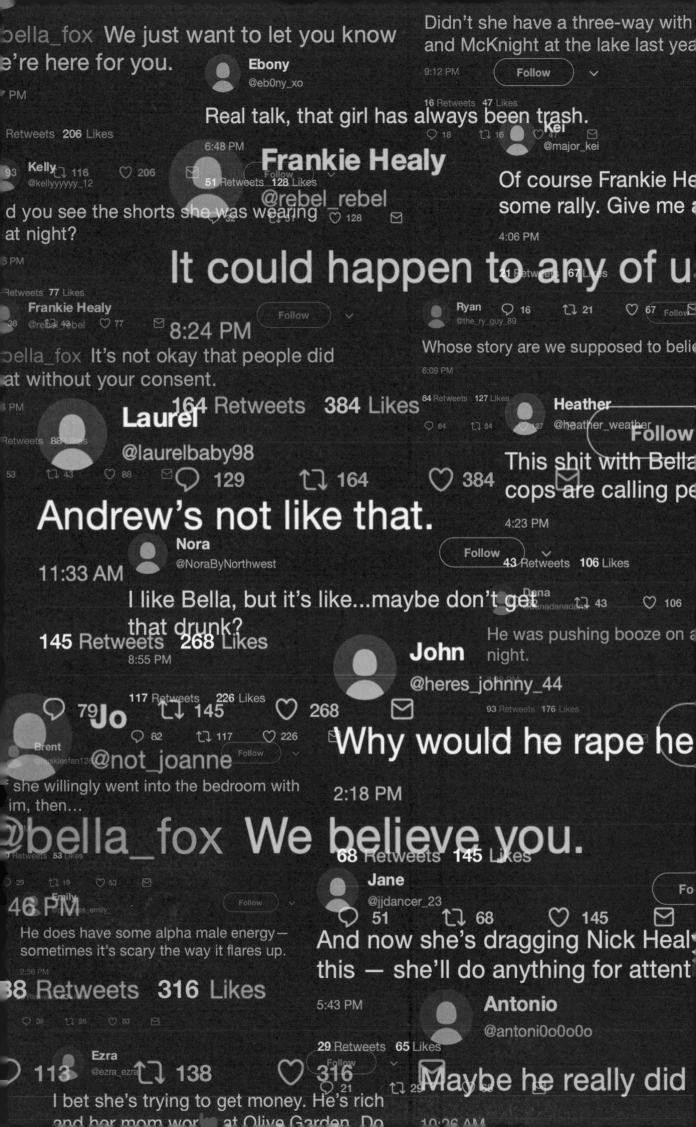

"This could get messy."

2

ENTR'ACTE

CHORUS: *Ooh this could get messy / But you don't seem to mind / Ooh don't go telling everybody / And overlook this obvious crime*

Instrumental

What part of your history's reinvented and under rug swept? / What part of your memory is selective and tends to forget? / With this distance it seems so obvious[1]

---

1   This bit comes from 'Hands Clean' off my 2002 album *Under Rug Swept*. Basically it was me talking about sexual abuse in a really pretty, harmonic song. I'm fascinated that only now are people really looking at this song. No one was really listening back then, because it just wasn't an era where sexual abuse was being taken seriously.

ACT 2 · SCENE 1

.... DR. GARDNER'S OFFICE — WAITING ROOM ....

Opening chords of "NOT THE DOCTOR." Mary Jane and Steve enter. Steve addresses the RECEPTIONIST as Mary Jane begins to sing "NOT THE DOCTOR."

STEVE: Hi. We're here to see Dr. Gardner.

MARY JANE: *I don't want to be the filler if the void is solely yours.*

STEVE: Steve and Mary Jane Healy.

MARY JANE: *And I don't want to share the secrets / That we've hidden well in our bottom drawer*[1]

STEVE: It's our first session.

MARY JANE: *And I don't want to be the bandage if the wound is not mine...*

STEVE: MJ?

MARY JANE: *Show me the back door!*

RECEPTIONIST: Just fill this out and she'll be right with you.

Steve chimes in with his own internal monologue as Mary Jane fills out the paperwork.

STEVE: *(to Mary Jane)* Why are you pouting?

MARY JANE: I'm not. *(then)* This wasn't my idea.

STEVE: I can't have ideas?

STEVE: *I don't want to be resented when I'm just trying to provide for you / I don't want to be berated for simply doing my best to reach you*[2] */ I don't want to be controlling, I just want our life to be normal again / What do you take me—*

MARY JANE AND STEVE: *What do you take me for?*

DR. GARDNER enters the waiting area at this awkward moment.

---

1 "In the original, these lyrics were: 'I don't want to be your glass of single malt whiskey / Hidden in the bottom drawer.'"
2 "I changed the lyrics for when the song switches to Steve's point of view. The original verse was: 'I don't want to be adored for what I merely represent to you / I don't want to be your babysitter / You're a very big boy now.'"

MARY JANE AND STEVE: *Visiting hours are nine to five*

STEVE: *And if I show up at ten past six, well I / I guarantee that there'll be no way she lets me in and oh*

MARY JANE AND STEVE: *Mind the awkward silence with our backs toward each other / You see it's too much to ask for and I / Am not the doctor*

DR. GARDNER: *(breezy)* Hello, I am the doctor. But you can call me Clare. Are you ready to open your hearts?

MARY JANE AND STEVE: *No I'm not the—*

DR. GARDNER: So, what brings you here?

MARY JANE: I guess I just don't see the point of this. I don't think we need counseling. I'd say we're probably the happiest of all our friends.

Steve buries his head in his hands.

STEVE: Oh boy...

MARY JANE: What?

STEVE: It's just that you turn everything into a contest, even when it isn't. We're the happiest. You made the front row at spin class. Our son got into the best school. It's like, we get it, Mary Jane, you're winning at Candy Land.

MARY JANE: Jesus, Steve, that's hostile! *(to Dr. Gardner)* I don't know where this is coming from.

STEVE: *(to Dr. Gardner)* We haven't had sex in almost a year.

MARY JANE: You're really just putting it all out there right away, huh?

STEVE: That's why we're here.

MARY JANE: I thought we were here to talk about our marriage and kids. Why does everything have to be about sex?

DR. GARDNER: Sex and marriage can be inextricably linked.

MARY JANE: *(exasperated)* My grandparents were married for 71 years. All those decades they spent caring for each other—that wasn't about sex. It was about family and about commitment and...

STEVE: Your grandparents had 12 kids, MJ. They were sex *fiends*.

DR. GARDNER: *(interrupting)* Okay, so we'll start here. Mary Jane, it looks like Steve is looking to re-establish a connection through physical touch. And Mary Jane, you require more of an emotional connection. And this is where we actually set each other up to win by knowing what touches your partner's heart the most.

MARY JANE: Apparently it's not Steve's heart that needs touching.[3]

DR. GARDNER: *(interrupting)* I see. So, Steve, you would describe yourself as the more high-libido partner? The initiator?

STEVE: ...And getting kicked in the head with a loafer.

MARY JANE: These are not loafers, they're drivers. Loafers have a sole.

DR. GARDNER: Mary Jane, you're reluctant to have sex. Has it always been this way?

STEVE: *(emphatic) Noooo*. Not at all! *(to Mary Jane, who looks offended)* It hasn't!

MARY JANE: Well, I got in a car accident. It would be nice if people were sensitive about that.

DR. GARDNER: *(to Mary Jane)* Sometimes physical injury can trigger past trauma, even sexual trauma—

STEVE: I would describe myself as a beagle under a table, begging for scraps...

MARY JANE: Oh, come on...

---

3 "When I wrote the original lyrics for the song behind this scene, I was basically saying, 'Get your shit together and call me; you're getting on my nerves.' Which is kind of an immature way of looking at long-term commitment. It was perfect for when I was nineteen because I wasn't ready for that yet. Now that I've been married ten years, I'm very clear on the fact that the epicenter of our relationship is my wanting to participate in the healing of his wounds and vice versa. So we're really actively participating. Sometimes I may feel like saying, 'You just deal with this with your fricking individual therapist; I don't have time.' But for the most part, with anything that comes up in my marriage, I feel inspired to be an active participant around the healing process, and Souleye is with me on that too.

One thing I was thinking about when I wrote this song was how, during the Second World War, all the men went to war and the women took over back at home. That spurred this movement towards autonomy, this realization: We can do anything a man can do, only better (and hey, look at my big bicep muscle!). We can do everything that we've been relying on our men for. It afforded empowerment, but it didn't afford love. That didn't help the romantic cause. So basically, 'Not the Doctor' is my talking from a very autonomous place, saying, 'Hey, you're over there, you have your wounds, you be responsible for those; I'll be over here, I'll take care of mine, we'll talk later.'"

MARY JANE: I don't have any sexual trauma. *(interrupting)* Look. I don't think having a lower sex drive is as bad as the alternative. There are people who are addicted and obsessed. For instance, Steve here looks at porn every single day.

STEVE: MJ!

DR. GARDNER: Why don't we go back to where we started.

MARY JANE: *(continuing)* You should see some of his search terms. They're *very* creative. Things I wouldn't even think of putting together! Redhead *and* MILF *and* outdoors. Nurse *and* shower *and* three-way...

STEVE: *(ashamed)* Mary Jane. Don't do this...

MARY JANE: Oh, you shouldn't be embarrassed. *I* should be embarrassed. Why would you even *want* to sleep with me when you already have such a vibrant sex life with Steve Healy?

DR. GARDNER: Whoa. Hold up. Let's talk this through...

STEVE: Maybe this was a mistake. Apparently I'm the only one with a problem.

DR. GARDNER: Your wounds are her wounds. And hers are yours. You need to learn to actively participate in each other's healing.

Not the Doctor

STEVE: Look, I'm sorry I'm not this perfect, disciplined person like you. I'm sorry I have needs. Don't you ever need anything?

Mary Jane is tempted to tell him the truth. But she can't.

DR. GARDNER: Everyone needs something, Steve.

STEVE: She doesn't. You don't know MJ. There's a reason everyone is jealous of her. She's the perfect mom, the perfect hostess—when she got in that car wreck last year, a day after her surgery she was up making quiche for the people that were supposed to be helping her. She's incredible. I *do* appreciate her.

MARY JANE: Well, you haven't been Googling "quiche."

STEVE: *(to Dr. Gardner)* She's funny, too. *(then, emotional)* We weren't always like this. There was a time when we were happy.[4]

---

4 "I love this moment when MJ makes this acerbic and cynical comment, and Steve responds by saying, 'See, she's funny.' It's so sweet. This is one of my favorite scenes. Working with Diablo, I based it on my own experience being a psychotherapeutic girl.

Frankie and Phoenix appear as though in a split screen. The music for "HEAD OVER FEET" begins.

STEVE: *(to Mary Jane)* I miss you. We were amazing once. Do you remember?

STEVE:
I had no choice

You stated your case

I thought about it

PHOENIX:
But to hear you

Time and again
I thought about it

MARY JANE:
You treat me like

I'm not used to

FRANKIE:
I'm a princess
Liking that

You ask how my
day was

MARY JANE: I'm just tired.

STEVE: You don't have to do so much, MJ.

FRANKIE:
You've already won me over[1]
In spite of me
And don't be alarmed
If I fall
Head over feet

MARY JANE:
And don't be alarmed
If I fall

1 Says orchestrator Tom Kitt, "The verse modulates up a step into the chorus, but because I was speaking to different characters and different places and times within the song, I modulated even more, so the song begins in one key, and then it modulates to another key for that first chorus. Putting it all together, I felt like a mad scientist."

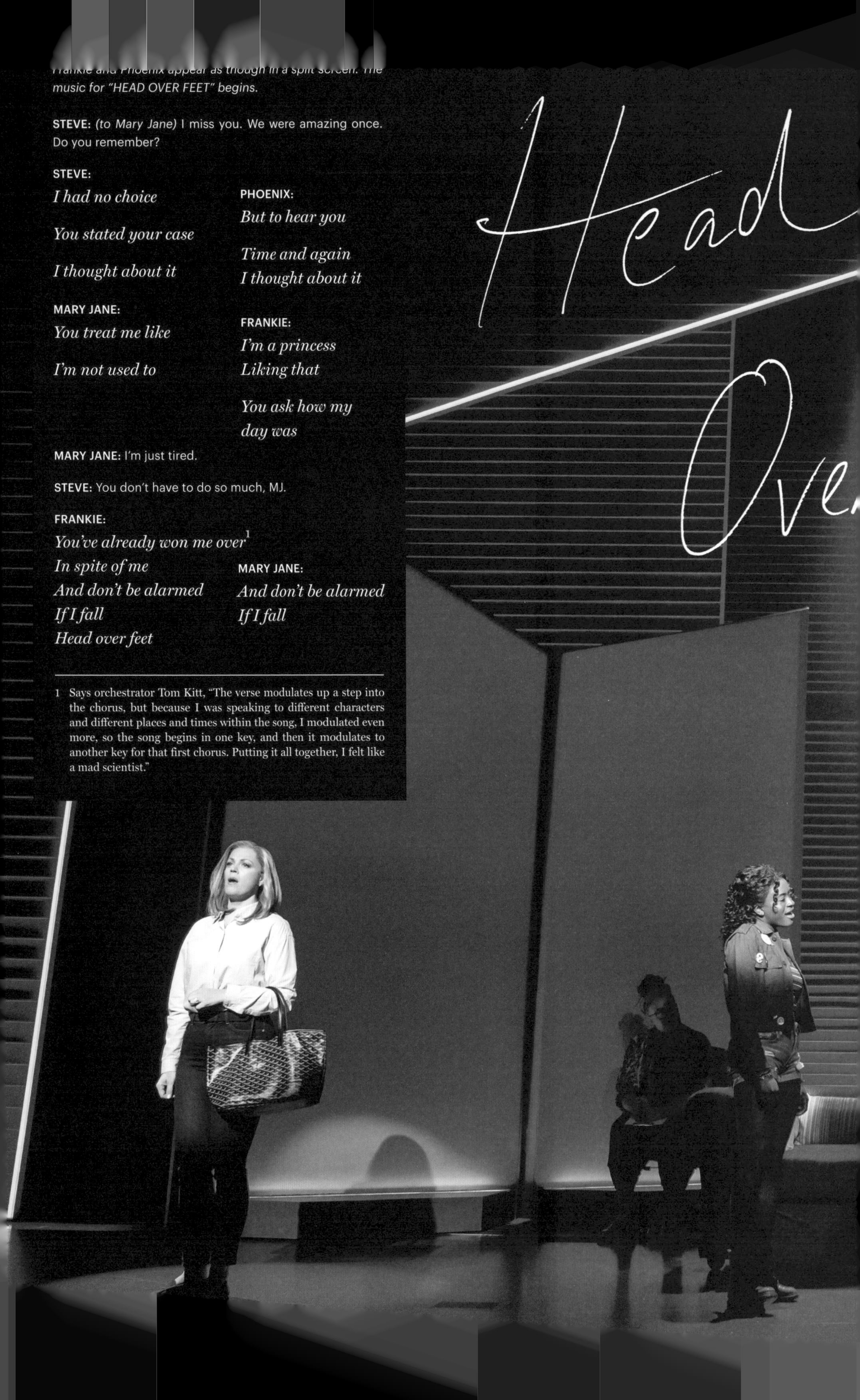

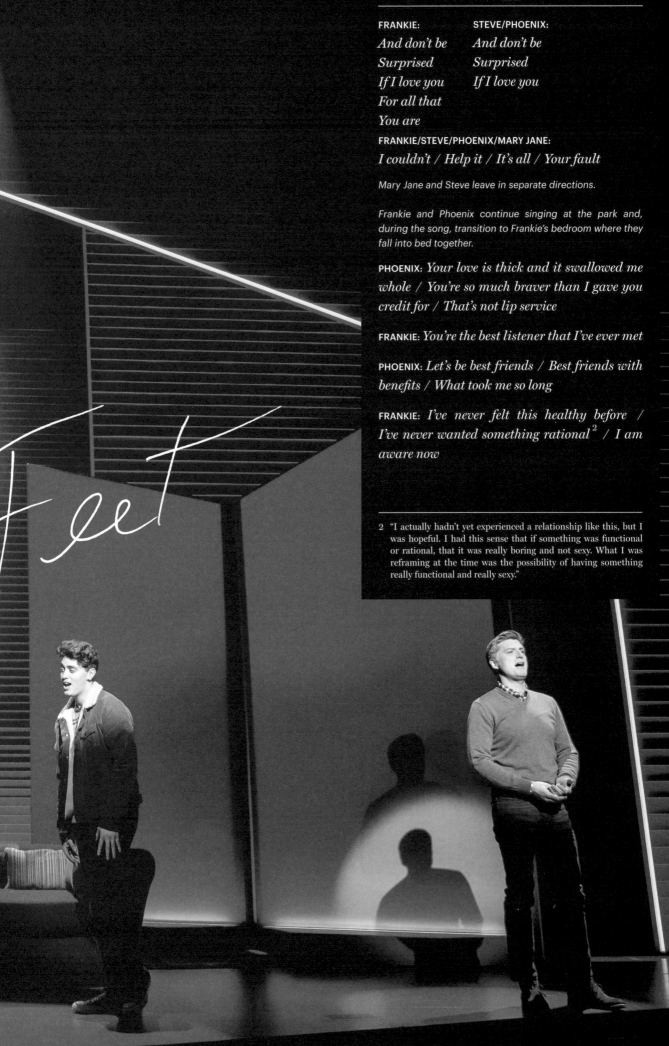

FRANKIE:	STEVE/PHOENIX:
And don't be	*And don't be*
Surprised	*Surprised*
If I love you	*If I love you*
For all that	
You are	

FRANKIE/STEVE/PHOENIX/MARY JANE:
I couldn't / Help it / It's all / Your fault

Mary Jane and Steve leave in separate directions.

Frankie and Phoenix continue singing at the park and, during the song, transition to Frankie's bedroom where they fall into bed together.

PHOENIX: *Your love is thick and it swallowed me whole / You're so much braver than I gave you credit for / That's not lip service*

FRANKIE: *You're the best listener that I've ever met*

PHOENIX: *Let's be best friends / Best friends with benefits / What took me so long*

FRANKIE: *I've never felt this healthy before / I've never wanted something rational [2] / I am aware now*

---

2 "I actually hadn't yet experienced a relationship like this, but I was hopeful. I had this sense that if something was functional or rational, that it was really boring and not sexy. What I was reframing at the time was the possibility of having something really functional and really sexy."

FRANKIE AND PHOENIX: *I am aware now / You've already won me over in spite of me / And don't be alarmed if I fall head over feet / And don't be surprised if I love you for all that you are / I couldn't help it / It's all your fault / You've already won me over in spite of me / And don't be alarmed if I fall head over feet / And don't be surprised if I love you for all that you are / I couldn't help it / It's all your fault*

FRANKIE: *Knot in my stomach and*

PHOENIX: *Lump in my throat*

We suddenly hear a voice. It's Jo, singing "YOUR HOUSE" as she approaches. Jo enters the Healy house like she's done a million times before.

JO: *I went to your house / Walked up the stairs / I opened your door without ringing the bell / I walked down the hall into your room / Where I could feel you / And I shouldn't be here without permission / Shouldn't be here...*[3]

Jo stares at Phoenix in the bed. He waves.

PHOENIX: Hi. Phoenix. You know me from biology class?

JO: *(in shock)* Right. We dissected an earthworm together.

PHOENIX: Yeah. *(awkward)* It had five hearts. They were all still beating.

Jo takes in the scene, wordless, then runs out of the bedroom.

FRANKIE: Jo!

Mary Jane and Steve enter.

MARY JANE: *(to Steve)* Actually, *you* violated *my* privacy by saying all that...

STEVE: That's kind of the point of therapy! *(startled)* Oh. Hi, Joanne.

Jo is trembling with rage and hurt. She begins babbling at Mary Jane.

JO: *(mock-cheerful)* Hi Steve. Hey, I thought you should know that Frankie is in her room with a boy in her bed! They've been having sexual intercourse while you were out. There's a condom on the floor...

STEVE: What?

MARY JANE: She has a boy in here?

JO: Yeah. I'm sure he's parkouring down the side of your house as we speak, but yeah. A guy was banging your daughter!

STEVE: Joanne!

---

3   "This song captures that moment of, 'Wow, I really love this person and I want to make this work, but their definition of monogamy is quite different from mine.' It's that sobering moment of, 'OK, not everyone is psyched about monogamy in the same way that I am.'"

JO: He was wearing dog tags with no shirt like a douche. Frankie barely knows this person. They met like five minutes ago. Also, please do not call me Joanne. I am not a fucking fabric store.

Jo runs out the door.

MARY JANE: *(yelling)* Frankie, what's going on here?

STEVE: You had a boy over here? In my house?

FRANKIE: I had a friend over.

He sees Phoenix take off.

STEVE: Yeah, there goes your "friend" running down Buttercup Drive with his pants falling down.

MARY JANE: Was this your first time?

FRANKIE: I don't have to tell you that! I have agency over my own body!

MARY JANE: Agency...what do you even mean?!

FRANKIE: Yeah, you *would* be unclear on "agency."

STEVE: Mary Frances. You are 16 years old. You're not ready.

MARY JANE: You're too young to be doing this. Especially with a boy you just met.

FRANKIE: What if it was a girl? I'm bisexual, did you know that?

STEVE: Whoa, okay...

MARY JANE: *(shocked)* Now you're just trying to shock us.

FRANKIE: You know, it's crazy how you don't have any problem with what happened to Bella, but when I *choose* to have sex with someone I care about it's a crime. I *chose* this.

MARY JANE: You didn't choose this. Some boy you just met talked you into it! I know how this works. And don't get me started on the situation with Bella. If you're not more careful, Frankie, that could happen to you too!

FRANKIE: *(stunned)* You don't get it.

Frankie begins throwing clothes in a duffel bag. Steve and Mary Jane continue their conversation.

MARY JANE: What are you doing?!

FRANKIE: None of your business.

STEVE: Actually it is. You're our child.

Frankie laughs at this.

FRANKIE: I'm not your child! Look at me! You don't own me just because you have a piece of paper in a file folder somewhere.

STEVE: Frankie!

FRANKIE: Is that even my real name? You thought you

could straighten my hair and erase all the parts of me you didn't like—

MARY JANE: *(stunned)* Honey, we—

FRANKIE: You thought if you raised me around all white kids that I'd turn out like you. Well, I'm glad I didn't. You guys, Nick...you live in a bubble. Or one of your perfect, stupid Christmas ornaments. You only see what you want to see.

STEVE: Sweetie—all we've ever done is love you.

FRANKIE: Oh yes, you're such wonderful people for "saving" a black child. Well, maybe I didn't need saving!

Frankie runs out of the house. Mary Jane longs to run after her, but hesitates. Steve comes up behind her.

MARY JANE: Frankie!

STEVE: Just let her go. She'll come back; she always does. She needs space.

MARY JANE: I told you I didn't want to go today. I didn't want to leave for two hours.

STEVE: What were we supposed to do, hire a sitter? She's not a baby anymore.

(awkward) Clearly.

MARY JANE: I don't know how she could say those things. I've never treated her differently...

STEVE: Maybe we should have. Maybe we should have let her meet her birth family.

MARY JANE: I wasn't going to expose her to that! I'm her mother; it's my job to protect her, and that's what I did.

STEVE: I think we made some mistakes.

MARY JANE: *(angry, defensive)* Who's "we"? You? You were barely there!

STEVE: What are you talking about?

MARY JANE: What do you think happened while you were gone 60 hours a week? A whole lot, let me tell you! Where were you when someone came up to Frankie and told her she was pretty for a black girl? Where were you when I had to answer a million rude questions from people at the playground: "Where did you get her? Was she abused? How much did she cost?"

STEVE: I got questions too, you know that—

MARY JANE: I did the work, Steve! I made every lunch, every dinner. I took care of her when she had strep throat, I was there 24/7. You've been gone for 90 percent of our kids' lives!

STEVE: So I could provide for them. And you...

MARY JANE: You weren't there for anything. You don't even know us.

STEVE: No wonder she hates you.

Even Steve is surprised by the cruelty of this comment. Mary Jane storms off.

AT THE TENDER HEART

In an interview with *Rolling Stone* in 1998, a then 24-year-old Alanis Morissette, who was already one of the best-selling female musicians of all time, sat down to discuss the many misperceptions that came with fame. To begin with, she wanted to let everyone know that she was not just—as *Rolling Stone* had once described her—"the stormy girl du jour." She was more than just her anger, or her temper, or her sadness. Her incandescent rages were a part of her—and they still are—but Morissette wanted people to understand that she was more than just the poster girl for pent-up Gen X angst, thrashing her long brown tendrils around while yodeling about revenge. If she came across as exasperated and incensed on her first record, she explained, it was because she wrote *Jagged Little Pill* as a direct response to the squeaky, polished image she had to project throughout her teenage years as a Canadian pop star. "When I was a teenager, I felt like I had to be positive and laughing and upbeat and maternal in all my friendships and interactions, and I felt that nobody would want to hear about any pain or difficulty that I was going through," she said. "If you hear the records that I did between when I was nine and when I was eighteen, there are some references to difficulties or pain, but I think, musically especially, it's very upbeat. It was very smiling-all-the-time, even when I wasn't happy."

She wrote the harsher songs on *Jagged Little Pill*, such as "Not the Doctor" (which dresses down a needy lover by saying "I don't want to be your mother, I didn't carry you in my womb for nine months"), as a kind of "self-protective" strike against those who would want to take advantage of her. She had spent her youth being told where to go, what to do, and when to smile by exploitative men. She would never let that happen again. "It's funny that the very lifestyle I entered into at the time *Jagged Little Pill* came out is the lifestyle where you have to, just for survival's sake, keep a lot of people at arm's length," Morissette said. "And I really think I threw the baby out with the bath water."

Still, Morissette's innate gentleness and sincerity are all over *Jagged Little Pill*, even as she was trying to project a tough exterior to the world. "Head Over Feet," the eighth song on the album, is a full-throated, unabashed love song and an homage to the giddy, carbonated rush of fresh infatuation. Along with "You Learn," it is part of the album's gooey, warm center—and a sign that Morissette was never really as angry as her critics made her out to be. She not only had a soft side, but also a schmaltzy side. She could be as gushy and sentimental as she could be growling and vengeful. And in a way, this rainbow of extreme emotion was the secret to the album's mass appeal. Had Morissette only expressed her disgust with sleazy men and her frustrations with draconian religious institutions, she might have been written off as a harpy or a shrew (as it was, several critics called her a "banshee" when *JLP* came out). Instead, she made a record that was howling and furious but also tender and idealistic and goofy. What the album was trying to do was map the complex, prismatic landscape of a young woman's mind, which is an unpredictable landscape full of righteous fury, existential questions, and heart-shaped doodles. If listening to the songs on *Jagged Little Pill* makes you feel like a perpetual teenager, well, that is the point. They are supposed to be a little too much, a maximalist explosion of feelings that sounds like the aural equivalent of a collage that covers an entire bedroom wall.

"Head Over Feet" is a song about the irrational pull of a blossoming romance, about the craving one can have for another during the honeymoon phase of a relationship. From the first line, "I had no choice," Morissette makes it clear that falling in love was a fait accompli, a force she could not resist even if she tried. She has said she wrote the song about a person who was incredibly kind to her, and how her first instinct was to push him away because she wasn't used to being treated with respect. "That song

> "When you are young, falling in love can feel like a centrifugal force."

was about the conflict with wanting to embrace these kind moments, but there also being a disparity between what I thought I deserved, versus how I was being treated," she said in an interview. Morissette begins the song with a thick crust of doubt ("You stated your case, time and again, I thought about it," she says to her suitor), but ends it with a soaring vocalise that sounds like wide open arms, willing to risk getting hurt if it means not cutting herself off from human connection. "I've never felt this healthy before," she cooes. "I've never wanted something rational. I am aware now."

In the musical, the song becomes a quartet, contrasting old love with new, teenage infatuation with the challenges of a long-term marriage. At first, Mary Jane and Steve start singing the song to each other in couples' therapy, as they try to remember why they initially fell for each other. So much has happened since those early days, when they pursued each other in college. They are grasping for a way back to those feelings, for that hunger for each other. Steve pleads with Mary Jane on the therapist's couch, asking her to travel back in her mind to their former happiness. She tries to tell him what's going on inside her head, but cannot find the words. "You treat me like..." she says, but doesn't finish the sentence. She wants to tell Steve that his

devotion to her is not the balm she needs—she doesn't want to be worshipped, she wants someone to ask her the hard questions about what's really going on.

Meanwhile, Frankie and Phoenix's mutual curiosity is just starting to bloom into something more tangible. The two teenage characters appear from either end of the stage and take over the song, walking slowly toward each other during the first verse. "You've already won me over," Frankie sings to Phoenix. "In spite of me." By the time the chorus hits, the two are harmonizing while they grip onto a swing set that is rotating rapidly at the center of the stage. It looks like a dream ballet, or a swirling montage from a romantic comedy. When you are young, falling in love can feel like centrifugal force, like the whole world is spinning. It makes you dizzy and a little nauseous, but you hold on and try to enjoy the ride.

Tom Kitt, the show's musical director, says that in early versions of the show, "Head Over Feet" came in the first act, but "it just felt like Phoenix and Frankie went too far too fast." When Cody and Paulus decided to move the song to Act Two so that it dovetails with the therapy scene, Kitt said that the song immediately took on a heavier, more complex meaning.

> "It makes you dizzy and a little nauseous, but you hold on and try to enjoy the ride."

"That there are two people in love and two people in crisis at the same time, it doesn't make it so effusive," he said. "It gives some darkness to what is a beautiful, unabashed lyric."

He also noted that "Head Over Feet" is a deceptively sophisticated musical accomplishment. Three-quarters of the way through the song, the key changes, allowing Morissette to throw her voice into an even higher register, mimicking the sudden intensity of a burgeoning crush. "When I first heard that modulation, I remember thinking, God this is so complicated, and it feels effortless when you're listening to the song," Kitt said. "But it's actually a very complicated composition."

ACT 2 · SCENE 2

Frankie begins to sing "UNPRODIGAL DAUGHTER" as she travels to New York City.

FRANKIE:

I had disengaged to avoid being totaled[1]

I would run away and say	**CHORUS:**
Good riddance soon enough	*Ahh*
I had grown disgusted by your	
Small-minded ceiling	*Mmm*
To imagine myself bolting	
had not been difficult	

Soon be my life	*Soon be*
Soon be my pace	*Soon be*
Soon be my choice	*Soon*
Of which you'll have no part of	*Ahh*

Unprodigal daughter	
Heading out onto my quest	
Disenchanted daughter	
and this train	
Cannot move fast enough	*Ahh*
Unencumbered daughter	
hit the ground	
Running at last!	
I'd invite you but I'm busy	
Being unoppresssed	*Being unoppressed*

FRANKIE/SINGERS:

One day I'll saddle back and speak of foreign adventures / One day I'll double back / And tell you about these unfettered years / One day I'll look back and feel something other than relieved

ALL: *Glad that I left when I did / I know you, you can't get the best of me*

FRANKIE: *When I'd speak of artistry / You would roll your eyes skyward / When I'd speak of spirituality / You would label me absurd / When I spoke of possibility / You would frown and shake your head*

FRANKIE/CHORUS: *If I had stayed much longer I'd have surely / Imploded / These are my words / This is my house / These are my friends / Of which you've / Had no part of*

CHORUS: *Unprodigal daughter*

FRANKIE: *Heading out onto my quest*

CHORUS: *Disenchanted daughter*

FRANKIE: *And this train cannot move fast enough*

CHORUS: *Unencumbered daughter*

FRANKIE: *Hit the ground running at last!*

FRANKIE/CHORUS: *I'd invite you but I'm busy being unoppressed / Being unoppressed, being unoppressed*

FRANKIE: *Being unoppressed!*

A VOICE: *You from New York*[2] */ You are so relevant / You reduce me to cosmic tears*

Energized by her freedom, Frankie takes out her phone and calls Phoenix. He picks up.

FRANKIE: Phoenix, hey. Did you get my text?

PHOENIX: *(distracted)* No, sorry...

FRANKIE: I'm in New York! In the East Village! I think. Ugh, my parents won't stop calling.

PHOENIX: What?

FRANKIE: I just ran away from home.

---

1 "When I originally wrote this, it was partly about family, partly about education, and partly about the culture in general. Any idea I had as a teenager was met with, 'Oh, you can't do that,' 'That doesn't rhyme,' or 'Your record company's not going to be so happy with that song.' I felt as if no one had the right to give unsolicited feedback, which I think is one of the most violent kinds of communication."

2 "I actually wrote this song about L.A. Part of what I loved about Hollywood then was, there was no ceiling. Any idea I had was met with, 'Yeah, let's do that tomorrow. Let's shoot it. Fuck it.' Going there was my way of emancipating."

PASSERBY 1 (KEN): You're in the middle of the sidewalk!

FRANKIE: I couldn't take it anymore. I can't deal with any of them.

PHOENIX: Can I call you right back?

PASSERBY 2: *(to Frankie)* Do you have a minute to talk about the environment?

PHOENIX: My sister's having a problem with her G-tube.

FRANKIE: What?

PHOENIX: It's a thing. She can't eat normally. *(then, calling out)* Just a second, Mom.

FRANKIE: You should come here! You got your car fixed, right?

PHOENIX: Yeah, but I kind of...can't? It's, like, a Tuesday?

FRANKIE: Come on. We could go to the Great Lawn and look at the stars. *(then)* I think Central Park is somewhere around here?

PASSERBY 3 (LAUREL): If it's more than an hour I'm not flying coach.

PHOENIX: Look, I gotta go.

FRANKIE: Are you mad at me or something?

PHOENIX: No, of course not. It's just that things got kind of heavy for a minute there. Jo was pissed at us. Is she, like, your girlfriend?

FRANKIE: *(interrupting)* I don't want to talk about that. *(beat)* I love you. *(long beat)* Aren't you going to say it?

PHOENIX: I can't. Yet.

FRANKIE: What?   **PHOENIX:** Because it means a lot to me. I want it to be the right time...

FRANKIE: Can this be the right time? I kind of need to hear it.

PHOENIX: *(awkward)* This is so new.

FRANKIE: Right...I guess it was fun to hook up with me because I'm something different and exotic, but loving me—that's impossible, right?

PHOENIX: Frankie, you know I'm not like that! I think you're so beautiful, I just—

She hangs up.

FRANKIE: I should have known.

Unprodigal Daughter

Daughter / (Frankie)
— artist/
riot grrl
— source of shame — rebel
— is not working out like her
mother wanted — sibling who
is perfect
— she has rejected Perfection
— is putting herself into
bad love/addiction relationships;
serial dating, bad habits —
— is this a HS girl or a young woman
in her twenties — back at home...
how old?
— involved in protests / transracial
adopted
in a
white
family
— feeling like growing up on the
wrong planet —

I'll tell you the first moment that *Jagged Little Pill*, the musical came into my mind. It was right after a guitar lesson. My mom [the Broadway performer LaChanze] came home. And she's like, "Celia, they're looking for unknown black talent for this Alanis Morissette musical. Do you know 'You Oughta Know'?" And I started running around my kitchen island jumping up and down singing that song. So I asked my guitar teacher to stay for an extra hour and he accompanied me in my basement. And I sent in the video of me singing in terrible, terrible acoustics. It's been history since. I did the reading in 2017. I remember at the same time I did my reading, I took a day off to go to my junior prom.

You started playing Frankie when you were only seventeen years old. Is it safe to say you have kind of grown up with the character?
I was living through Frankie with the level of awareness that a seventeen-year-old person can have. Now two years later so much has happened, and there's been so much radical self-understanding that I've come to. I am able to use that to inform a young but incredibly wise black queer woman in a predominantly white space. I truly feel that I have been blessed with a wealth of knowledge to inform both myself and the audiences that come to the show. Looking out into the audience, not a lot of them look like me. It's a gift to be able to tell this story so that other people can understand what it's like to be in this body and to inhabit the space that I do.

The production team for the show is predominantly female, but also predominantly white. How did you feel you worked together to be able to accurately portray a woman of color's story on stage?

Celia Rose Gooding (Frankie Healy)

has performed on stage as Penelope Pennywise in *Urinetown* and Carmen Diaz in *Fame* at the Rosetta LeNoire Musical Theatre Academy in New York City. She studied acting and film at the Berridge Conservatory in Normandy, France, with a concentration in Shakespeare, as well as dance at the Ailey School. She is a graduate of Hackley School in Tarrytown, New York, with hours in performing arts. She is currently a student at Pace University in New York City, majoring in Musical Theater.

Tell me about your first experience with Jagged Little Pill, *the album.*
I knew of a lot of the music before I even knew who Alanis was. One of the first songs I learned how to play on guitar when I played it briefly was "You Oughta Know." I wasn't deeply wronged by a lover, but that song just felt really, really good. Looking back, I realize that it was the first time when I could find the intersection of anger and feminism. I think a lot of my femininity, being a black girl in a white space, was processed like daintiness and softness and how palatable I could be. But with "You Oughta Know," it was so outspoken and beautifully angry and deeply, deeply feminist. I realized that there was a way to be a really awesome, angry, powerful woman. And that idea has carried me throughout my whole life.

How did you get involved in the musical?
I grew up in Westchester in the Bronxville area. Frankie and Celia have very similar growing-up experiences. We intersect often. I can think back as Celia and say, "I've been there. I've been through the touching of the hair and the rejection from white guys and knowing what that deep hurt feels like."

"I am able to ... inform a young but incredibly wise black queer woman in a predominantly white space."

With Diablo Cody, there were so many instances where either she pulled me aside or I pulled her aside and we just talked about the truth of it. It's so easy for predominantly white production teams to overlook a black experience. Not on purpose, but just because they don't understand it and they don't want to speak on something they don't understand. So feeling that they gave me this space and they made me feel so safe and so comfortable that it just poured out of me. And they took everything, they took all of it. It was amazing because it was one of the first times when I shared my experience to a group of white people and they actually received it, and were like, "Okay. Let's put that in the show." I honestly can say that if it weren't for those moments of being around this group of people and sharing my truth and knowing that they actually heard it, I would not be nearly as outspoken as I am today.

What was one of those moments, when you felt Diablo and Diane included something from your own experience in the show?

So after the phone call with Phoenix, Frankie shares this really, really deep personal hurt and fear of being fetishized as a black woman, as being the thing that you can sort of play with and toy with because it's fun and it's new and it's different. I said, "This is what Frankie's thinking. Why doesn't she just say it? Why don't we just say it and be uncomfortable for a second because that's the discomfort we feel every single day?" And Diablo was like, "Great, we're keeping it, we're putting it in."

Frankie and Jo have a tumultuous relationship. They are best friends, and also lovers. Over the course of the show, Frankie betrays Jo and those bonds are severed. But they are so strong at the beginning. I'm thinking of the joy you and Lauren Patten radiate during "Hand in My Pocket."

With Frankie and Jo, it's very similar to the friendship that Lauren and I have. We love each other very deeply. Before every show I swing by, give her a kiss on the forehead, tell her I love her, and get ready to do the show. That's just my person in this cast.

What do you see as the meaning of "Hand in My Pocket," especially for your generation?

Frankie is so busy trying to save so many other people that she forgets the people who are trying to save her. And it's heartbreaking, but it's in high school. What can you do? I think with "Hand in My Pocket," though, the idea is that there's a whole bunch of stuff going on. We are in a really, really scary place, politically, emotionally, socially, mentally, physically, environmentally. It's really easy to get overwhelmed and think, "Oh God, there's nothing we can do." And no matter the level of truth in that, you have to understand that with whatever time we have, we've got to put a hand in the pocket and say, "You know what? Everything's going to be fine," and keep it pushing.

Especially for my generation, Gen Z, we've sort of been given the very bottom of the barrel. Life's only getting harder. Things are only getting more expensive. College is impossible. Student loans are terrifying. Our president's insane. The planet is dying. We've inherited a dying earth and we're the ones being told that we have to fix it, and we can't, because

we're kids. And the people who are supposed to be responsible aren't doing it anymore because they think now it's our job, and that's not the case. So we have to understand that we can't fix what we didn't break.

The show deals with the subject of transracial adoption and its many complexities—Mary Jane and Steve love Frankie, but they cannot always understand her experience. How did you prepare to tackle that issue?

It was a lot of conversation. It was a lot of reading on all of our parts of just what transracial adoption is and the emotional and mental effects it can have on both parties, the parent and the child. And it was a lot of me speaking on my black experience and Elizabeth speaking on her white experience, and knowing where they intersect and where they're different, and finding the places in which they can butt heads. We've given ourselves a map and we're navigating through that every day.

Your big solo number is "Unprodigal Daughter," a song that was not on Jagged Little Pill, *but still perfectly captures Frankie's exuberance after she runs away from home towards New York City.*

Frankie understands that she can't keep looking for other people to save her. That's what "Unprodigal" means to me. It's about Frankie saying that she is going to release herself from the bondage that she feels her hometown is keeping her in. She is the person who's going to just pack up and say, "You know what? This town is not built for me. This space is not something that I will be able to modify and fix and make comfortable for me. I'm not going to build a world that's safe for me when I know there's something out there that already is, so I'm just going to go there."

And that's where Frankie's mind is. Larbi has choreographed this incredible number for her. It's a lot of movements that open the chest. To be very technical about it, it's a lot of opening that heart space and opening that place where you keep all your tension and where you carry your truth. And that is so joyous and so fierce and so, so important for Frankie.

When Lauren Patten is singing "You Oughta Know," you as Frankie have to stand on stage and just kind of...take in Jo's hurt and rejection. What does it feel like to absorb that every night?
I think that moment when Lauren starts singing "You Oughta Know" is a moment of Frankie really understanding the effect she has on people. She grows up thinking that a lot of her actions don't have consequences. And that's not me saying that Frankie is reckless with her decisions. She just thinks that since no one really cares about her, no one's going to hold her accountable for what she does. So she's going to be yelling so someone can hear her and she's going to be the most outspoken person, and she's going to be the loudest in the room just so someone can hear her. And she doesn't really realize that Jo has heard her the whole time.

Frankie obviously doesn't think that she is a flawless person, but she is not really looking at herself when she is trying to fix a broken planet as one person. And when "You Oughta Know" starts, Frankie is still trying to excuse her actions, but it's when she actually starts listening to what Jo is saying that Frankie understands that Jo felt abandoned, and that Frankie just sort of dumped all of her problems on Jo and ran away with some boy. And that's a betrayal within itself. Especially in queer relationships—leaving a queer relationship for the safety and security and the cushiness of a straight relationship. And that's a problem within itself that Frankie didn't even understand. So when "You Oughta Know" starts, Frankie is hit with radical truth after radical truth after radical truth. And it's heartbreaking for Frankie, obviously, but it's really necessary.

Frankie is the outspoken activist of the show, always fighting for a cause. She presses her brother, Nick, into fighting for Bella after the assault. But it is interesting to see how, at the end of the show when you sing "No" during Bella's rally, Frankie steps back a bit and is not the loudest voice in the crowd.
I think "No" is Frankie taking not a backseat, but a side seat, to a movement. I think it's Frankie gathering all the materials

that she needs and then putting someone else at the forefront and saying, "This is your story. I'm going to do what I can to help, but this isn't something that I'm going to be able to do on my own." It used to be Bella and Frankie hand-in-hand. And in rehearsal it changed, because it's Frankie saying, "I have gathered as many people as I can. I have gotten all the signs, I've gotten the march map. Bella, go. Go tell your truth. Go and tell the truth and make sure everyone hears you."

Technically, what is it like to sing Alanis's songs? You have so many big belting moments throughout the show.
"Ironic" is such a fun song to sing, but it places my voice right at that point where my voice will break if I'm not really, really careful. So a lot of it is me reminding myself to "breathe from the wings." Whenever I sing, I feel like I have a big old expensive pair of wings on my back. Especially in "Unprodigal Daughter," where I'm thrashing my body around and also having to sing very difficult melody tracks. I try not to get so in my head, like, "Oh my God, I'm singing one of Alanis's most iconic songs. What am I going to do?" Because I can't panic. Then the story doesn't get told.

You don't sing like Alanis at all—nobody does—but do you still feel you are channeling her spirit when you sing her songs?
I think Alanis is everywhere in the show. The show is, ultimately, about the importance of communication and the importance of being honest with yourself and with the people around you for the greater good. And so much of that was communicated from Alanis herself. I think that's where Alanis is, in every moment when someone tells the truth for the first time.

I love that moment at the very end of the show, when in the final second of "You Learn," Frankie and Mary Jane clasp hands.
It's a summary of what we've just been through. It's not a bookend. It's a checkpoint. Frankie and MJ at the end, we inhale together. We don't exhale. It's very important, because it's very easy, especially after the two and a half hours, to be like, "We're done. Hooray! We did it. It's over." No, it can't be that. It has to be, "Great. What's next? What can we do? How do we keep going?"

FACING THE FACTS

TRANSRACIAL ADOPTION

When planning to adopt, many prospective parents say that the child's race or ethnicity does not matter. They believe "that they could love a child unconditionally, regardless of whether they look like them or share their cultural heritage and traditions," according to the adoption and foster care resource and support network AdoptUSKids. It's wonderful that adoptive parents feel they can care for any child in need, but it's a myth that race doesn't matter. "Learning about and respecting a child's culture—and finding ways to maintain their connections to it—are critical components to helping an adopted child thrive," says AdoptUSKids.

Invariably, children of a different race or ethnicity will have questions their parents cannot answer. Though there's no specific operating manual for how to raise children of a different race or ethnicity, experts advise that parents address the issue instead of ignoring it. To do so could cause long-lasting harm to the child. The multimedia journalist Kaylee Domzalski, who grew up as a transracial adoptee, recently wrote in Slate about how her parents failed to teach her about her Korean heritage or language: "That's left me with a sense of loss, placelessness, and sometimes regret that I will grapple with for the rest of my life."

Pepperdine University psychology professor Thema Bryant-Davis recommends that parents create a diverse environment, including identifying potential role models of the same race or ethnicity as their child. Additionally, she says that children must develop their own positive relationships with people of their race, see their parents interacting with people of their race as peers, and learn about the legacy of people who look like them.

Helping a child of another race cope with and respond to racism and discrimination is a hugely important aspect of transracial adoption, but doing so can be tricky for adoptive parents. White parents may be able to feel grief or sadness about incidents that cause racial trauma to their children, but they do not themselves feel vulnerable or targeted. Bryant-Davis believes the best approach is for parents to "honestly acknowledge that you cannot understand the incident in the same way, while also showing compassion."

Lay the foundation for productive discussions about race by reading books and articles by authors who represent various communities of color and cultures, including *Outsiders Within: Writing on Transracial Adoption* (2006). Movies about the topic include *Off and Running* (2010) and *Girl, Adopted* (2013).

ACT 2 · SCENES 3 & 4

SOCIAL MEDIA

ENSEMBLE #1 (HEATHER): This shit with Bella Fox is crazy. I hear the cops are calling people.

ENSEMBLE #2 (MAX): Didn't she have a three-way with Zack and McKnight at the lake last year???!

ENSEMBLE #3 (EBONY): Real talk, that girl has always been trash.

ENSEMBLE #4 (EZRA): I bet she's trying to get money. He's rich and her mom works at Olive Garden. Do the math.

ENSEMBLE #5 (ANTONIO): Maybe he really did it?

ENSEMBLE #6 (LAUREL): Andrew's not like that.

ENSEMBLE #7 (JOHN): Why would he rape *her*?

ENSEMBLE #8 (KEI): Of course Frankie Healy is organizing some rally. Give me a break.

ENSEMBLE #10 (NORA): I like Bella, but it's like...maybe don't get that drunk?

ENSEMBLE #12 (JANE): And now she's dragging Nick Healy into this—she'll do anything for attention.

THE HEALY HOUSE (KITCHEN)

Mary Jane is attempting to make a quiche. She seems scattered and frustrated. She texts her dealer. Bella enters, surprising Mary Jane.

BELLA: Hi, Mrs. Healy.

MARY JANE: *(startled)* Yes. Hi, Bella.

BELLA: Can I...talk to Nick?

MARY JANE: Nick's not home.

BELLA: Is he okay? He hasn't been returning my texts... I kinda need to talk to him.

MARY JANE: He's fine; he's just not here. *(then)* Can I help you?

Bella almost laughs at the absurdity of this.

BELLA: NO. No no no...It's uh, a complicated situation...

MARY JANE: Bella, I've heard the talk about what happened, and—

BELLA: *Of course you did.*

MARY JANE: I know how you feel right now.

BELLA: I doubt that.

MARY JANE: *(with difficulty)* Something similar actually happened to me, once. Same story, really. And afterwards, I felt very angry. *(careful)* Mostly, I was angry at myself.

As Mary Jane begins to recount—however vaguely—her experience, we sense that it is extraordinarily difficult for her to talk about.

MARY JANE: Because I put myself in a dangerous situation. *(then)* In a perfect world, these things wouldn't happen. But—

BELLA: I'm not asking for perfect!

Mary Jane is thrown, but continues in her "steady lecture" voice.

MARY JANE: Bad things happen. And we have to be strong and accept our mistakes and move on.

BELLA: Okay. So you clearly moved on. When did it happen to you?

MARY JANE: *(waving it off)* It's not important.

BELLA: If it's not important, you can say it.

It's not any easier for Mary Jane to say it the second time.

MARY JANE: In college. It was a million years ago. Ancient history. Like I said, it doesn't matter anymore.

BELLA: Okay. Well, then when did you start to feel better?

This is a sincere, hopeful question from Bella. A long beat of silence from MJ.

BELLA: How long did it take?

Mary Jane is still unable to respond. Bella grows frustrated as she realizes...

BELLA: Tell me when I'm going to feel normal again.

It's clear the answer is never. And it's also clear that is the first time Mary Jane has realized that.

BELLA: Oh, that's great.

Bella charges out of the house in tears. Mary Jane is frozen in the kitchen for a beat. Nick enters.

NICK: What's going on?

MARY JANE: It's nothing. Your sister's upset. I'm making her favorite quiche; I'm sure she'll be home soon. She'll be hungry...

NICK: Was that Bella? *(beat)* I got a call from the police. They want to talk to me.

MARY JANE: No. You have nothing to do with this!

NICK: *(interrupting)* I have to tell you what happened at that party.

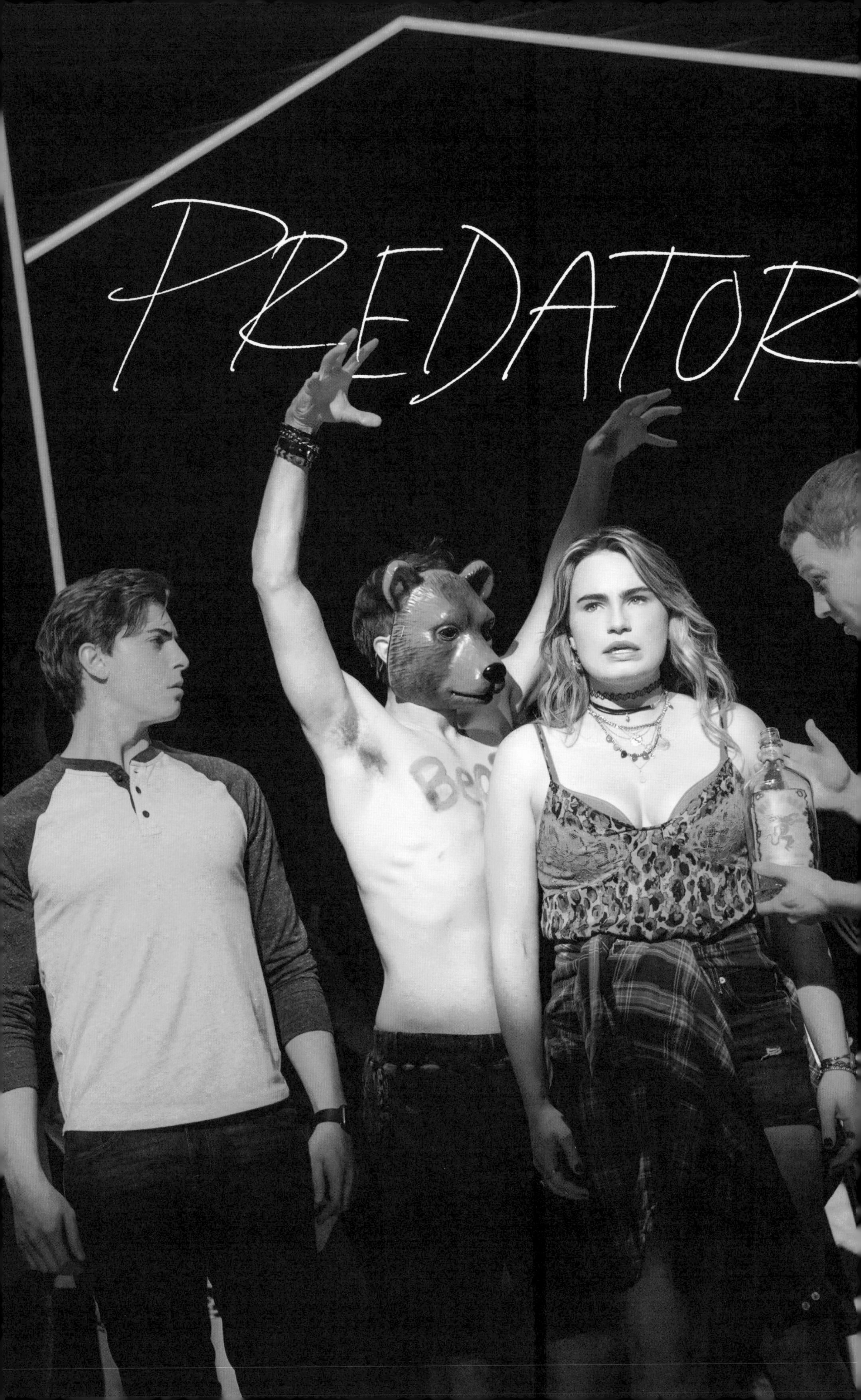
PREDATOR

A VOICE: *Ooh...*

NICK: I should have said something before... But it's like I blocked it out or something...

A VOICE: *Ooh...*

NICK: Andrew said he was gonna make sure she was okay. *(then)* Now I can't stop thinking about Bella...

BELLA slowly emerges from the background. She's making her way through a party. She sings "PREDATOR."

BELLA: *First I am spotted across the room / Sussed out for the degree of naivete / When I make the cut then all systems go / And you take your first step toward me / My eyes are invitations / My welcome sign is bright / My armor is porous enough / To be worked by your design / My goodness is commendable / But won't pull your heartstrings / This magnet for predators / Is dying to be discerning / Your system of madness to mimic connection / Then you engender my trust as you pounce / You isolate and then divert attention[1] / Distract from deception, keep me in the dark*

We see how Andrew manages to isolate Bella from the rest of the party, trying to claim her, earn her trust in her confused state. She steadies herself, laughs, tries to get away without offending him. A dance all women know. Nick is observing.

A VOICE:	CHORUS:
Ooh...	*Ahh...*[2]
Ooh...	*Ahh...*
	Ooh...ahh...
Ooh...	*Ooh...*

BELLA: *You kept me off balance / With your charming deflection / You kept me distracted / Couldn't pick this apart / What started as union / Turned to isolation / And you are obsessed with your prey*

CHORUS: *My eyes are invitations*

BELLA/CHORUS: *My welcome sign is bright / My armor is porous enough / To be worked by your design / My trusting's commendable / But won't pull your heartstrings*

BELLA: *This magnet for predators is learning to be discerning*

---

1 "This song is about the mechanics of date rape. Every circumstance is different, but it's almost predictable as to how this unfolds. They see that you're empathic and vulnerable, and they have a whole system where they do their thing."

2 Says orchestrator Tom Kitt, "Chorus member Jane Bruce acts as the voice of memory. You hear her before 'Predator' and also in the first act, when Bella is recounting what happened and when Mary Jane is in church. Her voice is like a string instrument."

BELLA:	CHORUS:
Ho ho...	*Ahh...*
Ah oh ho...	
Ho oh oh whoa...	*Oh...*

MARY JANE: *Wake up*

NICK: *Wake up*

MARY JANE: You saw that happening and did *nothing*?

NICK: I guess I kinda couldn't process what I was seeing. I just left.

MARY JANE: Did you forget she was a human being?

A beat. Nick finally reckons with the consequences of his inaction.

NICK: She was unconscious and I did nothing.

MARY JANE: How could you just walk away?

NICK: *(broken)* Mom, tell me what to do.

MARY JANE: You can't repeat this to anyone, I'll tell you that much!

NICK: People think Bella is lying! I'm her only witness.

MARY JANE: If you have to talk to the police, you tell them you were at the party and you left. You didn't see anything.

NICK: Why?

MARY JANE: Because if something like this goes public, it'll follow you for the rest of your life. Your admission could be rescinded! They do that, you know. I've read about it happening.

NICK: Why would they punish me for telling the truth?

MARY JANE: They wouldn't. They'd punish you for drinking, maybe they'd even call you an accomplice.

NICK: *(frustrated)* ...You're mad at me for not doing anything in the moment. But now I want to make it right and you're asking me not to! What about Bella?

MARY JANE: You can't help Bella now. You can't undo what happened. You'll just ruin another life. Yours.

NICK: And yours. Right? That's what you're scared of.

MARY JANE: *(shaking)* We worked too hard for this to lose it all overnight, Nick.

NICK: Fine, then I lose everything. I fucked up, Mom.

With a last sorrowful look, Mary Jane exits.

CHORUS: *Ahh... / This is the sound of me hitting*

CHORUS 1 (LAUREL):
Bottom
　　CHORUS 2 (JOHN):
　　　Bottom　CHORUS 3:
　　　　Bottom　CHORUS 4:
　　　　　Bottom

Vocal cacophony fades into NYC traffic sounds.

"This magnet for predators...

is learning..."

TELLING YOUR STORY

If you listen closely to *Jagged Little Pill*, the album, you will hear a rumbling sound bubbling just underneath the surface. It is an urgent growl, a low howl, the sound of a woman who won't be silent any longer. When *Jagged Little Pill* first came out, many critics—most of them male—picked up on this seething in her songs and used it to dismiss Morissette as histrionic; in 1996, one critic called her an "avenging banshee," suggesting that she was a jilted she-beast, out to destroy her ex-boyfriends. What these critics could not grasp in the music—but which so many of Morissette's young women fans understood implicitly—is that the anger towards men in her songs is not really about lost love or revenge. Instead, it is about something far more insidious and systemic; it is about abuse and silence, assault and power. Two decades before the #MeToo movement, Morissette and her contemporaries were singing about their own experiences with exploitation and harassment. In "Right Through You," Morissette sings "You took a long hard look at my ass and then played golf for a while."

It is not a subtle message. As a teenage pop musician in Canada, Morissette found herself surrounded by older men who not only tried to dictate her future, but were often inappropriate with their advances. "I mean, I was flying alone when I was 10," she told the *New York Times* in 2019. "I was going on a music-video shoot with four men to Europe when I was 14. I was always the one that everyone was like, 'She's going to be fine.' Meanwhile, I'm like chewing my nails down to the quick and throwing up and having sexual-abuse stories all through my teens."

While most of the songs on *Jagged Little Pill* are subtle in their treatment of abuse, Morissette began to address the subject more directly in later records. The song "Hands Clean," which originally appeared on her fifth album, *Under Rug Swept* (and appears in the musical at the top of the second act), is about a relationship between an underage woman and an older man. "That's the story of rape, basically," Morissette told *Self* magazine in 2019. "And the people who were addressing it at the time, they weren't being very supportive. Still now, women are *sort* of being supported. It—and I—were just straight-up ignored at best. Vilified and shamed and victimized and victim-attacked at worst."

Even though she was attacked for speaking out about her own abusive relationships, Morissette has continued to address the subject head-on in her work. When it came to the Broadway musical, she pushed hard for the show to include a plotline about a sexual assault and its aftermath. While there was some hesitancy at first from the creative team about showing a high-school rape on stage, Morissette felt that it was crucial to include Bella's story, and said she trusted Broadway audiences to handle the discomfort and heaviness of the situation. "I mean it's all over a lot of my songs, it's all over my history," she says. "And it's all over most fucking women's history. People say one in five women have been assaulted. I'm like, *every* woman's been subject to some version, covert or overt, of sexual harassment, abuse. Even just being a woman in a body you're going to be subject to something."

When it came to a song for Bella to sing as she recounts the night she was assaulted, Morissette realized that she could offer Paulus and Cody a song she had never released on an album before. "Predator," one of two new songs in the show (the other is "Smiling") is a song about feeling like prey in your own body, especially as a woman in a vulnerable situation. As Bella sings, "This magnet for predators is learning to be discerning," it is heartbreaking—her self-knowledge comes at a tragic price.

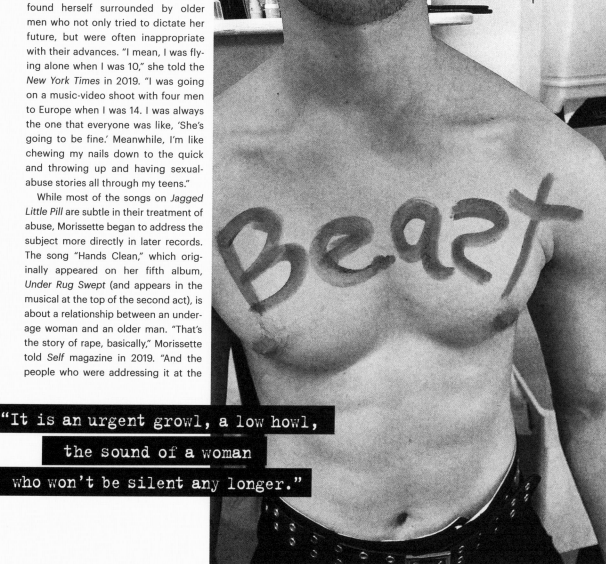

"It is an urgent growl, a low howl, the sound of a woman who won't be silent any longer."

In the show, as Kathryn Gallagher, who plays Bella, recounts the story of her rape at a drunken party, the dancer Heather Lang pantomimes the event, stumbling and flinging her body around the stage like a rag doll. It is clear how powerless Bella was that night, how unable to defend herself. "The first time I saw that choreography, nobody prepared me," said Diablo Cody, who wrote the show's book. "They hadn't told me that Heather was going to be mirroring Kathryn and that the scene was going to end with an actual depiction of what had happened, and it really blew me away."

This scene—where Bella gets to be fully in control of her narrative—was not always a part of the show. Kathryn Gallagher, who plays Bella, was in the chorus, and her abuse was just a smaller side plot to the larger Healy family drama. But during the course of developing the show, the #MeToo movement swelled and the Weinstein scandal broke, and suddenly the women on the creative team, including Morissette, felt a new urgency to expand Bella's role and make her a main character who gets to tell her story without shame. For Gallagher, "Predator" is a difficult song to sing night after night, but she feels that it is so important to show an audience that Bella was a victim who had nothing to do with her own assault. "What's really interesting about 'Predator' is it's a deep dive into the psyche of this endless conversation Bella is having with herself about why, because it doesn't make sense," Gallagher says. "But I think that it was important for the audience to see that this was a girl who had no way of saying anything. This was a girl who was physically almost lifeless. And he took advantage of that."

"What makes Bella's story so powerful is that she is angry and she is hurt and she has been silenced, but she is certain of what happened and she is certain of her deservedness to get to say that," Gallagher says. "She is worth her story being heard. I hope that by sharing our stories, we are telling younger girls that their story is theirs to share, to stand in, to be believed, to be heard, to be seen, to know that they have people who are here ready to listen, ready to hear them, and that they don't have to go the rest of their life thinking that they did something wrong when they didn't."

KATHRYN GALLAGHER (Bella)

plays Annika on Netflix's mega hit show *YOU* produced by Greg Berlanti and Sera Gamble, starring John Stamos, Penn Badgley, and Shay Mitchell. In 2015 Kathryn made her Broadway debut in the Tony-nominated revival of *Spring Awakening*. Kathryn's music has had placements in film and television such as *Younger*, *Covert Affairs*, and Stuart Blumberg's *Thanks for Sharing*.

Tell me about your first experience with Jagged Little Pill, *the album.*
Her albums have been my bibles since I was a little girl. I've known pretty much every word on this album since I was five years old. My mom used to play it around the house. Then I did a paper on Alanis in college (very poorly written). I already told her she will never, ever get her hands on it! Then I studied songwriting in music school and Glen Ballard [the producer of *Jagged Little Pill*] came to talk to us. At the end, I wrote a paper about Glen Ballard's creating *Jagged Little Pill* with Alanis. So it's a very full circle job for me.

It feels like Bella's story—of being sexually assaulted and learning how to tell her story without shame—is very relevant to this current moment.
I think that we didn't expect Bella's story to hit such a spot with so many different people in the way it did. I was getting messages from survivors; they were coming to me at the stage door. They were telling me about how, because of this story, they finally told their partner of what happened

to them twenty years ago and they had never told anyone. Someone I know told me that this had happened to her forty-five years ago, and she had never told a soul until she saw the show and finally went home and told her husband. And she's felt lighter ever since.

Do you feel a lot of responsibility, as you are the vessel for telling an assault survivor's story every night on the stage?
It's a huge responsibility. It's not a show I can phone in. It's not anything I would ever want to take lightly. It is not something that I feel I can do at even 98%. You have to bring absolutely everything to the table every time. I wear this bracelet every day—a survivor sent it to me. It says "survivor" on it. When you tell this story on a grand stage, you allow people to rid themselves of this level of shame that is not theirs to feel and it never was. I'm more proud of this than anything I've ever done.

You sing "Predator," one of two new Alanis Morrisette songs included in the show. It is a song all about a woman reckoning with abuse, and questioning her own role in what happened. Even though the assault is not her fault, she is definitely running through a complex tangle of emotions.
You replay that moment every single second in your head. You don't get a break from it. It affects your body in ways you never expected. Our brain has so many incredible survival tactics. When you hear a survivor go into court, the first question they are asked is, "Why didn't you scream? Why didn't you kick them?" But there's science beyond belief to back up why we freeze. It's an animal instinct. What's really interesting about "Predator" is it's this deep dive into the psyche of this endless conversation you're having with yourself, of *why*, because that's what doesn't make sense.

Alanis often sings about her own experiences with abuse and learning how to own her pain. Did her experiences inform your performance at all?
Absolutely, she's so deeply involved. And deeply knowledgeable about trauma and the psychology of it and where your body holds trauma. I know that the way that I sit on the couch in Bella's post-party scene is something that Alanis wrote to Diane about. She said, "she has to be sitting with a pillow on her lap" because a survivor would be protecting that area.

During the song, while you are replaying the memory of the party in your head, the dancer Heather Lang steps in and plays a drunk version of you while you watch. What do you think Larbi was trying to say with that choreography?
I think that something that so many survivors experience is dissociation. In the case of Bella, she blacked out. She doesn't remember. There are people that didn't drink and still black it out and have no memory of their assault years later. One of just the most genius things that Larbi and Diane created was that physical representation of dissociation, of being out of your body. And Heather is just one of the most incredible dancers I have ever seen in my life. In the first workshop, even during breaks, she would watch me walk. She said, "I just have to understand how your body moves."

Bella is such a heavy role to play night after night. How do you stay sane through it all?
There's a couple things that are pillars of my existence these days that helped me keep a level head on. It's been really like an exercise in willpower to give Bella and Kathryn entirely separate worlds. When the show starts, I have a little smudge spray. After the show I play music, and I dance around my dressing room. Claire Warden, our intimacy coach, told me to literally dance it out because our body traps trauma. So I jump around my dressing room and listen to badass female rock stars that I love.

"There's so much power in truth... Bella personifies that."

But then the rest of my life I just have to make sure is really simple. And I go to therapy, I call my friends, I walk my dog, I'm in the studio most days, making my own music. I eat well, sleep well, and have really wonderful people surrounding me. Then I'm getting more involved with the Joyful Heart Foundation, which is a foundation I've been obsessed with and supporting from afar for years now—they have done such incredible things with survivors.

When the show ends, Bella is getting to go to trial and tell her story, but it is not clear what her future holds.
Bella is a girl with no money, no promised future, no fall-back plan. Her mom is not around. Her going to trial is going to wipe out any finances she has. It's going to have her reputation torn to shreds. It is going to have every possible level of dignity she has left taken away from her. So that's Bella's future at the end of the show. It's not a happy story. She is brave, and by telling her story we are helping people. But for Bella, she has got a long road ahead. Even if she wins the trial, she still carries this trauma with her.

This is still something she is going to have every single day. And there will be days when it's better. There will be days when it's worse, but it's hers forever. There's so much power in truth and in not accepting shame or blame. Bella personifies that. She knows it's not pretty. She's already had the cop tell her she was drunk and it doesn't matter. She's already had every member of her community call her a slut. She's now at the point where she feels—you can call me whatever you want, it's still not right. Regardless of how messy it is, by not saying something, she would be condemned to a world of shame. I think in her brain that would be a lot harder for her to work through. She has this self-imposed isolation in the beginning and this community-imposed isolation in the middle. By the end, it's her finding power not in her isolation, but in herself and in her ability to believe her own story.

SEXUAL ASSAULT

FACING THE FACTS

EVERYONE'S ISSUE!

SEXUAL ASSAULT

The numbers are staggering and tragic. About 1 in 5 women American
women has been the victim of an attempted or completed rape, according
to government statistics from 2011. Every year, nearly half a million
people are sexually assaulted, and women of high school and college age
(12 to 24) are by far the most likely to experience sexual violence.

Fully 94 percent of women who are raped experience symptoms of
post-traumatic stress disorder (PTSD) during the two weeks following the crime, and 50 percent of women who've been sexually assaulted
experience PTSD throughout their lifetimes, a number that dwarfs the
average prevalence of less than 8 percent.

The long-term psychological and physical effects of rape are devastat-
ing. "People who experience PTSD may have persistent, frightening thoughts
and memories of the event(s), experience sleep problems, feel detached
or numb, or may be easily startled," according to the National Institutes
of Health. It's common for victims to experience life-long anxiety and
depression. One-third of women who are raped contemplate suicide.

Some effects of sexual violence are less obvious but no less heartbreaking. According to RAINN, the nation's largest anti-sexual violence
organization, these can include a tendency to get into arguments more
frequently than before, a feeling of mistrust towards family or friends,
increased problems at work or school, and significant professional or
emotional issues. Rape victims also have a higher risk of abusing drugs.
RAINN reports that they are six times more likely to use cocaine versus
the general public, and ten times more likely to use other major drugs.
There is no easy fix for coping with trauma and its aftermath.

Many victims do not report sexual violence to the police. The reasons
for not doing so include fear of retaliation, a belief that police would
not or could not take action, a desire to protect their privacy, and
worry that reporting the crime would harm the perpetrator. Ryan Leigh
Dostie, a veteran of the United States Army and a rape survivor, wrote
in the *New York Times*: "How exhausting rape is for everyone involved,
the paperwork and the sneers, followed by the investigation that ultimately will go nowhere." But, she added, "When we stay silent to protect
ourselves, we perpetuate our own isolation." According to Department of
Justice statistics, only 23 percent of incidents of sexual violence are
reported, and only .5 percent of rapists are incarcerated.

ACT 2 · SCENE 5

Frankie waits on the street. She looks up, relieved, as Jo approaches, barely looking at her. Frankie is appropriately effusive at the sight of her best friend, but there's also clearly something unresolved.

FRANKIE: *(grateful)* Oh God. Thanks for coming. I didn't have money for the train, and then my debit card didn't work, and I wasn't about to break down and call home... Where's Dottie the Datsun?

Jo's voice is low, subdued.

JO: I'm parked right around the corner.

FRANKIE: Awesome. *(hurrying after her)* That was pretty crazy. Back at my house. *(off Jo's silence)* I'm surprised you even showed up.

JO: I'm your best friend. I'm not going to leave you stranded in a neighborhood you can't even name.

FRANKIE: But you're mad.

JO: Can you guess why? Or are you so far up your own ass these days that you don't even know?

FRANKIE: I'm really sorry. I was going to tell you—

JO: And yet you didn't. Because you knew what you were doing was wrong.

FRANKIE: I didn't think I was going to fall in love with him...

JO: *Love*. Well, congratulations, Frankie. I'm glad you found something *healthy* and *rational*. I'm clearly not as legit as your fuckboy Phoenix.

FRANKIE: That's not what I'm saying, Jo. I just didn't think you and I were in an exclusive relationship.

JO: Right. Why would you take "this" seriously?

FRANKIE: *(frantic)* You know I didn't mean it like that...

Jo whips around and turns to face Frankie. Jo sings "YOU OUGHTA KNOW."

JO: *I want you to know, / That I'm happy for you / I wish nothing but the best for you both / The perfect version of me / Is he perverted like me? / Would he go down on you in a theater? / So he speaks eloquently / And you can have his baby*[1] */ I'm sure you'd make a really excellent mother / 'Cause the love that you gave that we made / Wasn't able to make it enough for you / To be open wide / And every time you speak his name / Does he know how you told me / You'd be there until you died / 'Til you died, but you're still alive / And I'm here, to remind you / Of the mess you left when you went away / It's not fair, to deny me / Of the cross I bear that you gave to me / You, you, you oughta know*[2] */ You seem very well, things look peaceful / I'm not quite as well, I thought you should know / Did you forget about me, / Mrs. Duplicity? / I hate to give him so much to live up to / It was a slap in the face / How quickly I was replaced / And are you thinking of me when he fucks you? / 'Cause the love that you gave that we made / Wasn't able to make it enough for you to be open wide, no / And every time you speak his name / Does he know how you told me / You'd be there until you died*[3] */ 'Til you died, but you're still alive / And I'm here, to remind you / Of the mess you left when you went away / It's not fair, to deny me / Of the cross I bear that you gave to me / You, you, you oughta know*

---

1 "I love this gender-skewed version of the song. The original lyrics are: 'An older version of me / Is she perverted like me? / Would she go down on you in a theater? Does she speak eloquently? / And would she have your baby? / I'm sure she'd make an excellent mother.'"

2 "It sounds like an angry song, but underneath that is vulnerability and devastation. Especially when I do an acoustic version, it's just so clear to me how devastated I was."

3 "People always thought it was about revenge, but there's a difference between revenge *fantasy* and the actual acting out of revenge. Think about it. Write about it. Punch about it in your kickboxing class. Write poems and songs and cathart your face off. But don't really seek revenge."

YOU OUGHTA

"IT WAS A SLAP IN THE FACE HOW QUICKLY I WAS REPLACED

KNOW

"ARE YOU THINKING OF ME WHEN HE F*CKS YOU?"

JO:
Uhh
Uhh
Uhh
Uhh Uh

CHORUS:
Uhh
Uhh
Uhh nuh nuh nuhnuh nuhnuh
Nuh nuhnuhnuh nuhnuh
Nuhnuh nuh nuh nuhnuh uhh

JO: *'Cause the joke that you laid in the bed / That was me and I'm not gonna fade / As soon as you close your eyes*

JO/CHORUS: *And you know it*

CHORUS: *And you know it and you*

JO:
And every time
I scratch my nails
Down someone else's back I hope you feel it

CHORUS:
Ahh

JO/CHORUS: *Well, can you feel it? / And I'm here, to remind you*

JO: *Of the mess you left when you went away*

JO/CHORUS: *It's not fair, to deny me*

JO: *Of the cross I bear*
That you gave to me
You, you, you
oughta know

CHORUS:
You, you, you, you, you

JO/CHORUS 1:
Well I'm here to
remind you
Of the mess you left
when you went away
It's not fair, to deny me
Of the cross I bear
That you gave to me
You, you, you

CHORUS 2:
Oh...

Oh...

JO: *Oughta know*

Frankie stares at Jo, wanting to explain herself; suddenly, Frankie's phone buzzes in her hand. She looks down and blanches in shock.

FRANKIE: Jo—

JO: *(angry)* What? Is it him?

FRANKIE: *(trembling)* No.

JO: Do you even give a shit—

FRANKIE: *(screaming)* No, it's my mom! Something's wrong!

Darkness.

POWER

"You Oughta Know" was the lead single off of *Jagged Little Pill*—which means that it is how much of the world first met Alanis Morissette. When Morissette warbles that first line—"I want you to know, that I'm happy for you"—her intense, laser-like vocal tone sounds like a hot knife slicing through the speakers. The "I" in the song is undeniable; Morissette is so instantly present in her lyrics that you cling to her every word. You instantly want to know who broke her heart, and moreover, you want them to pay. Morissette, with her cheeky profanity (who hasn't joyfully belted the words "go down on you in a theater" in karaoke?), seemed suddenly different than the other women on the radio. She was not just singing about lost love; she was out for epic revenge. She wasn't going to let her ex go gently into that good night; instead she was here to remind him of the mess he left, and she wasn't going anywhere. It was such a bold statement to make on a debut album, and a risky one at that—the single could have easily backfired; critics could have written Morissette off as a hysteric with anger issues. In fact, even the producers at Maverick assumed that "You Oughta Know" might not take off; they released the single with the hope that it would be just popular enough that Morissette could do a small tour and begin working on a follow-up record.

Of course, what happened next is another story. KROQ, Los Angeles's biggest alternative station, began spinning "You Oughta Know" day and night. The song sounded

> "It is not a song about spite; it is a song about being heard. It is a song about a woman asserting her right to speak and stand up for herself."

crunchy and addictive on rock radio (thanks to the addition of a thumping new bassline and drum track from Flea and Dave Navarro of the Red Hot Chili Peppers) and listeners were immediately drawn to Morissette's eccentric, edgy wordplay. The critics soon took notice. David Browne of *Rolling Stone* wrote in 1995 that "You Oughta Know" had "a throbbing-gristle beat that grabs your collar and rips it off." Still, early reviews like Browne's also carried a not-so-subtle whiff of misogyny when it came to characterizing Morissette's outlook on relationships. "In her songs, men take her for granted and mentally abuse her, and she retaliates by threatening to leave one of her exes' names off her album credits (talk about a career-minded individual). Morissette needs to make new friends."

But (mostly male) critics like Browne, who wrote that "You Oughta Know" is "spiteful and seething," were missing the point of the song. It is not a song about spite, it is a song about being heard. It is a song about a woman asserting her right to speak and stand up for herself, even after she has been terribly hurt. When Morissette sings about "the cross I bear that you gave to me," she is singing about more than just a personal vendetta; she is talking about the burden of being a woman in a world that consistently tries to

disenfranchise women and deny them agency in their own stories. In "You Oughta Know," Morissette casts herself as the main character of a blighted romance, the one who gets to set the terms. She gets to interrupt her ex's dinner on her schedule; she gets to remind him of all of his broken promises. For many young women, the song sounded less like a petty complaint and more like a rallying cry: you don't just have to sit there and accept betrayal. You have choices. You can put on your best leather pants and stand in a desert and yodel about what you deserve at the top of your lungs.

In a 1995 interview with MTV, a young Morissette smiled gently as a male reporter asked her about the meaning behind "You Oughta Know."

"Lots of people say, well, she's a man-hater," the reporter said. "How do you respond to people who say that?"

"I say no, I'm not," Morissette shot back. "This song was written for the sake of release, and sort of this really dysfunctional subconscious part of myself. It was a way for me to let go of that certain situation, of which I take part responsibility for what happened. I was the one who put my self-esteem in his hands and basically gave him free rein to do with it as he would. But I love men, and I'm now attracted to men who treat me very well, and I don't put myself in situations with men that don't." (As for the identity of the particular man she was singing about, Morissette has never come clean; over the years there have been many theories, and several men who have come forward arguing that they are the object of the song's ire, but she prefers to keep the truth a mystery.)

"You Oughta Know" may be Morissette's most popular, most iconic song—which is why director Diane Paulus knew she had to save it for the second act of *Jagged Little Pill*. "I knew structurally we'd have to withhold it," she said. "I

knew it was going to have to come somewhere in the middle to two-thirds of Act Two because you can't give that away too soon."

At first, Paulus thought that she might give the song to Mary Jane, as "one might think such a significant song should lie with the protagonist," but as the team developed the show, they realized that "You Oughta Know" could really shine as an anthem for Jo (Lauren Patten) to sing after Frankie cheats on her with Phoenix. It may seem like an unexpected choice to have a supporting character sing the musical's biggest number, but Paulus said that she felt strongly about giving Jo a moment to stand boldly in her own spotlight. The song took on a new dimension when it came out of the mouth of a queer woman who feels pushed aside, not only by her own family, but by the one person she thought truly accepted her. "Coming out of Jo, it could actually be more than just what people might reduce it to like a breakup song," Paulus said. "It could stand for being seen."

Paulus and her creative team worked together to ensure that "You Oughta Know" would feel like a star-is-born moment for Patten—the song starts out quiet and eerie (Tom Kitt took Morissette's version and slowed it down, adding an almost jazzy undertone) and then swells to a full explosion, with the chorus undulating around Patten in a sea of fiery red light. "It starts with a groove and then it's a slow build," Paulus said. "And then the whirling, swirling backgrounds that come in are like harpies."

At the first preview of *Jagged Little Pill* at A.R.T. in Boston, the song got an instant standing ovation. Then, no matter what Paulus did to tweak the number, the audiences continued standing up. To emphasize this crowd participation, Paulus and the lighting designer, Justin Townshend, decided for the Broadway production to bathe the audience in light at the end of the song. "We were saying," Paulus recalls, "this is a musical, you're here, if you want to scream and sing along or stand. Of course Lauren is delivering an unbelievable performance, but people are also saying, 'I'm here too.' It becomes a song where the audience is able to say, 'I've been there.' Whatever you are, 'You Oughta Know' hits: personal, political, psychological, emotional."

Patten, who is a queer woman herself, said that she feels that "You Oughta Know" was never a song about revenge or fury; instead "It was always a song about identity. It was never really a song about being cheated on or getting back at your ex or telling your ex to fuck off. I always wanted to find a way that honored the fact that that is some people's experience with the song, but that it also went deeper into the core of needing to be acknowledged and needing to be seen as valid."

"'You Oughta Know,'" Patten said, touches "such a primal core human experience that it doesn't feel like it's ever going to be done. Or like I'll ever finish mining it for new things, which is exciting and relieving because I'll be singing it for a long time."

LAUREN PATTEN (Jo)

has appeared in the Broadway production of *Fun Home*, *The Wolves* (Obie and Drama Desk winner), and Steven Levenson's *Days of Rage*. Her film and television credits include *Blue Bloods*, *The Good Fight*, *Succession*, and *The Big Sick*.

Tell me about your first experience with Jagged Little Pill, the album.

I was a little young for the album when it came out, but my sister loved the album. She's seven years older than me. So I never had listened to it all the way through until after I got the first reading of the show. And what surprised me was how many of the songs and how much of the album I had already downloaded into my brain because it's such a part of our cultural consciousness.

How did you get involved with the musical?

I was actually on my way to the Obie Awards in 2017 for a play that I was in called *The Wolves*. I got a call from my agent saying, "Hey, you have this last-minute audition for *Jagged Little Pill* tomorrow at noon." I'm like, "Great, so much time to prepare." I went in and there were a couple of sides for Jo, but the script was not completed yet. I was sort of going off of instinct with it. They asked me to prepare a rock song and I came in with "So What" by P!nk. And then they asked me in the audition, "Do you know 'You Oughta Know'?" Of course I said, "Yes, *I know that song*." They asked me if I felt like I could sing it in the audition room. And I remember going, "Sort of— I mean the verse has a lot of words." They said, "Here's the music for it. Just go out and listen to it for a little bit and then come in and do whatever you can, don't worry about it."

I remember in the very first audition, Bryan Perri, our music director, was in the room when I sang it. Before they had me sing it again with a couple of adjustments, he asked me, "Does it hurt you to sing like that or are you hurting yourself?" I said, "No, this is how I sing," but it's not how I sing everything. I mean, I've also done traditional musical theater and I also sing jazz and country and different genres. But when the music lends itself to the sort of darker, grittier side of my voice, it feels very natural to just slide into whatever the music is pulling out of me and my voice. So from the very first audition with no preparation, that was how I gravitated toward singing it.

193

In the version of "You Oughta Know" you sing in the show, the music director Tom Kitt changed the melody a bit in the last chorus.

During previews, Tom came to me and asked if I thought it might be helpful to take that last bridge up to a different melody line because it didn't make sense anymore dramatically to have me vocally go back down to the basement tones that Alanis hits in the record, after doing that big rock scream. Jo is at that point in the song when she's really letting it come out for the first time and really letting the rage hit. So Tom and I came up with a melody line that sounded right, and Alanis was super stoked about it.

The song comes after Jo has found her girlfriend, Frankie, in bed with Phoenix. This is a betrayal on so many levels—not only has Frankie cheated on you, but she cheated on you with a heterosexual male. It would make sense for Jo to start the song with wild anger, but you chose to start slowly, and softly. It's almost creepy.

I believe it was Diane Paulus's idea to have me not move for the first verse in the chorus, which I love and have always loved. Alanis starts the song kind of at an eight and then builds to a ten for the most of the rest of the song. And I never wanted to do that as an actor because it just wouldn't leave anywhere for the song to go dramatically. It's very different to perform the song in concert or to perform it on a

record than it is to use it as a narrative storytelling moment in the show.

I always saw "You Oughta Know" as the first moment that Jo is demanding to be seen and heard. And it always was a song about identity for me. It was never really a song about being cheated on or getting back at your ex. It wasn't divorced from that, but it went deeper to the core of needing to be seen as valid. When you sing it as an actor, there's a musical break in between the words "I'm here" and then "to remind you." The chorus always starts with a huge "I'm here." I feel like I've unlocked so many more variations of Jo's experience of finding a way to say, "I'm here."

I think we have to talk about the standing ovations. Starting with the Cambridge run, "You Oughta Know" has brought the audience to their feet almost every night.

Oh yeah. That's never something you expect. I think we always knew that it was going to be a big moment for the show. It's arguably her most famous song, or at least one of her most famous songs. I actually was quite nervous; the first preview in Cambridge was really the only time I felt pressure singing the song because I had been in such an incubated, loving, supportive environment in the development. It was the first time doing it in front of a paid audience. And we had heard that a lot of massive Alanis fans had flown in from all over the world to see the very first

"The song took on a new dimension when it came out of the mouth of a queer woman."

preview of the show. I mean people who came from Brazil and came from Japan. I remember warming up and it kind of hitting me that these people had been listening to her iconic version of it for twenty-five years. And I was about to do it really differently.

I got on stage and did the song and people stood up, and no one expected it at all. And then as previews continued, it kept happening to the point where there was some work done tech-wise of trying to change the lights.

"We put so much energy out from the stage that it gives people this permission to return it to us."

Yes, at first Diane Paulus and the lighting team tried to dim the lights so people wouldn't stand, but then they kept standing anyway! Now the moment is built into the show.
Now it's been adjusted so that it's a stage manager cue. Our stage manager Ira Mont susses out what the audience reaction is and then cues us to move forward with the next scene. I really didn't expect it to continue for Broadway. It's so rare and so kind of ludicrous for it to happen that, yeah, I just never expect it. And there've been audiences for the Broadway run who haven't stood and it doesn't feel like a letdown or a disappointment because there's always a huge wave of energy from the audience. I think we put so much energy out from the stage that it gives people permission to return it to us.

One of my other favorite moments of yours is when you sing "Your House," a secret, acapella track that Morissette put on Jagged Little Pill *about sneaking into an ex's house when he is away. In your case, Jo is sneaking into Frankie's room, where she finds her there with Phoenix.*
Yeah, it's like this slow motion horror movie. I love "Your House" so much. I know that there is no place for the full song in the show, and I also so much wish that there could be because it's so good. I think that it was always important to honor that Alanis was bad-ass enough to put this aca-pella number after three minutes of silence on her record. What a weird thing to do, and it is so great! It was sort of a mind fuck as an actor, because the song is naturally melancholy, and is written from the perspective of somebody who knows that the relationship is over. I finally was able to

tap into it as Jo by using the suggestion that Larbi and Diane gave me, which was thinking that I'm going to Frankie's to surprise her. Jo thinks, "I'm going to save it and I'm going to do something special for Frankie that makes her fall in love with me again." And then of course it's blown apart.

What makes Frankie's betrayal so searing that Jo is driven to sing the ultimate revenge anthem with "You Oughta Know"?
I think it is the particular betrayal of fleeing to a straight relationship from something that is queerer. I mean, there was an old line that used to be in the scene before "You Oughta Know," where Jo said, "Congratulations, Frankie, you finally fit in."

I remember the excitement of changing the lyric to "and you can have his baby" (from "would she have your baby") because I think it is really queering the song. It ties into that part of Jo who is a queer person who is not yet super comfy in their queer identity. That's been my own experience as I've come out. It's not like you come out and then it's like, now I'm queer and I feel super confident in it and I have no more questions! I think seeing Jo at this very vulnerable point in her experience of queerness being invalidated so callously by the one person who she thought understood is part of why the pain is so great, and why it was important to me to have the last line before going into the song, "Why would you take this seriously?" Why would you take this sort of nebulous queer person who isn't super confident and isn't super defined yet seriously, versus this charming, curly haired, cis-white-het dude?

As a queer woman yourself, what does it mean to bring a character like Jo so valiantly to the stage? She really gets to own her spotlight moment.
I think a lot of times media has a queer character dealing with external struggles that are very valid, but they know *how* they identify. They have known their identity since they were a kid, and they are dealing with a lot of pressure and blowbacks from that identity. What I don't see, and what I crave, are stories of queer people dealing with their internal struggles around being queer and understanding how they want to move through the world as a queer person. So it's a big joy for me to be able to bring a character like that to the stage.

And excuse me, but I think it's very powerful to give a song like "You Oughta Know" to the queer character. I've heard a lot of people say, "I never thought they'd give that song to a queer person." And getting to express the very specific pains and rage and needs to be heard by queer people through that song I think is deeply meaningful to audience members. I've gotten letters from people who have gotten the courage to come out to their parents by watching the show. I've gotten mothers and fathers and teachers at the stage door who are in tears because they finally understood something about their kids. So it's been quite the privilege.

Why do you think the songs from Jagged Little Pill *hold up after all this time?*
Because they just slap. They're just slapping bops! I think that more than anything, Alanis is an unbelievable lyricist, and that the songs touch something that is primal.

ANATOMY OF AN OVATION

Starting during the first Boston performance of *Jagged Little Pill*, audiences began to stand up and applaud after Lauren Patten and the ensemble performed "You Oughta Know." And then it...just kept happening. We spoke to the cast and creative team about the power of that moment.

ALANIS MORISSETTE: That song is such permission. Women weren't allowed to feel angry, depressed, and fearful. We're not allowed to feel fear. It is divine permission to feel vulnerable, feel rejected. To not be like, "Oh, no, it was a totally mutual decision." No, it wasn't, I was dumped. It wasn't mutual.

DIANE PAULUS: I'll never forget the first preview at A.R.T. We hit "You Oughta Know" and the audience stood up and the show completely stopped. And we were all dying. Like, what is happening? It was uncontrollable to the point that the next day we went back into rehearsal and I said to my stage manager, "All right, let's change the lighting cue." I said, "I don't want it to feel like we're holding for applause." So we changed some of the lighting cues and we went into the preview the next night, and it happened again. There was literally nothing we could do. And for the ten weeks we played at A.R.T., that happened every single performance.

LAUREN PATTEN: It was definitely a surprise. I also didn't expect it to continue for Broadway. You know, I remember going in for the first Broadway preview and thinking, "Okay, that might've just been a Cambridge thing" because it's so rare and so kind of ludicrous for it to happen.

PAULUS: Going into Broadway, it was really coaching Lauren like a sports coach. I think there was one early matinee where the audience didn't stand, and I was so relieved. I was like, "Okay, it's happened." Just for her to know that it's not about the standing ovation. That's not the point of the song. You've got to live in the not knowing. How do we keep the show on the edge and dare not to know about what's going to happen at any given show?

PATTEN: There've been audiences for the Broadway run who haven't stood, and it doesn't feel like a let down or a disappointment because every time there's a huge wave of energy from the audience. I think the moment unlocks something in people.

SIDI LARBI CHERKAOUI: I think it's the circumstance of stillness to total explosion, mixed with an iconic song.

DIABLO CODY: I knew that Jo would definitely be the comic relief in this show, which makes it all the more surprising and explosive when she's the one who has that volcanic, cathartic moment of rage.

ELIZABETH STANLEY: "You Oughta Know" is such a moment. And the audience is having such a moment. It feels like this hot, red flame. Like the lights are red. And you're like, "What's on fire?"

LARBI: You're clapping for the song's power, its twenty-five year history. You're clapping for Lauren's ability to convey this song, but also to finally release herself as Jo. That connects us again, which is a paradox. All of us saying screw the world makes us connect to the world. That's what's so beautiful about it. It's really interesting how our disconnect reconnects us.

TOM KITT: I've always come from the place where I want to feel like the standing ovation is earned. And what I feel with "You Oughta Know" is that people aren't just going, all right, I might as well stand. People stand right away. Whether you're clapping loudly at your seat whooping or you're standing, I feel like there is a huge catharsis. People who are

feeling what Lauren is doing in that moment, what the show has been saying. Those moments happen when something speaks to you.

GLEN BALLARD: It's the culmination of the whole show. That moment's pretty transcendent for me.

PATTEN: I think we put so much energy out from the stage that it gives people permission to return it to us. So whether people are standing or not, it's always a really beautiful moment of communion to me.

ACT 2 · SCENE 6

Mary Jane is alone in her room. We hear the beginning of "UNINVITED." She takes pills.

MARY JANE: *Like anyone would be / I am disturbed by my fascination with you[1] / Like any flesh-and-blood human / I have simply found an object to crave / But you, you're not allowed / You're uninvited*
An unfortunate slight

                            CHORUS:
                            Ohh...
                            Ohh...

---

1 "This song is about intimacy and lack of emotional safety. It's about not trusting myself, not trusting someone else, not feeling safe. If intimacy is anything, it's about creating safety—enough to be vulnerable and to speak transparently and to move through things together. It's also just my ambivalence about surrendering, being infatuated. I just want to be all-in."

MARY JANE/BELLA:
Must be strangely exciting
To watch the stoic squirm
Must be somewhat heartening
To watch the flawless fall from grace[2]

           CHORUS:
           Ahh...

           Ahh...

MARY JANE:
But you you're not allowed
You're uninvited
An unfortunate slight

           CHORUS:

           Ahh...

   CHORUS 1:   **CHORUS 2:**
   Ahh...   *Ahh ahh*
   Ahh...   *Ahh ahh*

---

2 "The original lyrics are, 'To watch shepherd meet shepherd,' a reference to *City of Angels*. I went to a screening of the movie. I never know if there's going to be a song yielded from having watched a screening, but I went home and wrote this song in about fifteen minutes."

FALL

FROM

GRACE

MARY JANE/BELLA: *Like any uncharted territory /
This must seem greatly intriguing / You speak
of my want like / You have experienced want /
Like mine before*

MARY JANE: *But this is not allowed*

You're uninvited [3]

An unfortunate slight

	CHORUS 1:	CHORUS 2:
	Ahh	*Ahh*
	Ahh ahh	*Ahh ahh*
	Ahh	*Ahh ahh*

MARY JANE: *Though I find this unnerving / I've
had my moment to deliberate*

CHORUS: *Ahh… / Ahh… / Ahh ahh*

---

3 "The final version of the song released on the album was actually
the original demo version of the song that we recorded on the first
day. Glen and I loved how spur-of-the-moment it felt and how
that seemed to jibe with the themes of the song. So we figured out
we really shouldn't make any major changes."

A DANCE WITH DEATH

During the song "Uninvited," Mary Jane Healy overdoses on fentanyl. In order to show her addiction spiraling into danger, director Diane Paulus and choreographer Sidi Larbi Cherkaoui came up with the idea of a duet, in which Elizabeth Stanley (Mary Jane) would dance with her alter-ego, played by Heather Lang. Lang thrashes around and fights with Stanley—showing the many ways that Mary Jane is battling her inner demons. We spoke to Stanley and Lang about developing this haunting scene.

How did you start developing "Uninvited" together?

HEATHER LANG: I was four or five months pregnant. I remember I just got out of that first trimester. And the team said, "Come early in the morning and we're going to develop this thing." Larbi was just throwing his body over a couch with reckless abandon. He said, "So can you try that?"

ELIZABETH STANLEY: I was working on another project, so the producers asked, "Can you stay late?" It was nighttime and they used iPhone flashlights to light us. They said, "Just sit on the couch and Heather's going to do some things around you. We'll feel it out."

What was Larbi's instruction like? The movement feels so wild and untethered.

LANG: I feel like that was very Larbi. A lot of the stuff that he's done I would say is highly structured improv. He's sitting there saying, "This is the essence, this is the shape." I go and do something, then we have a dialogue. The way that he moves is really exquisite. It's super risky and exciting.

STANLEY: Larbi said, "Everything that you do should look awkward, not elegant and not pretty." He would pull me back to being grounded in what's happening in the moment. You can't be concerned with what the result is, or how it looks from the outside. You can't think, "What face am I making?"

What research did you do to embody the physicality of an overdose?

LANG: My husband is over twenty years sober, and I have a lot of sober people in my life. And I am a person who has dealt with addiction. So I have an understanding for what that is, and I think all of us do on some level. I haven't had an overdose, but when I was growing up, my best friend's brother had an overdose. She found him in the bathroom, and I was there with her dealing with all that.

What are you both thinking about while performing the dance?

STANLEY: It truly feels like we're team partners in that moment. By the time we get to this moment it's layered with anger, or pain, or sorrow, or frustration, or struggle. It's so intimate. There's the moment of reaching for her. It is that wanting and yet also resisting it at the same time. Your ego wants to like all the parts of yourself. But, most of us have many parts of ourselves that we really hate, or don't want to acknowledge. We try to hide them, not only from ourselves, but from everybody else. But then we're also feeling, "No, but I love you. I want to keep you around. I need you."

LANG: It's so beautiful. It's actually gorgeous. But it's also so sad and painful.

STANLEY: The lyric "You're not allowed, you're uninvited" has morphed for me. I feel like when I first heard that, it was more of a rejection like, "You're not supposed to be here, get out." And now it's more like, "You haven't been invited, but here you are." But then the next lyric is, "an unfortunate slight." In that moment, we're reaching for each other.

Heather, you had surgery recently, and yet you really toss yourself around the sofa!

LANG: I got a hip replacement. Prior to that if someone had told me to do this dance, I would have said, "I don't know." But now I just feel like a phoenix rising from the ashes. It's a rebirth for me. I put my right knee up on the edge of the couch, and I have to put all my brute force into it. Larbi actually didn't give me tons of direction on that. I just had this instinct inside of me that said, "I feel like it should just be like flying."

STANLEY (TO LANG): It's very clear to me that you're a life-long artist. You've spent your lifetime training in this craft. It only comes with years of experience and really hard technical work, that you can have that kind of surrender in your performance.

The dance gets quite violent at times! You are almost brawling with each other.

LANG: I secretly want to be in superhero fight movies. I just want to be in Kung Fu movies.

STANLEY: It is scary. And good. As a woman, there have not been very many moments when I've gotten to behave that way on stage. To actually be complicatedly rageful and passionately fighting about survival, and life.

ACT 2 · SCENE 7

Steve and Nick are in the hallway outside of Mary Jane's room. A DOCTOR enters. Steve is desperate for answers.

STEVE: Are you Dr. Woodson?

DR. WOODSON: Yes.

STEVE: I'm Steve. Healy. Can you please give me an update on my wife?

DR. WOODSON: In addition to oxycodone, she also had fentanyl in her system.

STEVE: What?!

DR. WOODSON: It's a very powerful opiate, stronger than heroin.

STEVE: That's not possible.

DR. WOODSON: Oxycodone is often contaminated with fentanyl. She might have gotten counterfeit pills off the street.

STEVE: No, she had a prescription. She got in a car accident; she was still having trouble with her back.

DR. WOODSON: Actually, she doesn't have a current prescription with either of the doctors that you wrote down.

STEVE: Could this be a mistake? She's an amazing mother. She's obsessed with her health. Does she look like a drug addict to you?

DR. WOODSON: What do you think a drug addict looks like? *(an awkward beat, then)* Did you notice any erratic behavior?

STEVE: *(breaking)* Yes.

NICK: *(taking over)* Is she going to be okay?

DR. WOODSON: We have a lot to discuss.

STEVE: Nick, why don't you go wait for Frankie?

Nick hesitates, then leaves.

DR. WOODSON: We have her on buprenorphine to help with withdrawals, but there could be serious long-term consequences from an overdose like this. Once she's discharged, I would suggest she goes to inpatient recovery.

STEVE: She won't do that.

DR. WOODSON: We strongly recommend it. I'll be back in a few minutes.

Steve is relieved and terrified all at once. He addresses Mary Jane.

STEVE: Remember when we were younger before the kids, we'd party and drink too much and we would joke about going to rehab someday? Well, you did it! *(to himself)* Not funny.

No response, of course. Steve strokes her hair gingerly, takes a deep breath.

STEVE: I thought after all this time we were done surprising each other.

Steve sings "MARY JANE."

STEVE: *What's the matter Mary Jane, you had a hard day[1] / As you place the don't disturb sign on the door / You lost your place in line again, what a pity / You never seem to want to dance anymore / Well it's full speed baby in the wrong direction / There's a few more bruises if that's the way / You insist on heading / Please be honest Mary Jane / Are you happy / Please don't censor your tears[2]*

We see Nick bringing Frankie into the hospital. They are both distraught.

FRANKIE: *(to Steve)* This is my fault.

STEVE: No, it's not.

He embraces Frankie. She turns to Nick, crying, and he leads her out of the room.

CHORUS:
Aah ee yah

STEVE: *Ooh...*

You're the sweet crusader   *Sweet crusader*
And you're on your way   *Ahh... hey...*

---

1 "This song is just an opportunity to be intensely empathic. It's saying: 'I hear you. I see you.' It's the most beautiful thing for me to hear empathic words coming out of a male voice."

2 "When I moved to L.A., I was incredibly lonely. I didn't speak for six months, because in Canada, you don't speak unless someone asks me a question. I thought, 'At some point, someone's going to ask me a question.' But nobody did. No one really cared."

STEVE:
You're the last great
innocent
And that's why I love you

Mary Jane wakes up.

STEVE: *So take this moment Mary Jane and be self-ish / Worry not about the cars that go by / 'Cause all that matters Mary Jane / Is your freedom*

So keep warm my dear, keep dry

Tell me

Tell me

What's the
matter Mary Jane

CHORUS 1:

Tell me

Tell me

What's the
matter
Mary Jane

CHORUS:
Last great
innocent

CHORUS:
Dry

CHORUS 2:
Tell me

Tell me

What's the
matter
Mary Jane

Tell me

Tell me

Please be honest
Mary Jane

Tell me
Tell me / Tell me

CHORUS: *Ya ooh ooh*

CHORUS 1:
Tell me

Tell me

Please be
honest
Mary Jane
Tell me

CHORUS 2:

Tell me

Tell me

Please be
honest Mary
Jane
Tell me

Mary Jane has now spent several days in the hospital. Steve helps her prepare to leave.

MARY JANE: Are you embarrassed?

STEVE: Just that I wasn't paying attention.

MARY JANE: Even if you had been, I don't know if you would have noticed. I'm *really* good at hiding things. *(rueful)* We've been married for 20 years and there are still things I haven't told you.

STEVE: I want to know everything.

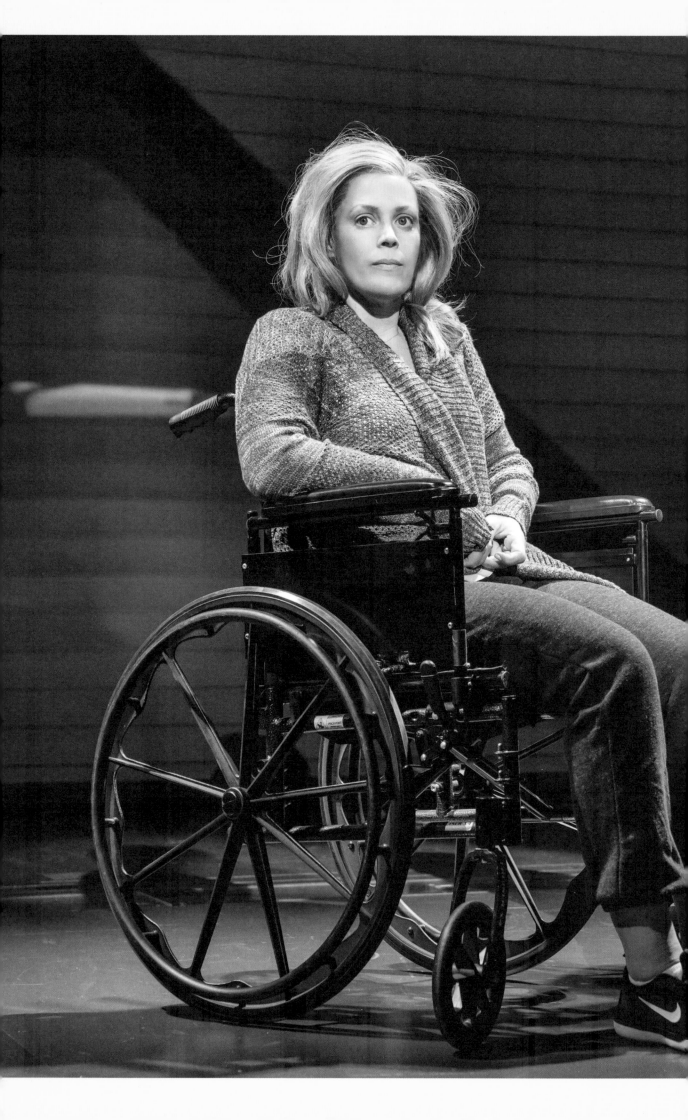

MARY JANE: I need help.

STEVE: Well, you're about to get 90 days of help. It's a nice place. They'll let the kids visit every Saturday. *(mock excited)* They even have a therapy dog named Curtis!

MARY JANE: Wow, can't wait! *(then)* What about after that? When I come home?

STEVE: Well, maybe we could try helping each other. Like the therapist said.

MARY JANE: Yeah. She said we could help heal each other.

STEVE: I never meant to make you feel like work was more important than you and the kids. I didn't realize how much I missed. I'm sorry. I've made so many mistakes. I'm such a mess.

MARY JANE: I'm detoxing from opiates. I win.

They hug. Nick enters (wearing different clothes, to show passage of time).

NICK: I pulled the car around.

MARY JANE: Where's Frankie?

NICK: She's downtown.

STEVE: She organized a big rally. It's today.

MARY JANE: A rally? For what?

NICK: *(hesitant)* For Bella.

MARY JANE: Nick. I was wrong. Forget about what people think of us. You have to go to the police. Tell them everything.

STEVE: *Mary Jane—he already did.*

MARY JANE: *(after a beat)* Have you talked to Bella? How is she?

NICK: I don't know if I can face her.

REACHING OUT

When Diablo Cody first began to think about turning *Jagged Little Pill*, the album, into a cohesive Broadway show, she started with the song "Mary Jane." The song, the ninth on the album, already feels cinematic, like it is part of a bigger story. It is one of the only songs on the record that Morissette sings in the third person, singing to a woman other than herself. "Alanis had a very clear idea of this character," Glen Ballard said in an interview about the process of writing "Mary Jane." "Of her standing in the night rain, worrying not about the cars that go by. It haunts me like an Edward Hopper painting. I love this song."

When Cody heard the lyrics to Mary Jane, she pictured a lonely woman, just as Morissette had, but she saw her as the isolated matriarch of a fractured family. "If that song wasn't on *Jagged Little Pill*, I couldn't begin to tell you what the show would be about," Cody said. "Because that was the beginning of all of it and it wound up informing the entire production. 'Mary Jane' had always intrigued me. It wasn't a single, it wasn't one of those songs that everyone knows. And I always wondered who it was about, and to be honest, I still don't know. I've never asked Alanis. I've never looked it up. So, to me it was always about Mary Jane Healy."

In the show, Mary Jane does not get to sing her namesake number—instead, she hears it as a kind of lullaby. Her husband, Steve, begins to sing to her when she is lying sedated in a hospital bed after a near-death Fentanyl overdose, and he realizes that he never stopped to slow down and notice that his wife had a serious problem. They've stopped connecting on the most basic level, and he doesn't even understand the sadness and solitude that led to her drug problem. "What's the matter, Mary Jane?" he cooes from her bedside. "You had a hard day, as you place the don't disturb

sign on the door." Both Steve and Mary Jane have stopped showing up for one another and have put up walls between one another, but as Steve keeps singing, the boundaries and resentments slowly begin to crumble. Diane Paulus shows time elapsing during Mary Jane's recovery with inventive staging—her hospital bed spins as the days pass, and every day she gets a little bit stronger and brighter. And all the while, Steve keeps serenading her. "Take this moment, Mary Jane, and be selfish," he urges. "Keep warm my dear, keep dry."

"I think 'Mary Jane' is so beautifully placed in the show, because it's all questions," Sean Allan Krill, who plays Steve, said. "Steve has found out that she has become addicted to opioids, but I love that his instinct is that there's something underneath that. So what is it? What can we do? What can we do to at least try to begin to heal this for you? Please tell me. *Tell me*. I love the fact that that song ends with those words: tell me, tell me, tell me. Because, as I said, I do believe that the overall mantra of the show is share, communicate."

And as for the longstanding rumor that the title of the song is a reference to marijuana—Morissette swears that isn't true. "I was too busy being a work addict to be a drug addict," she said in an interview about writing the song. Plus, "I was decidedly Canadian during the writing of that record...I think I was the cleanest artist that I'd ever known." Instead, the name Mary Jane came to her from her youth in the Catholic church, and served as a kind of general stand-in for divine feminine energy. She based the character of Mary Jane off of a woman who helped her when she first moved to Los Angeles, but she said that she sang the song more generally to women everywhere who give selflessly and ask for little in return. "I mean it's a song just drenched in empathy," Morissette said. "Empathy is such a trendy word to be talking about right now but it's just the cornerstone of every stage of development."

When she first heard that the song would belong to Steve, Morissette was surprised—on the original record, the lyrics are about the secret and sacred communication between two women. But in the end, Morissette felt that it was exactly right that "a man was singing a profoundly empathic song to a woman." Because "Mary Jane" is about a universal concept: reaching across the expanse to understand another, be it a stranger, a friend, or the person you've shared a bed with for decades.

> "She sang the song more generally to women everywhere who give selflessly and ask for little in return."

ACT 2 · SCENE 8

.... A RALLY IN SUPPORT OF BELLA ....

People march with signs: "DO YOU BELIEVE HER NOW?" "TELL YOUR STORY" etc.

Phoenix enters. He has a sign.

We see Jo arrive at the other side of the rally—there's an awkward moment as she and Phoenix see each other. Then Phoenix steps forward and raises his sign, steadfast. Jo does the same. This is bigger than the three of them, and they know it.

Bella walks toward the group as the TESTIMONIES begin and begins to sing "NO."

BELLA: *My mind is invaded / My gates are ignored / My thoughts are negated / And you're on a roll*

PROTESTOR #1 (NORA): *And I am offended / By your acts of shamelessness*

PROTESTOR #2 (JANE): *Your lack of conscience / And your flagrant steamroll*

PROTESTOR #3 (EZRA): *What part of no do you not understand? / Do you not understand?*

PROTESTORS #1, #2, #3, AND BELLA:	**CHORUS:**
What part of no	*Oh...oh...*
do you not understand?	
Do you not understand?	*Hoo...*

Nick appears, hesitant. But Bella walks right up to him.

BELLA: Why didn't you stop him?

NICK: I don't know. But everyone knows the truth now.

BELLA: Because *you* said it. Why wasn't it enough for me to say it? You get to be the hero. Like always. Because of who you are, because of what you look like...they believe *you*.

NICK: *(tearful)* I'm sorry. If I could change anything about my life, Bella...I would go back...

BELLA: Yeah. So would I.

PROTESTER #4 (MAX): *My sorrow is laughed off / My rage is discounted*

BELLA: *My fears are founded / This dam is no more*

PROTESTORS:	**CHORUS:**
What part of no	*Oh...*
do you not understand?[1]	*Oh...*
Do you not understand?	

BELLA/PROTESTORS: *Don't touch me / My body is frozen / Thanks to you*

BELLA/NICK/PROTESTORS: *And I've sat with these secrets*

CHORUS: *I'm no longer willing to*

PROTESTORS: *What part of no do you not understand? / Do you not understand? / What part of no do you not understand? / Do you not understand?*

As we move into "EASY NOT TO" reprise.

BELLA/NICK:	**FRANKIE/JO:**		
It's easy not to			
So much easier	*And what goes around*		
Not to	*Never comes around*		
To you	*To you*	**CHORUS 3:**	
		It's easier	**CHORUS 4:**
	To you		*Get up!*

ALL: *Wake up... / What part of no do you not understand?*

---

1 "The chorus of voices turns the original song into a fierce, fist-pumping protest song."

IT TOOK ME 10 YEARS TO STOP BLAMING MYSELF #MeToo
BELIEVE BLACK WOMEN

ACT 2 · SCENE 9

The scene transitions into the Healy living room, complete with Christmas tree. Yes, it's the holidays again. And Mary Jane is writing her famous "Healy Holiday Letter."

MARY JANE: Welcome to the annual Healy Holiday Letter. I've decided to go digital this year to save the trees, Christmas or otherwise. *(then)* Where to begin...I'm in awe of my daughter, Frankie. It took me 40 years to be as brave as she is at 17. She has spent this past year doing everything she can to bring justice to her friend, Bella Fox, who is a rape survivor. *(beat)* Like myself. As you may have heard, Bella's case is going to trial. The defendant still got into a good college, even under the circumstances. He's sticking to his story. But Bella gets to tell *hers*. Most of us never do.

FRANKIE: I didn't know what you were going through, Mom. I just—never saw you as a person.

MARY JANE: You're my kid, that's normal. Most people don't know their parents until it's too late.

The chorus sings "THANK YOU."

A VOICE (NORA): *How 'bout me not blaming you for everything*

CHORUS: *I'm reaching out to make amends*[1]

THREE VOICES (NORA/EZRA/LAUREL): *How 'bout me enjoying the moment for once*

CHORUS: *No pressure for you to let me in*

MARY JANE: When we adopted you, I just wanted you to feel like you fit in here.

FRANKIE: Mom. I don't want to fit in here.

MARY JANE: I got it wrong. I'm going to start listening.

CHORUS 1: *How 'bout how good it feels to finally forgive you*[2]

CHORUS 2: *These are not times for the weak of heart*

CHORUS 1:	CHORUS 2:
One step, one prayer,	*One prayer,*
I soldier on	*I soldier on*

Nick appears and joins MJ and Frankie on the couch.

MARY JANE: Nick is making decisions for himself now. He's taking a year off, and he's going to appear as a witness in Bella's case. He can't change the past, but he's looking inside himself to understand why he didn't do something when he had the chance. It's been a year of figuring out for both of us and we're taking it day by day. *(beat)* Moving on to Steve—he's taking guitar lessons!

"I SEE RIGHT THROUGH YOU" vamp begins as Steve appears with his guitar.

MARY JANE: It's kind of hot, even though he can only play this one Alanis Morissette riff. We're also in marriage counseling—which I highly recommend, and also individual therapy, because we're both messed up, perfectly imperfect people just like you. We don't have any secrets anymore. *(deep breath)* What else? Oh yes, as you all know, I overdosed on fentanyl and oxycodone. I'm sure *that* was a hot topic at the coffee shop! Don't worry, it was as messy and humiliating as you all imagined it to be. After they pulled all the tubes out of my body, I was privileged enough to go to the Keystone Center for 90 days. That was the easy part—recovery will last the rest of my life. I didn't expect to make friends there, because I'm a stuck-up bitch from Connecticut. But you know what? I met some of the kindest, most intelligent human beings I've ever known. I've lived among all of you in this town for so long that I forgot people could be genuine and actually have empathy! xoxo, MJ

STEVE: You're not actually going to send that, are you?

MARY JANE: What do I have to lose?

STEVE: You're not at rock bottom anymore. I know you think you are, but you're not.

MARY JANE: Where am I, then?

STEVE/NICK/FRANKIE: Rock middle.

MARY JANE: I'll take it.

STEVE: Next year's letter is going to be different. Maybe not amazing. Maybe not spectacular. But a little bit better. It's gotta be.

MARY JANE: I think this is my final letter.

NICK: You're not going to do it anymore?

FRANKIE: Why not?

---

1 "A longer version of the song was cut before the show opened in New York, but we recorded it for the album."
2 "One of the quickest ways to feeling a sense of spirit, for me, is through gratitude. It's important to mark and name and ritualize that which I'm grateful for."

MARY JANE: Because Christmas letters are for assholes.

FRANKIE: I dare you to send it.

NICK: Yeah. Just like that.

Then. Holding his gaze, she drops her finger dramatically (and deliberately) onto the keyboard, hitting SEND. Steve is shocked. So is Mary Jane.

MARY JANE: Merry Fucking Christmas.

STEVE: Who did that go to?

MARY JANE: *Everyone!*

Their laughter is bittersweet, cathartic, liberated, melancholy, real...

Mary Jane sings "YOU LEARN." Frankie, Nick, and Steve join her.

MARY JANE: *I, recommend getting your heart trampled on to anyone, yeah / I, recommend walking around naked in your living room, yeah / Swallow it down*

FRANKIE: *What a jagged little pill*

MARY JANE: *It feels so good*

NICK: *Swimming in your stomach*

STEVE: *Wait until the dust settles*[3]

MARY JANE/FRANKIE/NICK/STEVE: *You live you learn, you love you learn / You cry you learn, you lose you learn / You bleed you learn, you scream you learn*[4]

Frankie turns to Jo.

FRANKIE: Hey. I miss hanging out with you.

JO: Of course you do. I'm the only interesting person in this town and my sex appeal is off the charts.

FRANKIE: Why do you always have to make *everything* a joke?

JO: It's called a defense mechanism.

FRANKIE: I guess I'm just wondering how you're doing.

JO: I'm figuring things out. I have a girlfriend.

FRANKIE: Yeah, I noticed. Chelsea, from the soccer team.

JO: Kelsey. Her name is *Kelsey.*

Frankie nods. Jo shifts gears back to the previous awkward topic.

JO: What about you? How are things with Phoenix?

---

3 "Reflection and processing are everything. 'You Learn' is really processing how even the most challenging times and the biggest conflicts and the strangest chapters yield beauty."

4 Says orchestrator Tom Kitt, "It's so wonderful how Alanis is able to find humility and gratitude for the pain that we all have to go through."

FRANKIE: He's good. We're just friends.

JO: It's probably for the best. You're a lot to handle.

FRANKIE: Hey!

JO: *I, recommend biting off more than you can chew to anyone*

FRANKIE: *I certainly do*

Phoenix and Bella enter.

PHOENIX: *I, recommend sticking your foot in your mouth at any time*

JO: *Feel free*

BELLA: *Throw it down*

NICK: *The caution blocks you from the wind*

BELLA: *Hold it up*

NICK: *To the rays*

FRANKIE/JO/BELLA/PHOENIX/NICK: *You wait and see when the smoke clears*

FRANKIE: *You live*

FRANKIE/NICK/BELLA/JO/PHOENIX: *You learn*

PHOENIX: *You love*

FRANKIE/NICK/BELLA/JO/PHOENIX: *You learn*

BELLA: *You cry you learn*

NICK: *You lose*

NICK/PHOENIX: *You learn*

FRANKIE: *You bleed*

FRANKIE/NICK/BELLA/JO/PHOENIX: *You learn*

JO: *You scream*

FRANKIE/NICK/BELLA/JO/PHOENIX:
You learn

MARY JANE:
La-ah-hi

Ya-ah-hi-yi

MARY JANE/FRANKIE:
La-ah-hi

Ya-ah-hi-yi

MARY JANE/FRANKIE/JO/NICK:
La-ah-hi

Ya-ah-hi-yi

CHORUS:
Lai-la lai-la

Lai-la

Lai-la

Lai-la

Lai-la

Lai-la

Lai-la

STEVE/MARY JANE: *Wear it out*

FRANKIE: *The way a three-year-old would do*

JO/NICK: *Melt it down*

MARY JANE: *You're gonna have to eventually anyway*

CHORUS: *The fire trucks are*

FRANKIE/JO/MARY JANE/PHOENIX/STEVE/NICK/BELLA:
Coming up around the bend

FRANKIE/JO/MARY JANE/PHOENIX/STEVE/NICK/BELLA

CHORUS: *You live you learn, you love you learn / You cry you learn, you lose you learn / You bleed you learn, you scream / You learn*

MARY JANE/STEVE/ FRANKIE/NICK/ JO/PHOENIX/BELLA:
You grieve, you learn

You choke, you learn

You laugh, you learn

You choose, you learn

You pray, you learn

You ask, you learn

You live

CHORUS:
You learn

Thank you India

Thank you Providence

Thank you

Disillusionment

Thank you clarity

Thank you consequence

Thank you

Thank you[5]

FRANKIE/MARY JANE:
You learn[6]

Silence

FRANKIE:
Ah hi ya aye

MARY JANE: *Aye*

---

5 "Gratitude has become one of the top five spiritual practices for me. Anytime there's anything going on that's really challenging, I take a moment of stillness, which can be tough as a mom of three—it might even be three in the morning."

6 "When you're in the middle of challenging, difficult times, it's tough to conjure the 'You Learn' energy. It's only in retrospect, through the evolution of consciousness, the evolution of our own spirits, that you reach this level of awareness. That's what it's all about, even when it's not fun."

The End

GRATITUDE

After the raging success of *Jagged Little Pill*, Morissette needed a break. She could have spent several years touring and running herself ragged, but instead she decided to travel and step away from public life. She went to India and Cuba, and decided not to start writing her second record until she felt less like she *had* to have a follow-up to her smash debut, and more like she had something real and necessary to express. The first song she wrote after her travels was "That I Would Be Good," a ballad about yearning for unconditional acceptance, no matter the circumstances. Morissette, who had almost overnight become galactically famous, struggled with having a high-profile public persona, and what that meant about who she could trust and what people expected of her. She wanted to know that she could be *good*, even if she wasn't an arena-filling rock star.

Morissette's travels, especially "a goddess trip" she took with her aunts to India, helped her to come to terms with the bizarre and sudden ways that her life had changed, and gave her space to step back from an industry she had been in for most of her life. "Ever since I was nine, I've been very focused on my music, and that was always my number one priority," she told *Rolling Stone* in 1998. "I had never really investigated what life would be like if I switched the priorities around. So I just got away from the public world and read and traveled." She said that she wanted to have a blank slate, to reconnect with her primal love of music.

One of the songs that grew out of that unlearning process was "Thank U," in which she expresses gratitude for all of the forces that shape her, both good and bad. "Thank you, frailty," she sings. "Thank you, consequence. Thank you, silence."

Diane Paulus knew she wanted to include "Thank U" at the end of the show—mixed into the chorus of "You Learn"—even though it is not on the original *Jagged Little Pill* recording. "It just has that hit status," she said. She also encouraged Tom Kitt to weave in bits of other Morissette songs into "You Learn/ Thank U," as a way to give a special thanks to diehard fans (for example, the line "These are not times for the weak at heart" comes from the song "Torch," off of Morissette's 2008 album *Flavors of Entanglement*).

Morissette's message about being grateful even for hardship is, in a way, at the heart of the Healy family's journey throughout the show. Each character must pass through a crucible—addiction, isolation, sexual abandonment, parental pressures, heartbreak, moral failure—in order to end up in a position to appreciate and value the bonds that hold the family together.

As Mary Jane Healy sits down at the end of the show to write her final Christmas letter—*ever*, because, as she admits, "Christmas letters are for assholes"—she is finally able to be honest, not just with her family and the hundreds of friends she sends the letter to, but with herself. She is open about her overdose, her rape, and her marital troubles. Steve, for his part, realizes he has been a disengaged, absentee father, an action that may have led to both of his children making choices that hurt others. Nick has taken a gap year before college to grapple with his inability to help Bella when she was in need. And Frankie finally understands that while she may never fully fit in in Greenport, she needs her family for support and guidance. These are not neat, clean endings. Mary Jane is still in recovery—she's not at rock bottom, but she's definitely, as her family says, at "rock middle." Nick is still confronting hard truths about his mistakes. And Frankie never fully mends fences with Jo, who has moved on with a new girlfriend and a cool new ear piercing. As Mary Jane writes, "It's been a year of figuring-out...and we are taking it day by day."

It is only fitting that the story of the Healys should end with "You Learn," the most hopeful, and yet nakedly human, song on *Jagged Little Pill*. It is a song about how the only way forward is through, even if the path is rocky and full of

"Sometimes growth feels like swallowing down a jagged little pill."

brambles, and you stumble along the way. "I recommend getting your heart trampled on to anyone," Morissette sings. It is advice that feels soft and lived-in, like a beloved T-shirt. Paulus said that when she first heard those lyrics, she could not believe that Morissette had written them when she was only a teenager. "Alanis was way ahead of her time and I think she was a prophetess," Paulus said. "She was tapping into something in herself that was transcending time. It was going backwards and forwards out of this nineteen-year-old self. She was tapping into something so primal about who we are as human beings."

"You Learn" is really the mission statement of *Jagged Little Pill*—both the album and the musical. In the end, Morissette's larger vision was never about anger or suffering; it was about harnessing those emotions and twisting them into new shapes, about owning what you have done, and forgiving yourself for what you cannot control. Life

hands you lemons, but it also hands you lessons. You bleed, you learn. You cry, you learn.

"What I love about 'You Learn' is that it feels like we've all learned that we also can return this unconditional love," said Sean Allan Krill, who plays Steve. "But it's existential, it's bigger than that too. It's all about how we can take all this pain and heartache that we've been through and learn from it and grow and become better versions of ourselves."

"We all go through our own trials and conflicts," said Celia Rose Gooding, who plays Frankie. "Because of the dysfunction early on in the family, and because people aren't communicating and having that support system in place, we're all kind of left alone to deal with these issues. And I think one of the morals of the show is, you have to help yourself before you can help somebody else. One of the beautiful things about our show was there really is no concrete solution. There's just constant improvement and you can only try to be the best person you can be and support those around you the best you can."

In the very last moment of "You Learn," right before the lights go out, Frankie and Mary Jane stand on stage by themselves. The show began with the two talking past each other, screaming over each other during "All I Really

Want." But in the show's final moments, we see that the two women have learned how to be a support system for each other, even when there are no clear right answers. Loving someone is about trying, and failing, and trying harder, and failing better. As Morissette sings, sometimes growth feels like swallowing down a jagged little pill. As the song ends, Frankie grabs Mary Jane's hand.

"I think my favorite part of the show is the very end," Gooding said. "Where Frankie is looking out into her future and realizing that due to the world we live in, being a black woman never gets any easier. And so she's looking out into this universe and saying, this is the world that I'm going to inherit. I cannot do this alone. And she reaches out for her mother. Frankie accepts the fact that not being able to do something on her own is not a weakness. It's a part of being human."

DECEMBER 7, 2019

St Mary Mother of Sorrows Parish

29 Willow Cove Boulevard † Greenport, CT 06839
www.SMMSP.org

Special Intentions This Week:
Forgiveness

We invite you to light a votive in the Blessed Sacrament Nave to have your very special intentions remembered for a week. Today we are asking that you think of those who have done you wrong as well as those to whom you have done wrong, and then send up a prayer that forgiveness may be granted to all. To reserve a candle, please call or visit the church office after Mass.

TODAY'S SCRIPTURE FOCUS READING:

Confess [your] faults one to another, and pray one for another, that ye may be healed. The effectual fervent prayer of a righteous man availeth much.   James 5:16

PASTOR

Fr. Joseph Payne, P
Fr. Paul Murphy, Pa
Fr. Andrew Wilk, P
Deacon John Peters

WEEKEN

Saturday Evening:
Sunday Morning: 7

WEEKDAY MA

Monday, Tuesday, W
Friday: 6:30 am & N
Thursday: 6:30, 8:4
Noon
Saturday: 7:00 am

ADORAT
BLESSED S

Monday - Friday: 7:
First Friday: 8:00 am
First Saturday: 7:30

SACRA
RECONC

Monday - Friday: A
0:45 - 11:45 am
aturday: After the
0 - 10:00 am; 4:00
er times for Conf

OFFERTORY

This week's altar bread and wine were donated by the Mary Jane and Steve Healy, family in memory of their mothers. The following weeks are still available: Dec 14, 21, and 28.

2ND ANNUAL FALL FASHION SHOW

This year our Fashion Show will be held Tuesday, January 21, at Nico's Restaurant. 7600 N. Metropolitan. Tickets are $20.00 per person. Cocktails at 6:30. Dinner at 7:30. For reservations, contact Courtney Slonsky 542-2779. Only tables of ten will be reserved. If you purchase your tickets before Thursday, Jan 9th, you could be the lucky winner of $50.00. Drawing will be held the evening of the fashion show.

ANNUAL COAT DRIVE

Saturday, December 13th and Sunday December 21st. Please bring any coats/jackets you wish to donate to church December 13th and December 21st.

ST VINCENT DE PAUL FOOD DRIVE

This weekend before & after the Masses Your non-perishable food items (please check expiration dates) will be donated to St. Thomas of Canterbury Parish Food Pantry. Any monetary donations will be distributed to the following Food Pantries: Ascension, Incarnation, St. Mary Virgin Mother & St. Stanislaus Kostka, who are in great need of assistance. We thank you in advance for your continuous generosity.

ALCOHOLICS ANONYMOUS/ NARCOTICS ANONYMOUS

Regular meetings are held in the Parish Hall on Tuesday at 8pm.

PARENTS' GROUP

The Parents Group is meeting to attend parenting lectures at Humana Hospital on Wednesday evenings through March 18. For More information call Jill Kane, 241-8350.

OPPORTUNITY

Would you be willing to be a Boy Scout leader at All Souls? This is a wonderful opportunity for a man or woman. Call Charles Montefiore, 546-6002. Note: Two of our older Scouts (Nick Healy and Aaron Smith) would be on hand to assist you.

NEW DIRECTORIES READY

Our handsome new church directories are ready for pick up, and to save us the cost of mailing, your cooperation in this respect will be much appreciated.

M.J. Healy   4:31 PM
The Annual Healy Holiday Letter!
Welcome to the annual Healy
holiday letter. I've decided to go d...

Kelly O'Connor   12:36 PM
RE: Brunch Plans
Ladies, it's time we hammer these
final details out. This brunch won't

CheckOut Co.   9:14 AM
Your Order is Ready
Get excited! The time has come.
Your gift will be ready in just a few

Headspace Monthly   Yesterday
The Month of You
No more distractions. No more
excuses. This month, you have one

Karen Killington   Yesterday
Call for Chaperones
Hello all! As we all know, the week of
the long-awaited celebratory trip to

SpiritWheel   Yesterday
Get Back on the Bike
Hey girl! We noticed you haven't
been to class in a couple days, just

Sassy Quotes Daily   Yesterday
Start Your Day With Some Sass
We get it. You haven't had your
coffee yet. But after you read this

Diane Elwood   Yesterday
PTA Meeting
Hey everyone, please take a minute
to fill out this snack form for our ne

LetMeKnow App   Yesterday
Calendar Notifcation
Notice: Upcoming event at 2:00 PM,
titled "Scheduled Self-Care". To tu...

Neighborhood Mes... Yesterday
Dog droppings on my sidewalk??
To whoever cannot find the decency
to pick up after their dog, I say this...

Kelly O'Connor   Wednesday
Brunch Plans
Ladies, let's do it! This weekend must
be the one, the family is travelling...

Squeaky   Wednesday
Your Order Has Been Shipped!
Let's get squeaking! Tell your pup to
start wagging that tail, because yo...

Craftsy   Wednesday
FREE DIY Embroidery Templates
Looking for a lazy sunday activity?

☆ **M.J. Healy**

The Annual Healy Holiday Letter!

To: Denise Fulton

Welcome to the annual Healy holiday letter. I've decided to go digital

Where to begin...

I'm in awe of my daughter, Frankie. It took me 40 years to be as brave
friend, Bella Fox, who is a rape survivor. Like myself. As you may have h
the circumstances. He's sticking to his story. But Bella gets to tell hers. M

Nick is making decisions for himself now. He's taking a year off, and he
inside himself to understand why he didn't do something when he had

Moving on to Steve—He's taking guitar lessons! It's kind of hot, even tho
I highly recommend, and also individual therapy, because we're both

What else? Oh yes, as you all know, I overdosed on Fentanyl and Oxyc
humiliating as you all imagined it to be. After they pulled all the tubes
the easy part—recovery will last the rest of my life. I didn't expect to m
met some of the kindest, most intelligent human beings I've ever know
and actually have empathy!

xoxo, M.J.

ɔm the Healys

e the trees, Christmas or otherwise.

he has spent this past year doing everything she can to bring justice to her
e is going to trial. The defendant still got into a good college, even under
do.

ɔr as a witness in Bella's case. He can't change the past, but he's looking
been a year of figuring out for both of us and we're taking it day by day.

play this one Alanis Morissette riff. We're also in marriage counseling—which
ɔctly imperfect people just like you. We don't have any secrets anymore.

that was a hot topic at the coffee shop! Don't worry, it was as messy and
was privileged enough to go to the Keystone Center for 90 days. That was
, because I'm a stuck up bitch from Connecticut. But you know what? I
ng all of you in this town for so long that I forgot people could be genuine

AFTERWORD

by Diablo Cody

I was sixteen years old the first time I heard the voice of Alanis Morissette. Well, technically that isn't true—I grew up watching *You Can't Do That on Television*, the Canadian kiddie show on which a young Alanis starred. But when I say "the voice of Alanis Morissette," I'm not referring to the literal vibrations created by her laryngeal folds. I'm talking about the powerful and primal flow of essential Alanis-ness that is her legendary album, *Jagged Little Pill*. This was not just a collection of songs, you understand. This was a seismic event that shifted the plates of pop culture and redefined irony for a generation. Alanis Morissette, rock star, was more than a voice. She was a Voice.

It was 1995 and I was hanging out in my bedroom in Lemont, Illinois, a small town with nine churches and zero bookstores. I was listening to Q-101, "Chicago's Rock Alternative," like I did every day after school. Though the grunge trend had expired like a tub of old yogurt, rock radio was still dominated by growling, lank-haired dudes with low-slung guitars and Big Muff distortion pedals. Kurt Cobain and Eddie Vedder had changed the game by championing feminist causes, but the rock scene in general still felt like the same old macho circlejerk it had been since forever. The "girl bands" that did get airplay at the time were all punk bravado and defiance—very necessary, but not always relatable to me as a vulnerable and confused Catholic girl who had *so many feelings* and was often afraid to express them. There was an Alanis-shaped hole in my heart; I just didn't know it yet.

So there I was, in my bedroom, flipping through *Sassy* magazine and painting my nails with Wite-Out as I listened to the radio. As the song ended—let's say it was "Cumbersome" by Seven Mary Three—the DJ broke in, sounding way more enthusiastic than usual. "I am so psyched to play this next song," the DJ said—again, this type of editorializing was rare on Q-101, a big corporate radio station. "It's from a new singer named Alanis Morissette and it's going to blow your mind. Here's 'You Oughta Know.'"

Curiosity piqued, I twisted the volume knob on my Sony boombox. A trembling voice filled the room, not just a voice, but a Voice: Alanis's brave, forceful, naked Voice revealing itself for the first time. It was an immediate shock to the system. After a parade of grunge singers cocooning themselves in flannel and mumbling purposely vague lyrics, here, at last, was someone ready to expose her soul. And "You Oughta Know" was just the beginning—the beginning of the beginning. As we would soon discover, there was so much more to this artist than just spite and rage; on *Jagged Little Pill* she revealed herself to be tender, spiritual, shameless, kindhearted, eternally questioning and utterly assured all at once. Shockingly, Alanis was only nineteen years old when she wrote these songs with producer Glen Ballard—just a skip ahead of me, age-wise, but miles beyond in terms of artistic maturity.

The music delighted and inspired me, as it did so many people in my generation, but I assumed my relationship with it would remain simple: Fan and album. Until … twenty-three years later: I was approaching my fortieth birthday and got a call from my agent about adapting *Jagged Little Pill* as a musical. Of course, I immediately and enthusiastically said yes. In retrospect, it's funny that I didn't take a beat to consider the proposition. I'd never written a play, let alone the book for a major musical. I wasn't a theater kid in high school; I'd been too "cool" at the time to express enthusiasm for anything beyond Marlboro Lights and peach-flavored wine cooler. Now, I was blithely signing on to write a story that needed to measure up to the brilliance of an iconic and beloved album. (But as one of my favorite songs says: "I recommend biting off more than you can chew to anyone. I certainly do.")

At this point, I had been working in Hollywood for around fifteen years. As a writer, I had become so jaded and crusty, that I might as well have been walking around with a wooden leg and an eyepatch. It had been a long time since I'd felt "wet behind the ears" or whatever slightly icky metaphor one might use to describe the feeling of having *no idea what you are doing*. Now, here I was in the new world of Broadway, entirely clueless. And, unlike when I was twenty-five and started writing movies, I was no longer fueled by the arrogance of youth. I was old enough to know that I could make some serious mistakes. I knew—as an investor cheerfully reminded me at a cocktail party—that most Broadway musicals fail. As I began the creative process in earnest, it dawned on me that writing the book for *Jagged Little Pill* was more than just a cool story to tell my friends or a retroactive treat for my teenage self—it was a tremendous responsibility.

I didn't make it any easier by deciding the show would deal with the opioid epidemic, sexual assault, political activism, and religion. This was not a dance-in-the-aisles jukebox musical with a featherweight story; as much as I enjoy those shows, I wanted *Jagged Little Pill* to be as real and provocative as the album that inspired it. Everyone on the creative team was committed to fully understanding every issue we explored in the show. We also all agreed that while this complex tangle of topics might seem like "too much" to some critics or audience members, it was an accurate reflection of modern life.

In the run-up to our first Broadway previews, the *New York Times* asked "Has Alanis Morissette Made the Most Woke Musical Since *Hair*?" I was proud to have helped prompt that query. After all, the idea of awareness—of waking up, morally and ideologically—is a major theme in our show. The album that Alanis and Glen Ballard wrote together was never a simple, catchy pop record. It was epic, it was messy, it was fearless, it was heroic. While the glory of a Broadway debut is unforgettable, my favorite part of this journey was the work itself—the priceless opportunity to connect with our creative team including, of course, Alanis Morissette, who is both the goddess my sixteen-year-old self dreamed she would be, and the accessible, gracious, hilarious collaborator my adult self needed her to be. Somewhere along the way, I caught "the bug" and realized I was a theater kid after all!

Writing my first Broadway show wasn't easy. I was admittedly naive when I jumped onboard without a second thought. And I didn't realize how much (often uncomfortable) personal work and introspection I'd have to do in order to successfully tell the story of the Healy family. But the result was the ultimate reward. *Jagged Little Pill* tells us that growth is uncomfortable but necessary for us to thrive. Watching this show come alive is something I'll never forget, and being a part of the album's legacy is the ultimate privilege.

Producing *Jagged Little Pill* has been the greatest professional journey of our lives. It's been a humbling privilege, a happy responsibility, and a genuine joy to collaborate with our Jagged Little Company and our entire extended Jagged Little Family—from attorneys and agencies to fans and friends, and everyone in between. We've all worked together to expand the legacy of Alanis's game-changing 1995 album and create a show that would both entertain and inspire. This journey has taken us from a humble downtown NYC rehearsal studio, to the venerable American Repertory Theater in Cambridge, MA, to Broadway's historic Broadhurst Theatre, to an outdoor stage in Times Square for *Dick Clark's New Year's Rockin' Eve 2020*, to recent protest marches for Black Lives Matter and LGBTQ Pride. We are so grateful to everyone who's stood with us—including you, dear reader—and we look forward to the future. Together, in solidarity, we know the journey is just getting started.

—VIVEK J. TIWARY, ARVIND ETHAN DAVID, AND EVA PRICE,
on behalf of all the producers, June 2020

Melcher Media and the producers would like to gratefully acknowledge the cast and crew listed on page 38, as well as the photographers listed below, who so graciously shared their time, photos, and ideas. In addition we would like to extend our sincere thanks to the following for their contributions to the book: Joshua Altman, Chika Azuma, Jennifer Bell, Greg Brunswick, Brittany Chapman, Sean Chia, Rebecca Curtiss, Ana Deboo, E.J. Devokaitis, Kate Elliott, Laura Ellis, Michelle Figueroa, Luke Gernert, Alia Habib, John Albert Harris, Halle Kilman, Gene Lee, Iris Lynch, Michele McGonigle De Young, Mary McGowan, Gina McIntyre, Anne Montavon, Leslie Papa, Cheryl Della Pietra, Nola Romano, Leda Scheintaub, Jonas Schildermans, David Schmerler, Roseanna M. Sharrow, Lenora Sumerling, Ryan M. Sweeney, Albert Tang, Angela Tucker / The Adopted Life, Anna Wahrman, Haley Weaver, Lee Wilcox, Nancy Wolff, Gretchen Young, Evan Zimmerman.

IMAGE CREDITS:
All photographs in the book were taken by *Matthew Murphy* except those listed below. *Alamy/Zuma Press, Inc.*: 16 (MJ); *Molly Barnett / grapevine PR*: 142c; *Alex Bruce*: 140–141, 222–223; *Antonio Cipriano*: 116b; *Evgenia Eliseeva, Eve Photography*: 6t; *Shannon Fanuko, backgrounds*: 29c, 142t; *Kathryn Gallagher*: 143b; *Alexandra Gavillet (art direction: RPM)*: 12, 13, 20, 21, 24, 25, 32, 33, 138, 139, 146–149; *Celia Rose Gooding*: 29t, 30, 94; *iStock*: 10 pen (Radionphoto), 144–145 desk (Josh Laverty); *J. Jared Janas*: 179; *Nathan Johnson / Drift Studio*: 74; *Paul Kepple*: 2–3, 10–11, 15, 16, 18–19, 27, 144–145, 220–221; *Derek Klena*: 28t, 28b, 111t; *Chad David Kraus*: 28c, 62, 70, 71, 88–89 (rehearsal shots), 95, 110, 116t, 142t, 143t, 143c, 95, 97t, 110, 116t, 142t, 143t (figs.), 143c, 190; *Sean Allan Krill*: 6c, 7c, 7b, 16r, 29c, 40, 100, 102b; *Michele Laurita*: 42–45; *Susan Lynch*: 34–35t; *Lucy Mackinnon*: 17, 26, 140 (inset), 151; *Sophie Ming, @sophiemingphoto*: 29b; *Lauren Patten*: 7c, 84b, 142b, 143b, 195; *Diane Paulus*: 60, 61, 166; *Courtesy of Rhino Entertainment Company, a Warner Music Group Company*: 41; *Finn Ross*: 40; *Shutterstock*: 3 Christmas border (Iolya 1988), 4–5 (Konstantin L), 15 clipboard (mihalec), 16 wedding (Billion Photos), 31 border (ESB Basic), 49, 83, 104–105, 212 patterns (Rawpixel. com), 101 pattern (Malinovskaya Yulia), 142 lockers (Stacey Newman), 222–223 red type (Vik Y), 222–223 Christmas border (artist Elizaveta); *Elizabeth Stanley*: 8; *Christopher Steighner*: 22–23; © *Liza Voll Photography*: 7t; *Wikimedia Commons*: 7 castle (CrispyCream27). INSERT: *Alamy*: 2b (Shelly Rivoli), 5t (Scootercaster), 5c (Erik McGregor/Zuma Wire), 5b (Gerry Rousseau), 9c (Michael Kemp), 10t (Matthew Kaplan), 10b (Jasper Chamber), 13c (Bob Korn), 13b (Jim West); *Annelise Baker*: 13t; *James Gallagher / @gallagherwalks*: 9t; *Getty / Emma McIntyre*: 2t; *Laurel Harris*: 9b; *Sean Allan Krill*: 6tl; *Courtesy Lauren Patten*: 6b; *Nora Schell*: 6tr.

A portion of the essay on page 224 originally appeared in the *Guide*, a publication of the American Repertory Theater.

JAGGED LITTLE PILL
Book by Diablo Cody
Lyrics by Alanis Morissette
Music by Alanis Morissette and Glen Ballard
Additional music by by Michael Farrell & Guy Sigsworth
Directed by Diane Paulus

Published by
GRAND CENTRAL PUBLISHING
Hachette Book Group
1290 Avenue of the Americas
New York, NY 10104
grandcentralpublishing.com
twitter.com/grandcentralpub

First Edition: October 2020

Grand Central Publishing is a division of Hachette Book Group, Inc. The Grand Central Publishing name and logo is a trademark of Hachette Book Group, Inc.

The publisher is not responsible for websites (or their content) that are not owned by the publisher.

The Hachette Speakers Bureau provides a wide range of authors for speaking events. To find out more, go to www.hachettespeakersbureau.com or call (866) 376-6591.

This book was produced by
MELCHER MEDIA, INC.
124 West 13th Street
New York, NY 10011
www.melcher.com

President, CEO: Charles Melcher
VP, COO: Bonnie Eldon
Editorial Director: Lauren Nathan
Executive Editor / Producer: Christopher Steighner
Production Director: Susan Lynch
Senior Editor: Megan Worman
Senior Digital Producer: Shannon Fanuko
Editorial Assistant: Zoe Margolis

Design by Paul Kepple and Alex Bruce at
HEADCASE DESIGN
www.headcasedesign.com

Library of Congress Cataloging-in-Publication Data has been applied for.

ISBNs:
978-1-5387-3699-9 (hardcover)
978-1-5387-3698-2 (ebook)
978-1-5491-0679-8 (audiobook CD)
978-1-5491-5884-1 (downloadable audiobook)

Printed in China

10 9 8 7 6 5 4 3 2 1